SERGE GAINSBOURG: A FISTFUL OF GITANES

Requiem for a Twister

by Sylvie Simmons

Helter
Skelter

Publishing

First published in 2001 by Helter Skelter Publishing
4 Denmark Street, London WC2H 8LL
First edition
Text copyright Sylvie Simmons © 2001
The moral right of the author has been asserted
Photographs copyright see picture credits page

Design by Bold; Typesetting by Caroline Walker
Printed by The Bath Press

Every effort has been made to contact the copyright holders of the photographs in this book, but one or two were unreachable. The publishers would be grateful if those concerned would contact Helter Skelter Publishing.

A CIP record for this book is available from the British Library

ISBN 1-900924-28-5

All Serge Gainsbourg lyrics quoted are copyright Warner-Chappell, France. They are quoted for review, study or critical purposes.

Front cover photograph by J.L. Rancruel / O. Medias
Back cover photograph by Patrick Duval, reprinted with his kind permission

SERGE GAINSBOURG:
A FISTFUL OF GITANES

Requiem for a Twister

by Sylvie Simmons

Helter
Skelter
Publishing

Contents

For Stan, who loved music

Foreword by Jane Birkin

In England you're discovering him… Like opening a Pharaoh's tomb, you see wonderful things… We stand outside whilst bright new faces shine lamps onto his brilliant world… Our perfumed flowers have faded in the air… You flash wild torches to light his gold sarcophagus… Hieroglyphs, treasured words, his painted throne, guarded by silent leopards… for years… And in the dark his sweet face has always smiled at you, waiting, patiently, for you to find the door.

Jane Birkin, January 2001

INTRODUCTION

"It's disgusting!" An immaculately coiffed matron with matching mini-dog pushes past me as I stop on the narrow pavement to photograph the revolving art gallery outside number 5 Rue de Verneuil. In a display of fellow-feeling, the stunted animal cocks a tiny back leg to deposit a pipette of piss on the stubbly face that someone has lovingly painted on an empty spot at the bottom of the wall. The residents of this respectable street in the Saint-Germain area of Paris, a stone's throw from the Seine – the kind of place where the corner shops sell old masters and scarily priced antiques – paid to have the walls whitewashed over just a matter of months ago, only for someone to sneak by in the night and spray-paint a slogan that marked the start of another round.

Ten years after Serge Gainsbourg's death, the palimpsest of paintings and graffiti that still covers every millimetre of his small, two-storey house has taken on a life of its own; it even has its own website and coffee-table book. A tossed salad of colours, styles and languages where messages of love sit alongside puns and poetry, comic-book caricatures of the artist nudge up against Realist portraits and phallic line-drawings of the Tube-Poster School, and an ongoing metaphysical debate as to the credibility of Einstein's proof of the existence of the soul after death concludes that Serge is not dead, he has ascended into heaven where he sits on the right hand of God The Hashish Smoker. If it weren't already his house, Gainsbourg would feel entirely at home.

When he died here in his bedroom on 2 March 1991, a month short of his 63rd birthday, France went into mourning. Brigitte Bardot, who'd slept with him, gave a eulogy; President Mitterand, who hadn't, gave one too. He was "our Baudelaire, our Apollinaire", said the head of state. "He elevated the song to the level of *art*". Flags were flown at half-mast – a less fitting symbol for the priapic pop genius than the bottles of whisky and Pastis and packets of Gitanes cigarettes left as tributes by the crowds who descended, à la Princess Di, on the police barricades erected around the Rue de Vernueil.

"Ask anyone in Paris," said Nicolas Godin of French group Air, "and they can remember what they were doing when they heard Gainsbourg had died. It was such a shock. Because he was always there, part of our culture. He was always on the television doing something crazy. He was a poet. He was a punk. And he wanted to fuck Whitney Houston."

The man who looked like an elegant turtle, cross-bred with a particularly louche, chain-smoking wolf was also a singer, songwriter, cutting-edge soundtrack composer, Eurovision Song Contest winner, novelist, photographer, actor, artist, drunk, director, screenwriter, populist, provocateur, sentimentalist, clown, lover, intellectual, and the man who single-handedly liberated French pop. In spite – or because – of a singular dedication to cigarettes, alcohol, sensuality and provocation (the then rheumy-eyed 56-year-old's infamous "I want to fuck you" offer to fellow-guest

Whitney, in perfect English, on a live, prime-time French TV family-variety show, combined all four) his musical output over more than three decades was staggeringly prodigious. It encompassed a variety of reinventions that made David Bowie look stagnant – classical, *chanson*, jazz, girl-pop, rock, reggae, disco, rap – and displayed a profound knowledge of, and respect for, tradition while simultaneously giving it two fingers, then using them to remodel it into something entirely unique.

His lyrics were mind-boggling exercises in Franglais triple-entendres and rhythmic, onomatopoeic word-percussion. Literature, coprophagy, sexual obsession, farting, incest, philosophy, grammar, cabbages, Nazi death camps and the Torrey Canyon disaster were all considered perfectly reasonable subject-matter for songs – songs both whistled in the street by *l'homme dans la rue* and printed in poetry books and studied in universities. And yet on this side of the Channel, Gainsbourg has really been known for just one song. His 1969 number one with the English actress Jane Birkin, 'Je T'Aime, Moi Non Plus'. As Robert Chalmers wrote in *The Independent*, "Gainsbourg has been cursed by an attribute which has proved "a more powerful hindrance to rock stardom than being blind, tone-deaf or dead: that most fatal of adjectives, *French*."

The British prejudice against French pop music – which runs every bit as deep and wide as the French prejudice against British food – stems back to the Swinging Sixites when we had The Beatles, the Stones and scampi in a basket and France had (or at least all we got to hear of what they had was) Sacha Distel, the Singing Nun and pâté de foie gras. It's a habit, sadly, that some Anglo music writers have found hard to shake off. (Witness *The Guardian*'s posthumous take on Gainsbourg: "He had a typical French feel for rock: he was hopeless at it".)

The fact that we're notoriously bad at foreign languages of course doesn't help, but, a bigger block is our wildly differing cultures and sense of *cool*. The international music business, which is dominated by the English-speaking countries, guarantees a highly honed and constantly changing sense of cooldom by its ongoing marketing assault of hip new fashions and sounds. By operating outside of those parameters, Gainsbourg may have been denied a large Anglophonic audience but as a by-product, by being able to safely ignore the orthodoxy of cool and its inbuilt rules and formalities, he was left to do whatever he wanted, and in the process produced a fascinating body of work, which music fans in Britain and the U.S are finally starting to discover.

Gainsbourg's renown and reconstruction has grown in the past ten or fifteen years via Jimmy Sommerville, Mick Harvey, St Etienne, Stereolab, Momus, Black Grape, Sonic Youth, Luscious Jackson and Divine Comedy, through to the kitsch young Easy Listening audience. And even on to commercially successful acts like Pulp, Suede and Beck, who passed the baton onto contemporary hit/hip artists from the dance culture (where French lyrics aren't a problem, but just another texture and sound to sample) like David Holmes, Mirwais and Air – those last two French acts that have been lionised in Britain; things *are* changing. And in a recent article in *Q* magazine on 'The 100 Greatest Stars Of The 20th Century', Serge – the sole French entry – made it to number 88, topping Damon Albarn of Blur. "Serge Gainsbourg is a French national institution," wrote David Quantick. "A fact that fills us with immense respect for the French." My sentiments exactly.

While writing this book, stumbling blindly around Paris through a blue fog of Gitane smoke, trying to find my way through the minefield of French pop and culture, I was fortunate to receive enormous assistance from a number of French writers, musicians, producers and Sergeologists who did their damnedest to guide me in the right direction. Special thanks to Jane Birkin, the actress, singer, playwright and Serge's former partner, who, in spite of a 30-year relationship with the British press in which "all I got was, 'What dirty records have you made, Jane?'", invited me to her home, made me the best cup of tea I've had in Paris, and spent hours providing detailed insights into his life and his work.

Thanks also to Philippe Lerichomme, Serge's celebrated record producer, the notoriously modest 'Man In The Shadows', as Gainsbourg dubbed him in one of his songs, who agreed to a very rare interview about his old friend. "I am always being asked by French journalists to talk about Serge and I always say no," he said. "But if it helps him get the respect he deserved in England, *d'accord*." Serge's former studio engineer Dominique Blanc-Francard shed important light on Gainsbourg's recording practices; François Ravard, Serge's friend and producer of his last film *Stan The Flasher*, had some fine stories to tell about Gainsbourg the film-maker, artist, and *Homo Aestheticus*; and Nicolas Godin of Air and Françoise Hardy helped contextualise Serge's influence on two generations of French pop musicians.

Meanwhile, answers to what must have seemed an endless bombardment of questions about the strange (to a Londoner) names and places I encountered during my research were generously provided by vinyl collector Daniel Vandel; TV presenter and journalist Laurence Romance; Serge collector and expert Daniel Vanderdonckt; writer-producer Jean-William Thoury; Philippe Thieyre, from the fine Paris bookshop Parallèle; and Serge Vincendet, from record shop Monster Melodies around the corner. Very special thanks to journalist/broadcaster Christian Eudeline for his positively valiant, ongoing explanations and insights into everything from the history of French pop music and culture to the history of France. And to Gilles Verlant, author of the 760-page definitive French-language biography *Gainsbourg* (published by Albin Michel; highly recommended if your French is up to it) for his painstaking efforts in ensuring that this book contains the minimum of errors, *"parce que Gainsbourg le mérite, et le public anglo-saxon aussi !"*.

A number of English-speaking musicians who knew, worked with, sampled, covered or were influenced by Serge, were also kind enough to grant me interviews. A big hand, then, to Marianne Faithfull, Sly Dunbar, Robbie Shakespeare, Beck, Mick Harvey, Alan Hawkshaw, Nick Currie (Momus), Bob Stanley (St Etienne), Sean O'Hagan (High Llamas), Steve Wynn and David Holmes. And a final thanks to *MOJO* magazine for starting *la boule* rolling, to Sean Body and Helter Skelter for picking it up and running with it, and to Nick Kent, Fred Dellar, Sue Smith, Martin Cobb, Peter Silverton and Neil Adams for their invaluable help and support.

As for Serge, I'm only sorry I arrived too late to add him to my list of interviews. A biographer could not ask for a more fascinating subject – a shy extrovert, a surreal realist, an iconoclast who craved being an icon, a man who would hang out drinking with policemen one day, frequent porn films with Dali another, make love with some of the world's most beautiful actresses (without ever letting them see him naked) and die alone in his own bed after a lifetime of positively heroic, or at least indisputably artistic, self-abuse. To quote his epitaph in French newspaper *Libération*, Serge had *"bu trop de cigarettes"* – drank too many cigarettes.

Though, if we're to believe the writing on the wall at no. 5 Rue de Verneuil, "Serge is not dead. He's in heaven, fucking". In fact, shortly after his death, the French satirical magazine *La Grosse Bertha* pictured him on its cover – stubbled chin, loose-lipped smile – standing on a cloud, straddling the blessed Mother of Jesus who was down on all fours, her butt beaming beatifically up at him. "Hey, Mary," murmured cartoon-Serge in the speech bubble, "You know, I could write you some great songs…"

Now, could you see the Brits doing that with John Lennon? I raise a glass (and in the words of the French national anthem): *"Allons enfants de la patrie, le jour de gloire est arrivé!"*

Author's note. Songs, albums, films etc. appear with their original titles, be they French, English, Franglais, or a language of Gainsbourg's imaginings. What follows in brackets is the author's English translation, except in the rare instances where an English title already exists. Quotes, however, have been translated into English, and, to avoid a complete take-over by brackets, the original French quotations have been exiled to the source note section at the back of the book.

Chapter One
LULU

Serge Gainsbourg owed his life to dirt. It was filth that quite literally came to his rescue on the hot summer's afternoon in 1927 when Olia Ginsburg knocked at the door of a grimy back-street building in the Pigalle, the red light district of Paris. Olia, 32 years old, a Russian-Jewish immigrant, wife of a musician, mother of a baby girl and pregnant once again, was led inside the makeshift abortion clinic. Her eyes quickly took in the room – the sink, the stool, the table in the middle of the room with the instruments all lined up on it – before coming to rest on the small metal bowl glinting in the sunlight, still wet and crudded with something unspeakable from the woman who had been there last. Serge's mother took one look and turned tail and ran. "He always said that his one good fortune in life," Jane Birkin recalled, "had been a dirty kidney bowl."

Nearly ten years had passed since Olia Besman and Joseph Ginsburg were married in the Ukraine. The dapper and talented young pianist – first-prize winner at the Conservatory of Music – had been employed and housed by Olia's parents to give music lessons to their eight children. Joseph was emotional and romantic, a fusion of Slav sentimentality and dramatic Jewish melancholia; Olia was caustically funny, practical and a fine mezzo-soprano. He fell immediately in love, courting her while the Bolshevik uprising raged around them. After one too many close calls – he'd had to hide from the troops, à la *Tin Drum*, under a peasant woman's voluminous skirts – they decided to escape. Using false papers, they made their way to Georgia, where they took a ship across the Black Sea to Constantinople, then via the Mediterranean to Marseille, stopping only when they reached Paris. Olia's older brother had already moved there, as had a growing population of Russian refugees. Joseph found work as a jobbing musician, and after a series of moves the family – as they became when Olia gave birth to a son, Marcel, in 1922 – installed themselves in a small apartment at 35 Rue de Chine.

Still one of the least well-to-do areas in the capital, the 20th arondissement in the 1920s was a run-down if almost villagey neighbourhood, with children playing in the streets and barrow-boys hawking their wares. What it wasn't was a Jewish neighbourhood. Jews driven out of Russia more by the pogroms than the communist revolution, had mostly congregated in the *quartiers* near Republique, Porte de Saint-Cloud and Hôtel de Ville. But Joseph was a liberal Jew, a free-thinker and, having been officially naturalised as citizens, he resolved that the Ginsburgs would be wholeheartedly and unreservedly *French*.

And so life went on – except for the unfortunate little Marcel, who died of bronchitis at age 16 months. A second child was born, a daughter, Jacqueline, who was a healthy 18-month-old when on 2 April 1928 Olia went into labour in the Hôtel Dieu hospital by the Seine to give birth to what she already knew would be twins.

"When the first one came out – Liliane – she started to cry," said Jane, "because she thought she was going to be the mother of three girls. And who should pop out a minute or two afterwards but Serge – who, of course, their mother doted on immediately." They named him – "to be very French and *integré*" – Lucien. And nicknamed him, to his great chagrin, Lulu.

The photos show a tiny baby with a bar-code of black hair and dark, sleepily hooded eyes; a miniature of his father, who was still out playing piano in Parisian theatres and clubs by night, and by day playing the upright that had pride of place in the apartment. Lulu and Liliane really had no choice but to suck in the music that surrounded them as if it were just another flavour of milk. And there was quite a selection: up-to-the minute stuff, like American-in-Paris Cole Porter, and American Russian-Jew George Gershwin (Joseph would play 'Rhapsody In Blue' by heart), as well as the classics – Bach, Scarlatti, Vivaldi and, always, Joseph's beloved Chopin. Lulu absorbed it all, and started playing piano, rudimentarily, himself, even before Joseph imposed the same mandatory lessons on the twins when they reached the age of four that their older sister had endured. The lessons continued when the pair started school – every day, an hour a day, as soon as they got home and before they started their homework.

He was a strict father, Serge would recall later, and quite the disciplinarian, which counterbalanced Olia's obvious doting on her little boy. ("My mother adores me, idolises me" he told French magazine *Actuel*).[1] When Lulu misbehaved, he'd get a belt across his bare buttocks from Joseph, who would always apologise afterwards, sentimentally, extravagantly, unable to bear that the boy would think him cruel. It was one of several things Lucien inherited from his father, along with his easy flair for music and a talent for art. But there was no murmur of rebellion: Lucien was a good boy and, like Jacqueline, very smart, good at his studies. He loved school, even if he was a shy timid child, small for his age and sometimes mistaken for a girl. Easily scared, Lucien would not go to sleep unless his big sister looked behind the curtains to check no-one was hiding.

The steady improvement in income from Joseph's work spurred a move in the mid 1930s to a bigger flat on Rue Caulaincourt in the 18th arondissement. They were now a stone's throw from music business mecca S.A.C.E.M (Société Des Auteurs-Compositeurs, the Writers-Composers Society) and a convenient ten minutes walk from the *marché des musiciens* (musician's market) in the Pigalle. Every evening at around five or six o'clock, Joseph would join the other musicians who gathered there in the hope of being hired for the night – a negative-image of the Mexican labourers in Los Angeles who'd congregate at the same hour of morning in search of a day's work. The improved lifestyle also brought Joseph and his wife the means to more easily indulge their profound love of Art. Art, wrote Joseph in his memoirs, for him had a capital A. Back in Russia, before he had become a musician, Joseph had planned to be an artist. He would paint all the time, until a fateful day when, travelling on the Trans-Siberian railway, the portrait he carried with him of a girl he had once loved passionately from afar, was stolen. In dramatic Slav fashion he swore he would not touch a paintbrush again, and he never did. Instead the couple went to every exhibition they could, hung framed art prints on the apartment wall, and took pride in their son's burgeoning artistic abilities.

Musical, artistic, intelligent – the one missing element separating Lucien Ginsburg and Serge Gainsbourg was *girls*. But patience, he was getting there. It was the summer of 1936 and the family were on a seaside holiday. Lucien was eight years old. Playing in the sand, humming along to the music playing over the tannoy – which he recognised as Charles Trenet, whose irrepressible, ebullient *varieté* songs ('Boum', for instance, which cineastes might recognise from *Toto The Hero*) were wildly popular in the optimistic period before the Second World War – he looked up and saw a pretty girl walking across the beach. The combination of the girl's beauty, the warmth of the sun shot through with the breeze off the sea, and the musical accompaniment fused in him like a nuclear reaction. At that very moment, he would later claim, he acquired a taste for female beauty that would remain tattooed inside him, inextricably linked with sensuality, visual image, and the sound of music. This seaside aesthetics lesson would develop further over the coming years, especially when his father performed in increasingly upmarket resort areas like Deauville and Biarritz. Lucien, getting his first real visions of luxury, witnessed what wealth could add to taste.

It was a secure, structured childhood – remarkably so for an immigrant family with a musician as head of the household – and, as he often told Jane, a happy one. "When I came over to Paris to do my first film and met Serge, he used to take me to all these incredible places in Pigalle where the men were all dressed up as women and he said, 'It's where my father used to play'. And he always used to say that the big *fête* in the house was on the first of January because on New Year's Eve his father would play all those joints until three in the morning and he would come back – in a marvellous mood, because people gave him big tips – with paper hats and confetti and blowers and the children would wake up to that."

For some years now, Joseph had fronted his own orchestra, Les Blue Star Boys. But before long, it would be a yellow star that had the biggest impact on the Ginsburg family's life.

* * * * * *

When France declared war on Germany in the summer of 1939, Lucien did not really notice. He was 11 years old, and the family had left Paris to live in Dinard on the Normandy coast, a resort where Joseph had landed a long residency. For Lulu it was one big summer holiday – not as exciting as when his father had a six-month assignment in Algiers and took his wife and children to be with him, perhaps – but Dinard had the bonus of a huge bonfire and fireworks display. Or that's how the sight of British troops setting fire to the coastal petrol reserves appeared to the boy at the time. But back in Paris by the following summer, things were very different. The Germans had taken the city. Government-sanctioned anti-semitism was officially launched. A law was passed requiring all Jews to register. The practical Olia hadn't wanted to, but Joseph insisted that since they were now French – which despite their strong Russian accents and taste for borscht and vodka he considered them to be – they should respect their adoptive country's laws. There were murmurs among the

Jewish community of disappearances; work – especially in the more visible jobs like journalism, art, theatre – was becoming harder for Jews to get as graffiti appeared across the city accusing them of stealing Frenchmen's jobs. The Ginsburgs didn't live in a Jewish community, they didn't keep a kosher house or go to synagogue; for a while at least, Joseph must have thought he was immune. Certainly life went on for the family with some semblance of normality. Joseph was still being paid to play piano at the Cabane Cubaine, and was earning enough to encourage his son's growing interest in painting by enrolling him in an art school in Montmartre.

Lulu's first year at the Academy coincidentally encouraged another of his growing interests. At the age of 13, he was too young to attend the nude life-drawing class but, passing by an open door one day, he saw the female model taking off her clothes. Hiding behind it he gazed, open-mouthed, at what he called her "striptease". It was absolutely overwhelming – whatever 'it' was. "I told myself, 'Something must happen with a girl, I just don't know what it is'," he told Bayon – the French author and journalist who published a book of two extraordinary interviews he did with Gainsbourg on the subjet of sex and death, *Mort Ou Vices*.[2] He was still a complete sexual innocent, he said. His father hadn't told him anything about the facts of life; the nearest to anything of a personal nature he'd imparted had been instructions on how to aim when pissing by keeping a firm grip on his *zizi*. When Joseph caught his son using the technique to different effect, aided by the airbrushed photos of women in the tame men's mag of the time, *Paris-Hollywood*, he merely ordered him to stop at once without any explanation why.

It was lucky Joseph hadn't told his son that wanking made you ill, otherwise the future *érotomane* might have turned out very differently. Because, not long after, Lulu was struck with a mystery illness, wasting away to a bag of bones. For a while it looked like he would go the way of his brother, until France's leading paediatrician – Olia was not going to settle for anything less for her darling boy – said that his only hope was to leave Paris and take the cure in the countryside. Not easy when the latest round of anti-semitic measures had banned Jews from travelling in trains (although, within the city limits, the last carriage of every metro had considerably been reserved for their exclusive use) or leaving town. But somehow the Ginsburgs managed, setting up temporary home on a farm in Courgenard – without Joseph, who was in Paris, earning the money to keep them there.

But while Lulu got better, Paris got worse. In 1942 the government issued the directive that all Jews over the age of six had to wear a yellow star – the size of a hand with 'Juif' written on it in black – clearly visible on their outer garments whenever they left the house. "His father would make them iron them so that they would look clean and proper for the French government," said Jane. "Serge would say that wearing the Jewish star was like being the sheriff and that he'd grown up under a good star, yellow." He might have joked about it later, but in truth it cut the sensitive adolescent to the core. "For me," he said in an interview more than 30 years later, "it is indelible. A young boy wearing the star – it was like you were a bull, branded with a red-hot iron."[3] It was a humiliation; a sign to everyone to see that you were part of a powerless group, officially despised, increasingly vilified in the press and open to physical attack from strangers. "Even at 13, 14 years old, I had already become an outsider, because the tough guy thing wasn't me." He fled into a smoky fantasy world of literature and cheap cigarettes (a heavy adolescent P4 habit – the French equivalent of Players No 6). "By reading the great story-tellers, Perrault, Grimm, Anderson, Hoffman", he said, "I had already escaped."

In Serge's memory of the sheriff's badge years, the French were worse than the Germans. At least, he reasoned, *les Boches* were only acting under orders. He remembered that day at the Art Academy – a safe haven of sanity in all the madness going on around it – and sitting in a classroom, drawing, right next to a German officer. Despite the yellow star, his fellow student gave him no trouble – quite the opposite, there was a sense of camaraderie, until they left the building and he stiffened back up into a German officer. And he spoke with bitterness of the way some of his father's fellow-musicians had begun to treat him, telling him, "'You, you've no right to be in this orchestra – you're a Jew, get lost.' They just wanted to take his place."[4] In the end they had their way. When an 8pm curfew was imposed on Jews, working as a nightclub pianist in Paris was impossible for Joseph. In desperation, he and another Jewish musician decided to illicitly make for the free zone in the South West.

After a long and dangerous journey, Joseph eventually made it to Limoges. He started working with a five-piece orchestra and sent money home via a network of friends and supporters. For almost eighteen months the family lived their separate lives, until one day a package arrived with false papers. The Guimbards, as they would now have to call themselves, should take the train, like any good gentile French family, and join him at his apartment on the Rue des Combes in the centre of Limoges.

Despite the risk of being caught, Olia was delighted to be leaving Paris. The food shortages were getting so bad that she had hidden her star in order to take a train to the countryside to get provisions for the children, and was very nearly arrested in the process. "She had worked out a way of putting little pins in the star so that she would pull a thread underneath her coat and all the pins would fall out so that she could go to the opera", said Jane, "because otherwise Jews weren't allowed in. She tried it when she was going out to buy food and a French policeman caught her and said, 'The next time you do that you're going to go straight into the train'." Olia's brother – the children's Uncle Michel – had gone into the train, winding up in Auschwitz, where he died. The deportations had increased, with Jacqueline very nearly among them.

Their journey to the South West, it turned out, was quite uneventful. There was an ecstatic reunion, and once again the family adjusted to a temporary new home. But even there they had to be careful what they did and who they spoke to. The Gestapo turned up at the apartment one day to check their papers and, knowing that the forgeries wouldn't stand up under close inspection, Olia had slipped them under the oilskin kitchen tablecloth where she sat on them, brazening it out and inviting them to search the place. Jacqueline's declaration that she wanted to join the Resistance didn't help matters – "much to their mother's horror", said Jane. "If it wasn't already dangerous enough being Jewish, to have her rush off and very possibly fall in love with someone from the Resistance – but she was the right age. So that was clamped down on immediately." Jacqueline and Liliane were sent off to a convent, while Lulu was packed off to a small free-school a dozen miles from Limoges.

One day, Lucien's headmaster learned that the military were coming back to make checks. He gave the boy an axe and sent him off to hide in the woods, telling him that if anyone should find him he should say he was the woodsman's son. "He said it was most exciting, like playing Robin Hood," said Jane. "He used to tell me he was hiding up this tree for a week, and I would imagine him up there with the children coming by with little food hampers for Serge, pretending they were going off on a picnic, but then Jacqueline said 'Oh, he was only up there for one night'. He romanticised many things."

Then, as every biographer knows, truth is an all too malleable concept, and doubly so with celebrities with a public history and image. Memory accidentally rearranges events; interviews often do it deliberately, and artists raised on fairy-tales do it better than anybody. So this is as good a place as any for an authorial declaration that any attempt, however sincere, however painstaking the detective work, to paint a completely faithful portrait of someone else's life is bound to end up more like a clumsy line-drawing, complete with spattered ink.

In 1944, the City of Lights was liberated and the Ginsburgs returned, slotting back as much as possible into their old way of life. But things had changed irrevocably for 16-year-old Lucien, when he went back to his old high school. Bad grades. Bad attitude. He had become a loner; he no longer felt part of the system. When he was in infant school they had given him a medal for being top of the class; he had worn it in the streets with pride; when he was at the *lycée* and equally good, they had given him a yellow star, which could have sent him to the camps.

It would be 30 years before he revisited the sherrif's badge era on *Rock Around The Bunker*. And, when he did, his approach was not pained or tortured but mischievous, scatological and caustically ironic. Nazibilly songs about Hitler, Eva and the Stormtroopers set to 50s American rock 'n' roll – wonderfully adolescent, a throwback to the age he was when he wore the yellow star. But the jokes were balanced with a black cover that bore a scrawled self-portrait. "I have never forgotten," he said, "that I ought to have died in 1941, '42, '43 or '44."[5]

But he had survived: the war, tuberculosis, the near-abortion. Life was a precarious business, and too short to waste in school. So he quit, just before his final exams (in later versions he would say they expelled him for bad behaviour). He was going, he announced to his family, to be an *artist*.

Chapter Two
DEATH OF A HAIRDRESSER

In 1945, the same year that he declared his intention to devote his life to art, Lucien lost his virginity. Alighting the metro at Barbès, he set off nervously to look for a prostitute. In addition to his natural shyness and timidity was an added element of guilt from having cadged the money from his unsuspecting mother. "The first ones he approached laughed at him and told to come back when he was old enough," said Jane. "Well he *was* old enough." Seventeen, but looking years younger, with not even the merest hint that he might one day need to shave.

The next group of women intimidated him so badly that he wound up picking the ugliest one who, on a grubby bed in a grubby room, chewed gum through the entire transaction. He found the experience so disgusting that he couldn't, or wouldn't, climax, waiting until he was home to take the matter in hand. Hardly surprising that he should later describe sex as *"onanisme, par personne interposée".*[1]

And yet there was something about paying for sex that appealed to Lucien and over the coming years he would continue to visit prostitutes, claiming to have had an affectionate relationship with several, even if only one of them had ever told him he was any good. "They mocked him," said Jane, "and he suffered terribly from that. So his vengeance later was to have the most beautiful girls in France."

There were plenty of beautiful women at the École Supérieure Des Beaux-Arts, the prestigious art school in which his father had enrolled him. (Although his decision to quit high school had horrified Olia, who saw her darling boy's future as a doctor or lawyer at the very least, it appeared to have stirred some latent painterly gene in Joseph.) If Lucien was slow on the uptake – by his own words a 'late starter', guaranteed by an almost puritanical attitude towards his body and a firm conviction of his ugliness – by 1947, two years into his studies, he had found a *personne interposée* that he didn't have to pay.

Although his attempts at an affair with an 18-year-old Russian aristocrat classmate – Olga Tolstoy, granddaughter of the celebrated writer – had ended in dismal failure, Lucien somehow found the confidence to approach another Russian aristocrat who was two years older than him (the same age difference that separated Joseph and the older Olia). Elisabeth Levitsky, a part-time model, was not only beautiful, thus answering Lucien's strict aesthetic requirements ("Painting has always been inextricably mixed into my sexual life," he said. "I've always had an *eye*"),[2] she was also more sexually forthcoming than La Tolstoy (of which, more later).

Elisabeth worked as secretary to the French surrealist poet Georges Hugnet, a friend of Salvador Dali. Dali's apartment on the Rue De L'Université was left unoccupied while the artist and his wife Gala were back at their home in Spain, and Hugnet had been given a set of keys to keep an eye on the place. Somehow Lucien and Elisabeth appropriated the keys and, on one delirious night that stayed tattooed in his memory, fucked in Dali's all-black living-room – its walls and ceiling covered in astrakhan, the curly black material used on old-fashioned coat collars – on a pile of priceless artworks by Miro, Ernst, Picasso and their unwitting host, scattered on the floor. Lucien left the apartment with a Gitane clamped between his lips, a future wife, a firm idea of the ideal in decor, a small black-and-white picture stolen from Dali's porn collection of two young girls eating each other out, and a reinforced belief that surrealism was the finest artistic movement there ever was.

In the year that had gone by since he'd switched his studies to painting from architecture (his original choice of a professionally oriented course might well have been a sop to his mother's future expectations for her only son) he had been experimenting in all kinds of movements – from figurative to impressionist to cubist and back again – in search of a style that fitted. But it was always the surrealists that drew him back. "My great regret," he said, "was not having lived during that time"[3] – the 1920s, when the literary-artistic movement led by poet André Breton flourished in France's capital. And although he later claimed he had never found his style as a painter, surrealism, with its surprise, shock and exaggeration, would have a major influence on his music.

In 1947, while continuing at Beaux-Arts, Lucien also enrolled in a simultaneous one-year course at music school to study composition, notation and theory – suggesting that even at this point he had some intuition that painting might not be the all-encompassing existence he had declared that it was. Elisabeth was also playing an increasingly prominent role in his life. Apart from anything else, she was keeping him – a fact which infuriated his father. When Joseph's lectures on fiscal responsibility and digs about having a gigolo for a son failed to have the desired effect, he hit on a more practical solution: he would hire a gypsy guitar player to teach his son to play guitar. It would be simple for someone of Lucien's musical skills to pick up, easy for him to carry around, and a good way of making some money at weddings and bar mitzvahs. He was right. Lucien loved the passionate, melancholic music the gypsy played, which had a good deal in common, he felt, with Slavic and Jewish music. And he was quick to adapt what he had learned to his own style – part Django Reinhardt, and a bigger part basic strum. With Joseph acting as unpaid agent, Lucien was set up on the party circuit, which he continued to play until, in the day in 1948 when the postman arrived at Avenue Bugeaud – the Ginsburg family's latest apartment in the far more salubrious 16th arondissement – with a letter from the French government ordering him into the army. Like every other 20-year-old Frenchman, Lucien had to perform 12 months of compulsory military service.

"Serge was the only person I've ever known who liked the *service militaire*," said Jane. "He learnt to drink in the army. I think, timid thing that he was, that he found that if he had a little bit too much to drink he was funny – he was the one standing on the chair telling jokes whereas before he would have gone red with shyness – and that he could suddenly have chums and take a girl out without being too worried."

Lucien had been offered an officership, merely on the grounds of having been evidently better-educated than the other recruits, but he turned it down, preferring to stay in the rank and file. It might not have been as glamorous as the French Foreign

Legion that Cole Porter had once belonged to, but the 93rd Regiment at Charras was, he said, "a universe of men. We talked dirty, strummed our guitars, sang stupid stuff and visited whores."[4] And, since he didn't get sent off to Algeria to fight, he had the time and opportunity to hone his skills in all of the above areas. He would perform on the guitar for his fellow recruits, making up dirty songs as he went along. He would amuse his new pals with his art college skills, drawing *"hyper-réaliste"* erotic pictures for them, then sit down and write passionate love letters to Elisabeth – once getting so worked up by his own skilful prose and artwork that he made an abortive attempt at deserting in order to make love to her. A short spell in the cooler was the result. But the 12 months passed quickly and, despite his protestations that he had tired of the never-ending competition – who could fart the loudest, drink the most, tell the the filthiest jokes – and that the promiscuity there depressed him, it was almost with reluctance that he took off his uniform and left the universe of men to go back home. "I went into the French army having never touched a drop of alcohol in my life," he would later claim, "and I left 13 months later, an alcoholic."[5]

✱✱ ✱✱✱✱

After their marriage in November 1951, life for Lucien and Elisabeth was starting to get markedly less bohemian. Whereas in the past they had lived in hotel rooms, at one time finding the celebrated French singer Leo Ferré their temporary next-door neighbour, at another sleeping in the very same room where Verlaine had fucked Rimbaud, they were now settled into an apartment in the Maison Des Réfugies Israelites. Both were working as teachers, Lucien giving art lessons to the young children of holocaust survivors at the nearby school.

"It was a boarding school," said Jane, "and some of them couldn't go home, and he knew conjuring tricks and would make them all sing. He would also make little paintings for the class and he knew how to frame them. He was like the Pied Piper – the children followed him everywhere. They loved that he would do things other grown-ups would never have dared to do. Because he always stayed childlike; that's what the mischievous attempt to always shock people was all about."

He was still studying art, as well as teaching it, and making some extra money colourising black and white movie photos for the local cinema and decorating fake Louis XIII furniture. But this wasn't enough to stop the workaholic Joseph to continue to come to him with offers of jobs as a musician. And these jobs were somewhat more upmarket than the wedding-and-bar-mitzvah circuit he had played prior to doing military service – piano-playing gigs in Parisian bars and nightclubs that Joseph had taken on to do himself, only to find he had double-booked himself elsewhere.

Being his father's stand-in paid more than teaching and painting. It also, he quickly discovered, had several other advantages; among them drinking and smoking on the job, getting to hear some great performers (Billie Holiday, Dizzy Gillespie, Art Tatum, Django Reinhardt) and finding himself in what he must have felt was the unlikeliest of positions of becoming a sexual magnet for the female clientele. So it did not take much persuasion on his father's part for him to agree to sit the exam to join SACEM – the French songwriters' society – in 1954, the same year that his twin Liliane married and moved to Casablanca and became an English teacher. He passed, graduating to playing summer seasons at the smart Northern coastal resort of Le Touquet. Now that he was away from home, he had plucked up the courage to croon along on his repertoire of French and American standards, Gershwin and Cole Porter, Charles Aznavour and Leo Ferré. His performances went over particularly well with the women, who would approach his piano with requests, not all of them musical. "Being a bar-pianist," he said, "is the best education"[6] – musically, sexually and alcoholically.

The art teaching had long since fallen victim to Lucien's new way of life, as had his painting. Finally his marriage followed suit. In 1957, after his third summer in a row in the Club De La Fôret in Le Touquet, Elisabeth filed for divorce. The reason cited on her application to dissolve the marriage was Lucien's adultery (in particular with an unnamed Englishwoman, the wife of a wealthy sweets manufacturer). That the bohemian artist she had married now wore a sharp suit and no longer touched a paintbrush would probably not have been recognised by the French courts of the time as legitimate grounds for divorce.

His reason for giving up painting, he told *Rock & Folk* magazine, was "I wanted to have an artistic genius, and all I had was talent."[7] Said Jane, "He was a rather sweet painter, but he wanted to be avant-garde. He realised that it wasn't avant-garde, that it wasn't good enough, so he broke one of his paintings over his first wife's head. He gave me the half of it, which stupidly I've lost – it was on a piece of wood, not very thick, thankfully, so it wouldn't have hurt too much – and it was fairly classical with a rather beautiful, sort of Renoir-ish girl on it. But he had to be the best, and with painting he knew what was the best and that wasn't it.

"I think the thing he admired most was painting. I remember when I was in the Orangerie restaurant with Serge and my father and I said 'There's Francis Bacon over there'. Serge said 'How do *you* know?' I said, 'Because I've seen pictures of him in London and I've also seen his paintings and he looks exactly like one of his self-portraits.' Serge said, 'So go and ask him for an autograph then'. He gave me a 100F note, and I went up to his table and said 'Are you Francis Bacon?' and he said he was and very sweetly wrote his autograph for Serge. I think they would have got on very well; they were not dissimilar – both very shy and sweet – and Serge adored Bacon's paintings.' He especially adored their power – he had read once that after the opening of one of Bacon's exhibitions, two men killed themselves. 'He said if he couldn't be Francis Bacon he'd tear up his stuff. Serge was not a modest man, therefore he didn't want to be a second class painter; he wanted to be a first-class songwriter."

In the summer of 1954, Lucien registered the first six songs he had written – "sophisticated, cynical songs mostly, about not being loved, that he didn't dare to sing himself," said Jane. Among them were 'Les Amours Perdues' ('The Lost Loves') and 'Défense D'Afficher' ('No Bill Stickers') which would be covered in 1959 by Juliette Gréco and Pia Colombo respectively. The two women – Gréco the strikingly beautiful existentialist vamp, with her white face, black hair, heavy eye make-up, and big black, beatnik sweater and tapered pants; Colombo less successful but with the same sense of Left Bank cool – came out of the *Rive Gauche* scene which had sprung up, after Paris was liberated from the Germans, around the cellar nightclubs in Saint-Germain-des-Près to become the centrepoint of the post-war spirit of freedom and creativity. He adored Gréco, and was terrified of her too; in his early days of playing nightclubs he had spotted her in the audience but couldn't get the courage to approach her. He'd tried calling her office once in the hope she would sing a song of his, but he was given the brush-off; he was just another unknown.

As he was filling in the registration form at SACEM, Lucien decided he would change his name. "I never felt right in my name," he said.[8] People were always mispronouncing or misspelling Ginsburg – as they had done since Joseph had become a naturalised Frenchman. Doubtless there was still baggage too left over from the days when to have a Jewish name meant trouble. But his first name was the one he was happiest to lose. Before he could get anywhere as a serious songwriter, he concluded, Lucien – and Lulu – must die.

"He thought it was a loser's name," said Jane. "He said it reminded him of hairdressers – they were always called Lucien. Serge, he thought, sounded more Russian. And he chose Gainsbourg because he loved the English painter Gainsborough. Lucien Ginsburg was this shy Jewish refugee who thought he was ugly and who the prostitutes used to scream at because he looked so young. Serge Gainsbourg was like putting on a suit of armour. Afterwards, little by little, he started to sing his songs himself. He was very frightened. He couldn't remember his own words because they were so clever, so he wrote them down on a piece of paper, and when his hands would shake so much in front of the chic nightclub audiences he would roll the paper up into a little ball and chuck it at them and they'd burst into applause. He appeared arrogant, but it was because he was really so terribly shy."

Things had progressed to where he had a regular slot at Milord L'Arsouille (the Left Bank nightclub he would describe as "one of the last to hold onto the *Rive Gauche* spirit").[9] Not only was it the place where the French revolutionaries had first publicly sung their anthem, 'La Marseillaise', it was also where Charles Trenet had started out – the man whose song, played over the tannoy on the beach while the pretty girl walked past, had been responsible for little Lulu's epiphany all those years ago. Serge had the job of playing piano in between the acts.

Two of those acts would have a big effect on his music and career. The first was Boris Vian – novelist, producer, agitator and jazz fan, who had started out writing songs for his own amusement and had been persuaded to try performing them himself. When Serge heard him sing at Milord in 1957, he was bowled over by the man's attitude and his cruel, caustically funny songs. "Through Vian, I understood that the song might not be such a minor means of expression," he said, "but a vehicle for my aggressive potential to break through".[10] The second significant person was Michèle Arnaud, the popular *Rive Droite* singer (she had a hit in 1958 with a French cover of Paul Anka's 'Diana') whose Left Bank-flavoured songs appealed to liberals among the Right Bank crowd. Arnaud, who had a residency at Milord, was the first artist to have faith in Serge's songs. On a visit to his parents' apartment, where Serge had moved after his separation from Elisabeth, she spotted the manuscript paper on the piano. He confessed to being a songwriter and played her a batch of his latest compositions, including 'Douze Belles Dans La Peau' and 'La Recette De L'Amour Fou'. She declared her intention to sing them onstage, and did so for the first time at Bobino, a theatre near Montparnasse. A journalist covering the early 1958 performance namechecked Serge's songs in his article – Gainsbourg's first review, and a favourable one.

Word spread about this curious singer-songwriter and his sad, caustic songs. Among the Left Bank intellectuals nodding coolly in the audience was Denis Bourgeois, one of the house-producers at French record company, Philips (Boris Vian was another one), who was sufficiently impressed with what he was hearing to recommend that his bosses offer Serge a contract. Papers were signed, a studio was booked and an arranger brought in to work on the songs – film composer Alain Goraguer, who had previously collaborated with Vian. And in 1958, at the age of 30, Serge was no longer an unknown with the hairdresser's name but a recording artist, label-mates with Gréco and French institutions George Brassens and Jacques Brel.

Chapter Three
LOOKING AT THE SKY

Serge's debut album *Du Chant À La Une!* (Songs On Page One) – nine tracks on a ten inch record, the diameter of choice of that period – was released in September 1958. The cover shot depicted the artist with one raised eyebrow and a hard, heavy-lidded stare that was equal parts challenge and cool detachment. It was the face, said French newspaper *Libération*, of a killer.[1]

It was a remarkable record. The music – a combination of elegant cocktail jazz, cool, existentialist beatnik-jazz-pop, and French *chanson* – had an innate ease and fluidity; and the lyrics – all written by Serge, apart from 'Ronsard 58' a co-write with French economist Serge Barthelemy – were variously cynical, arrogant, vulnerable, scathing, sophisticated, provocative and cruel, but always fascinating. Equally, if not more, fascinating for the Anglo fan who discovered Gainsbourg via *Histoire De Melody Nelson* or even 'Je T'Aime, Moi Non Plus', was his singing. *Singing* – not the breathy, close-to-the microphone murmur that he would introduce on *Initials B.B.*, but a croon, somewhere between languid and limpid, shot through with an almost American (or at least, at that time, un-French) sense of rhythm and swing. "When I knew him", said Jane, "he would never once put on any of his early stuff because he couldn't bear hearing himself when he used to sing in that high voice."

There were songs about removal men ('Le Charleston Des Déménageurs De Piano'), booze ('L'Alcool'), a couple in a car crash ('Du Jazz Dans Le Ravin') and the ticket puncher at the metro station who shoots himself because he can no longer bear an existence filled with nothing but little holes ('Le Poinçonneur Des Lilas'), as well as the more expected subject matter of the opposite sex. But in these early songs of Serge's, women existed merely to be cheated on ('La Femme Des Uns Sous Le Corps Des Autres'), manipulated ('La Recette De L'Amour Fou'), shrugged off ('Douze Belles Dans La Peau') or tossed aside when the man was tired of them ('Ce Mortel Ennui'). That last song might well have been the story of Serge's failed marriage to Elisabeth; when Michèle Arnaud once asked him why they had broken up, he said it was because his wife – whose body was expanding rapidly – no longer conformed to his 'ideal of beauty'.

Serge was by no means the first to introduce misogyny to French, or any other, popular music (witness Jacques Brel's 'Les Biches', to name but one), it's just that they seemed incongruous from someone who seemed to so love women, and his words cut with the skill and precision of a surgeon wielding a scalpel. Surprisingly, the origins of Serge's misogyny were neither his early experiences with prostitutes nor his insecurity about his looks, but a thwarted love affair when he was 19 years old.

You might recall the first Russian aristocrat that Lucien had fallen for prior to

Elisabeth – Olga Tolstoy, granddaughter of Leo, the author of *War And Peace*. Serge certainly did. He never forgot how smitten he had been, how amazed he was that she seemed to like him too. He certainly never forgot that night when they wound up in bed together, when she told him she was a virgin, and he was ready to deflower her. Then at the last minute she got cold feet. She promised to come back the next night, but she didn't. He was inconsolable – furious that, as he saw it, he'd been duped, that he'd let her get away. As he told it to Bayon, he bore the grudge for years, until one night in 1960, when he was in Algeria to appear on a TV show, and Olga showed up at his door.

He barely recognised her, he said. In the 13 years that had passed, marriage, children and life had changed her for the worst. And, what was more, their positions were reversed – *he* was the one with the name now, and *she* was the one who wanted *him*. "In the end," he told Bayon, "she was nothing. And me? I was *me*." He turned her away. Finally he had his revenge. For what – a young girl's last-minute nerves or change of mind? "For her desertion," he said. The fact that she'd said she would come back and didn't. "The suffering! It was dreadful. Dreadful. That, perhaps, is where my misogyny came from: that Tolstoy woman. The bitch."[2] There are few unholier trinities than literature, rejection and sex.

The job of penning *Du Chant À La Une!*'s liner-notes was given to Marcel Aymé, Henry Miller's French translator and the author of cool, cynical modernist books. "Serge Gainsbourg is a 25 year old piano player," he wrote, conveniently lopping five years off the newcomer's age, "who became a songwriter, lyricist and singer. He sings about alcohol, girls, adultery, fast cars, poverty, miserable jobs. His songs – inspired by the experiences of a youth which life did not favour – have an accent of melancholy, bitterness and, above all, the directness of a police report. They are set to spare music" – six musicians including Serge, on piano, guitar, double bass, drums, saxophone and vibes – "in which, in contemporary fashion, the concern for rhythm eclipses the melody. My wish for Gainsbourg is that fate might shine on him, especially since he deserves it, and that it brings some splashes of sunlight into his songs."[3]

It was not a hit. Then no-one really thought it would be – except Serge. As biographer Gilles Verlant wrote, "you were not seduced by Gainsbourg's songs, you felt attacked by them." His producer Denis Bourgeois knew that the songs were not going to appeal to French radio, which – in spite of the rock 'n' roll anarchy reigning across the Atlantic, with D.J.s vying to play the latest Elvis and Jerry Lee, Chuck Berry or Fats Domino – had stayed resolutely stagnant, dictating a strict formula to the studios of clean, heavily orchestrated, nicely sung, unchallenging material. Not only did Serge not look like the average *chansonnier*, he did not sing like one. And unlike the more modern French singer-songwriters like Jacques Brel and Georges Brassens, who essentially set poetry to music, Serge's words, uniquely, were welded to the music. A part of the rhythm, with an inbuilt music of their own, while still managing to retain their intellectual content. His audience, Bourgeois figured, would be the sophisticated Left Bank club crowd who appreciated modern, cynical music. And Serge's music, in Bourgeois's opinion, was the most modern and cynical he'd heard. It was a sentiment shared by Bourgeois's fellow producer at Philips, Boris

Vian – the man whose own caustic, uncompromising songs had been such an inspiration to Serge at Milord's.

Vian wrote the first major article to appear on Serge Gainsbourg. Raving about *Du Chant À La Une!* in the magazine *Canard Enchaîné* (*Private Eye* is the nearest British equivalent), he ordered his readers to go out and buy it – "quite understandably," said Serge, "since I never hid the fact that I followed directly on from him. I had a fixation on Boris Vian. An hallucinatory charm. He wrote the first article about me. It ended with 'Damn, you're fools if you don't buy Gainsbourg's record.'"[4] Not long afterwards, when Vian invited him to his house behind the Moulin Rouge, his host took a book of Cole Porter's lyrics off the shelf, opened it up and told an ecstatic Serge, "You have the same patterns of stress and intonation, the same technique of pushing back and alliteration."[5]

But, Vian aside, Serge did not get too much support from the music press – not that there was much of a music press in France in the late 1950s in the first place. There were a couple of reviews ranging from lukewarm to largely favourable, a couple of fluff pieces planted by the record company, and a news item that his tale of the suicidal ticket-puncher in 'Le Poinçonneur Des Lilas' had raised the hackles of metro station staff at what they saw as an innacurate portrayal of one of their associates. Serge replied that the song had been inspired by a true conversation he'd had with the ticket-man at Lilas station. "What do you dream about all day when you're doing this?" Serge had asked him. His reply: "Of looking at the sky." The song – which would be covered by three different French artists within a year – became a post-war standard.

✳ ✳ ✳ ✳ ✳ ✳

It was partly the lack of other means of marketing their non-conformist new signing that resulted in Serge's appearance on another album that year. *Opus 109* was a compilation of new faces, unknown talent, recorded live at the Trois Baudets, a small, 350-seater theatre in Montmartre. Philips thought the record and its accompanying French tour – featuring a big star headliner, Jacques Brel – would help raise Gainsbourg's profile. To an extent it did, athough the first live review from the tour wouldn't have done much to entice an already indifferent record-buying public. While acknowledging the "poetry" of his songs, the critic from *Libération* wondered aloud if Serge, with his "wan face and washed-out voice"[6] had made the right decision to sing the songs himself. Still tormented by paralysing stage-fright, even brought on by his short, four-song slot near the bottom of the bill, you might wonder if Serge had wondered too. But when Yves Montand – the actor and seductive, velvet-voiced singer who'd covered songs by populists like Maurice Chevalier and poets like Jacques Prévert – once asked him if he wanted to be a composer, performer or writer, Serge answered *"Je veux tout"* – "I want it all."

He had the kind of enormous appetite for fame, success, recognition and love that you don't often find in the product of a structured and loving family; Serge could never quite fit the cliché of the pop star under the spotlight demanding the attention he never got in his childhood, or the clown making people laugh to mask a profound misery. Nor did writing songs appear to be a tortured business. Though the words might take a bit of work, the melodies, he said, came easy – a consequence of having to summon tunes out of the air in his years as a nightclub pianist. He gave birth to his songs *"comme une négresse"* in the bush, making a big hole in the earth, squatting down in it, watching the song just come tumbling right out. His feeling of being an outsider came from a different source. Asked to analyse it himself, he once said it was because when his parents left Russia, they had left behind his roots. They still showed in his music – "My music is Judeo-Russian; always something sad"[7] – but he had no grandparents, no ancestry, no land he felt was truly his. "I would have loved to have had roots. To be a man you need roots," he told *Actuel* magazine. "I am rootless."[8]

If his records weren't flying off the shelves, the recognition factor took a big step forward when, part way through the *Opus 109* tour, Serge learnt that *Du Chant À La Une!* had won the grand prize of *L'Academie Charles Cros* – a kind of cultural-artistic Grammy for songwriters crossed with a more grandiose version of Britain's Ivor Novello Award. And an even larger stride followed when, shaking so much from nerves that he dropped the glass of whisky she offered him, he found himself in Juliette Gréco's apartment clutching a pile of his songs. Gréco had taken a couple of years off to be with her lover, Darryl F. Zanuck, the filmmaker, and she had been scouting for the best new songwriters for her comeback record. Once again Serge grabbed the grand prize. In 1959 the EP *Juliette Gréco Chante Serge Gainsbourg* was released. (Extended Play records, four tracks with a nice picture sleeve-cover, were the prime medium for pop releases in France at the time; singles were mainly produced for jukeboxes.) Serge was overjoyed. He gave Gréco one of his paintings as a gift – two naked children on a beach. Although he had claimed to have destroyed all his canvases in that dramatic moment when, like Joseph before him, he had decided to give up painting, he'd evidently been shrewder than his father and kept a couple for emergencies.

Serge now had three women covering his material – Gréco, newcomer Pia Colombo, and Michèle Arnaud, who no doubt was feeling a little crowded out by her protegé's newfound popularity, though she faithfully continued to sing his songs. But it was Serge's friendship with Gréco that raised his fame quotient. Newspapers and magazines ran pictures of the pair on the town together, and journalists began their enduring practice of wondering what such a beauty was doing with such a "beast". They called him *"un monstre"*, *"un Neanderthal"*. Serge might well have agreed with them; Lucien certainly would have. He'd said that he didn't have mirrors in his room because he'd broken them all with his "ugly face". As Robert Chalmers (a supporter) wrote in *The Independent*, "Gainsbourg's self-image, in his less upbeat moods at least, resembled that of the French poet Tristan de Corbière, who for years kept a dead and flattened toad nailed to his bedroom wall: he said it saved him the trouble of looking at his reflection." Even the descriptions Serge's male friends gave of him painted a picture of E.T. dressed as a dandy with a cigarette. It would be quite some time before he could simply give a Gallic shrug and say, "Ugliness has more going for it than beauty does: it endures." His face, like his music, was unorthodox, unmainstream, uninterested in rules and formalities, and utterly distinctive.

And it did come with its own advantages. The director of a daft French film starring Brigitte Bardot, *Voulez-Vous Danser Avec Moi?* (*Would You Dance With Me*), was hunting around for someone to play the sleazy photographer who blackmails Brigitte's cheating husband – a dentist – with compromising pictures, when he spotted Serge on the sleeve of *Le Poinçonneur De Lilas* (one of two EPs that flanked *Du Chant À La Une!*). He knew at once he'd found his perfect

creep. It would be the first of many such bad-guy roles that Serge would undertake in his second, simultaneous career.

By the end of 1959 Serge had a second full album and its two satellite EPs (*Le Claqueur De Doigts* and *L'Anthracite*) in the shops. The prosaically (it probably wasn't scatologically) titled *Gainsbourg No 2* – mutant jazz-pop engaged in an unnatural act with *chanson*, French literature and Americana – wasn't quite up to the extraordinary standard of its predecessor; then again, he hadn't had much time to write it, having spent much of the year out on tour. But it had its moments. The cool, 'Fever'-esque 'Le Claqueur De Doigts' (The Finger-Popper) the guy standing by *le jukebox* snapping his fingers is given onomatopaeic, syncopated words with their own in-built snap and pop; Serge had taken his word-music fusion to another level. 'Mambo Miam Miam' was a nod to the exotic dances that were all the rage at the time, in Britain as well as in France, while, at the other extreme, 'La Nuit D'Octobre' (The Night In October) was based on poem by Alfred De Musset – one of his worst poems, Serge said later, which is how he dared to take the liberty of adapting it.

Again it was not a hit. "Aggressive, introverted jazz" as Gilles Verlant described it, with literary language, was not what the postman wanted to whistle on his rounds. There were some fans among the critics though; the leading newspaper *Le Monde* wrote of his "absolute frankness of tone, his obvious concern at never going along with something that has already been said or done", and the fearless way in which he looked at the world "through the piercing eye of a man who is not afraid of what people will say about him."

The sleeve photo portrayed a smart, besuited Serge with a gun in one hand and roses in the other (predating the L.A. heavy rock band by almost 30 years). He said that it perfectly encapsulated his outlook – a gun for his critics, roses for his women. Though it was also, clearly, an homage to his early mentor, the supreme wearer of the sharp Italian suit Boris Vian. In June 1959, during a preview of the movie based on his novel *J'irai Cracher Sur Vos Tombes* (*I Will Spit On Your Graves*), Vian suffered a heart attack and died. A low point in what was otherwise an exhilarating year for Gainsbourg, one which ended with his first magazine cover story.

LA SEMAINE Radiophonique

XXVIII⁻ ANNÉE
Nᵒ 43

HERDOMADAIRE
25/10/59

La Vedette de la SEMAINE
Serge GAINSBOURG
par Germaine RAMOS

C'EST un garçon qui ne ressemble à personne — et qui fait des chansons comme personne !

Il est grand, très frêle, timide d'aspect, de voix... vous parle si bas que vous l'entendez à peine. Rien, oh ! certes, du garçon fanfaron et content de lui. Mais il fait des chansons qui vous arrivent dans le cœur, et l'estomac « coupe le point ». Il y éprouve tout, rien ne l'arrête, ni la pudeur inutile, ni la peur de choquer. Il a toutes les audaces, mais il a l'originalité, et la maîtrise. Il n'imite personne, ne cherche jamais à faire joli, ou gentil, aimable ou commercial.

Avec lui, rien de banal, de convenu. L'idée est toujours étonnante et le mot celui qu'on n'attendait pas. Il vous donne, avec quelle ironie amère, la « recette de l'amour fou », raconte un accident mortel dans « le jazz du ravin », conte les malheurs du « conducteur des Lilas », chante l'alcool...

Mes illusions donnent sur la cour,
Mais dans les troquets des Ilmebourgs
J'ai des ardoises de rêverie
Et le sens de l'ironie !...

Sûrement que chez lui ce sens domine à plein ? Il évoque les femmes avec cruauté et on a l'impression que pour cet esprit audacieux, rien n'est sacré...

Qui, c'est un « type ». Il faut le prendre tel qu'il est avec son talent décongertant, provoquant, avec son « intelligence » destructrice. Il est sans concession, et ne veut pas « se faire » !

Ses sujets ? des problèmes éternels : l'amour, l'aventure, l'alcool, les aventures de la vie... mais il prend à sa manière, qui n'est pas celle des autres. Son auditeur est d'abord, parfois, choqué, incompréhensif, ou rébarbatif, puis il est peu à peu conquis. Parce qu'il est difficile de résister à l'intelligence ! Difficile aussi de résister au charme, curieux qui se dégage des enregistrements de ce garçon qui a l'air d'un chanteur, mais qui dit ses chansons mieux qu'une personne. « Tout » est surprenant, prenant, la voix murmurante, un peu rauque, bizarre, au souffle bref, le mélange d'ironie mordante et de désenchantement, l'élégance de la prononciation, unie à quelque chose d'indéfinissable, qui est le ton de la gouaille faubourienne... Il est implacable, sent-il, parce qu'il est, sans l'avouer, trop vulnérable, et qui sait ? trop tendre...

Serge Gainsbourg est russe d'origine et il a fait diverses études avant la chanson. Après avoir été élève à Condorcet, il a été aux Beaux-Arts où il a travaillé l'architecture « mais la peinture l'a tenté et retenu, et il a peint tant ans. Mais, arriver dans la peinture, en vivre, même, n'est pas facile. Il faudrait être aidé, trouver un mécène. Gainsbourg était musicien depuis l'enfance,

ayant beaucoup travaillé avec son père. Un jour, sur sa guitare il a composé des chansons ; on l'a encouragé. Des artistes les ont chantées et lui-même... Croit-il en lui ? On ne sait pas. Ce qu'il voudrait c'arriver à pouvoir peindre à nouveau, c'est sa passion ; s'il se libérait par le succès de ses chansons, il pourrait être son propre mécène...

Il fut pianiste de bar, puis guitariste ; il a accompagné Michèle Arnaud qui, toujours à l'affût des chansons de qualité et ne craignant pas de lutter pour les imposer, a été sa première interprète. Lui-même a fait son tour de chant à Milord l'Arsouille, aux Trois Baudets, en tournée, etc.

Ses premières chansons parlaient d'amour (*Nul ne le saura jamais... Ça vaut pas la peine d'en parler*). Il les estime sans intérêt. Il faut arriver au fameux « poinçonneur » pour qu'il commence à se reconnaître dans ses œuvres !

Il reconnaît qu'il a été très amer, en face de la vie, mais il l'est moins, ça va mieux ! Pour faire une chanson il part sur un titre qui doit tout contenir. Son grand défaut, c'est d'être « sceptique », il dit que c'est aussi sa principale qualité... Il est ambitieux à coup sûr, a de hautes aspirations. Il ne saurait souhaiter rien de médiocre et il croit au fond en son destin...

Étrange artiste, étrange garçon, qui préfère à toute autre la phrase de Baudelaire : « L'étrangeté est une des parties intégrantes du Beau ». Savez-vous ce qu'il aime ? « Beaucoup les orages, beaucoup le whisky aussi, passionnément les amours contrariées » (en général à ce point de vue, tout humain est gâté !...) À la folie, les femmes hautaines et réfrigérantes. Pas du tout : l'académisme de l'art contemporain ».

Il nous apporte quelque chose — quelque chose de nouveau, de bizarre, de tourmenté, de profond, d'ultra-moderne. Car chez lui la musique veut les paroles, parfois il doute, parfois brutale, « implacable dans sa ligne mélodique », « le choque, sarte, sconce, boulverse. On ne demeure pas indifférent en l'écoutant ; on l'adore ou on le déteste. Mais même alors, on doit reconnaître : « Gainsbourg, c'est quelqu'un ! »

PETITE NOUVELLE

LA R.T.F. remettra au Pape Jean XXIII pour le premier anniversaire de son couronnement un disque comprenant des extraits de ses discours durant sa nonciature à Paris, et des déclarations de personnalités françaises ayant connu le Souverain Pontife.

VIENT DE PARAITRE

L'ALMANACH 1960 de Radio-Télé-Luxembourg. Abondamment illustré, il comprend des confidences, des enquêtes, des nouvelles, de nombreux échos sur les émissions de Radio-Luxembourg ou de Télé-Luxembourg, des jeux, des reportages et le grand Test psychologique d'André Robs.

Pierre Destailles (à gauche) et Maurice Teynec, dans « Les Aventures de Sherlock Holmes », tous les lundis, à 21 h. 20, sur le Régional.
(Photo R.T.F.)

les idées et les faits

« Il a remporté tous les suffrages de celui qui a su mêler l'utile à l'agréable », écrivait Horace dans son « Art poétique ».

C'est parce qu'ils cherchent à remporter tous les suffrages que les directeurs de programmes, dans les stations radiophoniques, s'emploient à organiser des émissions agréables à entendre et utiles à écouter. Service public, la Radio tend de plus en plus à se devoir pour toutes ses antennes, qu'elles soient officielles ou qu'elles soient privées. De plus en plus, entre un tiré de jeux et une retransmission d'opéra-comique, se glissera à longueur de journée des conseils pratiques et des renseignements utiles qui s'adressent à tous les milieux, à tous les sexes et à tous les âges.

Depuis « Le passe-temps des dames et des demoiselles » et la « Rendez-vous à cinq heures », en passant par « La route en direct », « Europe-Santé » et « Enquête à la médecine », tout ce que peut si doit savoir un auditeur conscient et organisé pour faire face aux multiples problèmes de la vie quotidienne, lui est dispensé, expliqué, détaillé par petites tranches facilement assimilables. C'est une manière d'école universelle sur les ondes, et nombreux sont les élèves qui en suivent les cours avec assiduité.

À l'intention de ces derniers, signalons deux chroniques nouvelles qui vont prendre place dans les émissions « Vous et nous » diffusées par France II. Chaque semaine, M. Pierre Gazotte répondra aux auditeurs qui signaleront les incorrections de langage qu'ils auront relevées dans leurs écoutes. M. Pierre Gazotte étant, comme chacun sait, membre de l'Académie française, on ne contestera pas sa compétence pour discuter prononciation et syntaxe et rendre des verdicts autorisés.

D'autre part, chaque semaine également, Mme Gisèle Dasailly, femme de lettres et femme du monde, donnera aux auditeurs des conseils de savoir-vivre ou, plus exactement, de savoir écouter. Non pas pour diriger les auditeurs dans le choix des programmes, mais pour leur indiquer la manière de se comporter dans leurs écoutes quotidiennes. Car il en est de la Radio comme de l'automobile : il y a cent manières de conduire et toutes ne sont pas bonnes. C'est pour choisir la meilleure que Gisèle Dasailly entend prodiguer ses conseils et ses avis. Heureuse manière d'adapter « l'art radiophonique » les règles préceptes de l'art poétique du poète latin.

Dans ce numéro :

La Semaine Radiophonique wrote of their 'Star of the Week', "He's a guy who's not like anyone else and whose songs are like no-one else either. He is tall, very frail, shy, with a voice that speaks to you so softly you can scarcely hear it... But the songs he writes hit you in the heart and stomach like a punch. In them he expresses every-thing – nothing stops him, not useless modesty nor fear of shocking... He imitates no-one, never tries to make things pretty or sweet, likeable or commercial." Serge would have nodded when he read that; he had always said he "detested" sentimen-tal songs. "With him there's nothing banal, nothing conventional. The ideas are always stunning and the words unexpected." Although concurring that he "wasn't much of a singer", the writer, Germaine Ramos, concluded that what he had was "something new, bizarre, tormented, deep and ultra-modern. Love him or hate him, you're going to have to recognise that Serge Gainsbourg is *somebody*."[9]

Somebody, though, who, at the age of 31 – just eight years younger than Vian when he died – was still living at home with his parents, sitting at Joseph's piano; Gitane *sans filtre* in hand, black coffee and a bottle by his side, reshaping the songs that would change the face of French pop music, even if the French pop music audi-ence were only interested in hearing them sung by somebody other than Serge.

Chapter 4
LE TWISTEUR

In 1986, the singer Françoise Hardy and the broadcaster Anne-Marie Simmond – the latter a professional graphologist, the former an amateur astrologist – published their joint opus *Entre Les Lignes Et Les Signes* (*Between The Lines And The Signs*) which analysed the charts and the handwriting of various French celebrities. Mme Simmond, endorsing the *Semaine Radiophonique* journalist's views, wrote that Serge's penmanship (which Jane Birkin had said was deliberately elaborate and stylish; "He liked the writing to be just so; he'd decided at a very young age, as an aesthetic idea, that he wouldn't bar any of the 't's or use any punctuation – he thought commas and full-stops were vulgar – so it was quite difficult to read his letters") indicated a man who knew he was somebody. It also showed a man, she averred, who was proud and vain but did not really like himself, and who was haunted by the idea of another more interesting life that he had managed to miss out on. Françoise Hardy's study of the constellations on 2 April 1928 pointed to above-average ambivalences and contradictions, an eager, egocentric and sometimes immature nature, and a tendency towards defeatism that was fortunately balanced by an ability to boldly venture into all of life's strange and funny possibilities.

This could be one of the reasons why the finest pop writer France has produced found himself starting the '60s, the Golden Age of pop and rock, dressed as an unmusical first century A.D. official of Ancient Rome in dreadful Franco-Italian sword-and-sandal epics like *La Révolte Des Esclaves* (Revolt Of The Slaves), *Hercule Se Déchaine* (Hercules Unchained) and *Samson Contre Hercule* (Samson v Hercules). Nasty characters, all of them. "No-one knew how to employ me as an actor," he said. "They always gave me bad-guy roles because of my ugly face."[1]

The first acting job his new agent had found him was as Corvino, the man who sent the Christians to the lions, in 1961's *La Révolte Des Esclaves*. After killing Sebastian (the future Saint), Serge's character ended up being ripped apart by his dogs (a canine acting feat aided by the insertion of a piece of raw meat down his breastplate). Years later, when Jane went with Serge to see *Des Esclaves* at a cinema in Barbès – the *quartier* he had once scoured in search of a prostitute, and which now had a large immigrant population – the audience cheered mightily when Corvino/Serge was savaged. As Jane turned to tell him what a great acting job he had done to have got such a strong crowd reaction, she saw that he had shrunk down into his jacket like a turtle into its shell and suggested they sneak out before the credits in case the audience attacked him too.

His first release of the new decade, in January 1960, was likewise a film-related project. The EP *L'Eau À La Bouche* (Mouth-Watering) came from Serge's first film soundtrack; it also brought him his first real commercial semi-success. The popularity of the comedy by Jacques Doniol-Valcroze, one of the new wave of French directors, about two sisters, their boyfriends, a dead grandmother and an inherited manor, pushed sales of the EP (on which he worked with arranger Alain Goraguer) to the 100,000 mark. Serge released a second soundtrack EP – from another film that year, *Les Loups Dans La Bergerie* (Wolves In The Sheep-fold) – before his real '60s debut, *Romantique 60*, appeared. Surprisingly not an album but another EP. Between them, the three 1960 EPs displayed what would become something of a Serge Gainsbourg trademark: the creative recycling, reshaping and collageing of his own titles, words and songs. *L'Eau À La Bouche*'s instrumental 'Judith' reappeared as a vocal ballad on *Romantique 60*, while 'Cha Cha Cha Du Loup' was a title that had made its initial appearance on *Les Loups Dans La Bergerie*.

Serge's third album, *L'Étonnant Serge Gainsbourg* (The Astonishing Serge Gainsbourg), finally came out the following year, in 1961. The information on the album sleeve that it was *"bon pour la danse"* (good for dancing) wasn't what was astonishing about it; working on the theory that music was to dance, not listen to, French records at the time were tagged with whatever movement of arms, legs and body some anonymous music business star-chamber had deemed appropriate. 'Judith', for instance, on *Romantique 60*, had been designated 'un slow'. (It was a custom that continued well into the mid '60s, if this writer's French vinyl compilations of British and American acts is anything to go by; Dylan's 'Just Like A Woman', for example, is another 'slow', while The Troggs' 'Wild Thing' and The Walker Brothers' 'Living Above Your Head' are each allocated the 'jerk').

Why anyone would choose this album to dance to, though, is rather hard to say. And if musically it wasn't as immediately astonishing as *Du Chant À La Une!*, lyrically it most certainly was. Less hard-edged and scathing, his words this time were either cynically cerebral – 'En Relisant Ta Lettre' (On Re-reading Your Letter), where the protagonist reads his lover's suicide note and comments on her grammatical errors – or romantic and literary. French literature students will have observed references in the songs 'Le Rock De Nerval', 'La Chanson De Prévert' and 'La Chanson De Maglia' (after Victor Hugo).

There was something of a tradition in France of fusing pop and literature – Charles Trenet had set some of Verlaine's poems to music, Leo Ferré did the same with Apollinaire, even the po-faced Jean-Paul Sartre had been set to music by Jospeh Kosma for Juliette Gréco to sing – but if Serge couldn't take credit for being the first, he might well have been the most extraordinary with his textual variations on literary themes. He had decided to go to Jacques Prévert's house himself to ask permission to use his name – maybe an outbreak of insecurity about his own writing, which he insisted wasn't literature; more likely grabbing the excuse to meet him. He knocked on the door at ten o'clock in the morning, to find the poet – no stranger to the pop world (Gréco and Yves Montand had already sung his 'lyrics') – merrily quaffing champagne, which he was happy to share. A man after Serge's own heart.

The tour that followed the album garnered some good reviews, but didn't win over the crowds or help his record sales, which stuck at around the 5,000 mark. In spite of a small but loyal following – intellectual students and collegiate *Rive Gaucheurs* mostly – and a growing number of singers wanting to interpret his songs,

Serge's audience appeared to have bottomed out. And, with the '60s invasion of France by the Americans and the Brits – first *Le Twist*, with *Les Yé-Yé* following close behind – it seemed ever more likely that Serge would stay way out on the side-lines.

Rock 'n' roll had been in full-swing in the U.S. and U.K. for years. Bill Haley – three years older and with less hair and more body fat than Serge – had already had 14 rock 'n' roll chart hits on both sides of the Atlantic by the mid 1950s, *and* played a Royal command performance in front of the Queen; and Buddy Holly had lived and died (the same year as Vian, in a plane crash) while France was still listening to cocktail-jazz and *chansons*. But things were about to change, and the man taking chief responsibility was the moon-faced Pennsylvanian, Chubby Checker. After 'The Twist' topped the U.S. singles chart twice in 1960 and 1961, followed by the international hit 'Let's Twist Again' and, albums *Twist With Chubby Checker*, *For Twisters Only*, *Let's Twist Again*, *Twistin' Round The World*, *For Teen Twisters Only* and a film *Don't Knock The Twist*, *le Twist* writhed its way into the Gallic con-sciousness as it had done in the rest of the world.

What had started out as another dance craze had taken on a new dimension. The Twist was like God, it was everywhere – Sam Cooke's 'Twisting The Night Away', Bobby Rydell's 'Teach Me To Twist', the Isley Brothers' 'Twist And Shout' – soon to become The Beatles' 'Twist And Shout' – the list goes on and on. The Twist, Leonard Cohen once said, was "the greatest ritual since circumcision." As for Serge, "He didn't talk about 'rock', he talked about 'twist'," said journalist Christian Eudeline. "He liked the word. To him it meant rebellious pop – which had been made so antiseptic. But also he knew wasn't part of this big *la vague Twist* – Twist Wave – the pop scene of the early '60s."

The *Twisteurs* and the *yé-yés* (named for the seemingly compulsive inclusion of the words 'yeah yeah' in British pop songs) struck terror into the heart of the con-servative French music business. Kids of 15 or 16 years of age were hauled off the street and into the studios to flood the country with French versions of Gerry & The Pacemakers and Cliff Richard songs. The 19-year-old Françoise Hardy made an album called *C'est Fab*. The teenage hit-maker Johnny Hallyday had been poached from Vogue and signed to Philips, guaranteeing an even further descent for Serge down his record label's list of priorities. Even French radio, a mighty bulwark against change, had surrendered and added a yé-yé show for the kids, *Salut Les Copains* (Hi, Pals), soon to spawn an enormously popular teenzine of the same name. Television followed, adding a number of adolescent-friendly programmes.

Serge – by now in his 30s – was wretched. "When these guys with their electric guitars arrived," he said, "I felt, it's all over for me." He seriously considered, he told France-Inter radio, giving up the music business and going back to painting where there were "no contracts and no compromises" – although there was never really a question of quitting the music business since he was never really a part of it in the first place. He had always done things the things the way he wanted to do them; and, since no-one was quite sure what to do with him, he was generally left to get on with it unmolested. Instead he went back home to his parents' flat, sat at Joseph's piano and and wrote the resolutely un-twistable 'Requiem Pour Un Twisteur'. A song, he

explained, about "a guy who twists so much he dies from it."

'Requiem Pour Un Twisteur', with its cool Hammond organ, was one of the highlights of Serge's fourth album, 1962's *No 4*. Others were the jazzy 'Ce Grand Méchant Vous' (That Big Bad You), the bluesy 'Black Trombone', 'Les Cigarillos' – which he described as "a tribute to the smoke that allows me to isolate myself" and 'Intoxicated Man', another nod to Boris Vian via his song 'Je Bois', and the title chosen by Mick Harvey of Nick Cave's Bad Seeds for one of his two '90s Serge tribute albums. Years later, when it reappeared in Gainsbourg's retrospective box-set, *The Guardian* described the original version of the song pretty accurately as "the James Bond song rewritten by Baudelaire".

It came out the same year that The Beatles released 'Love Me Do'. So, another non-hit. If sales were never great for Gainsbourg, yé-yé made things worse. Even if his lyrics had incorporated the now-trendy Franglais and had namechecked hip

American consumables when these new French acts were still in nappies, he looked like these kids' fathers. And his music and words had a substance and intelligence that no-one appeared to want – except singers of the old school, like Gréco, for whom he had written the lovely 'L'Accordeon', and Catherine Sauvage, who had followed Gréco's lead by recording her own EP of Gainsbourg songs.

Then Serge had a brainwave. If it was the English sound that the French people wanted to hear, he would make his next record in England. "He was always very bright," said Jane, "he twigged onto things before anybody else, and he liked the English sound better." He recorded his first made-in-England EP, 1963's *Vilaine Fille, Mauvaise Garcon* (Bad Girl, Naughty Boy) in London with Harry Robinson.

"A lot of the French guys used English musicians", said Alan Hawkshaw, composer of the theme tunes to *Grange Hill*, *The Champ* and *Countdown* among many others, and in the '60s and '70s one of Britain's leading British keyboard session players. "And Serge always used the cream of the session musicians."

Though it avoided absorbing too much of 'Swinging London', *Vilaine Fille, Mauvaise Garcon* was a big leap forward. The title track was a hit for Petula Clark – though not for Serge; 'L'Appareil À Sous' (Slot Machine) was a hit for Brigitte Bardot – again not for Serge; 'La Javanaise' (several meanings: the people of Java, a rave-up, a popular waltz and tribute to Boris Vian's 'La Java Javanaise') with its superb lyrics with their own in-built rhythm and musicality, was covered by Juliette Gréco; the only one of the four tracks that appears to have remained untouched was the gleefully rhythmic and surreally titled 'Un Violon, Un Jambon' (A Violin, A Ham).

Meanwhile, the actor's life beckoned once again, this time in *L'Inconnue De Hong Kong* (The Unknown Woman From Hong Kong). An apt title, since few ever heard of the film, and Serge's only memories of it, were accompanying its director to the red-light district to see a particularly gruesome porn film starring a girl and a dog, and the plane in which they flew back to Paris hitting a typhoon and very nearly coming down in the sea (a handy experience, no doubt, when eight years later he would get around to writing *Histoire De Melody Nelson*).

Serge released two other EPs in 1963, *Strip-Tease* and *Chez Les Yé-Yé*, the latter taking a dig at the mindless teen pop that had shunned him in 'Chez Les Yé-Yé' (With The Yé-Yés) and 'Les Temps Des Yoyos' (The Time Of The Yoyos).

Strip-Tease – a jazzy EP featuring arrangements by Alain Goraguer and the Anglo titles 'Some Small Chance', 'Wake Me At Five' and 'Safari' – was lifted from the soundtrack Serge wrote to the 1963 film *Strip-Tease*. Its director Jacques Poitrenaud, a friend of Serge's, asked him to appear in the film as the piano player in a jazz band in addition to writing the score. Banned in France for its nudity, it starred Christa Paffgen as a dancer desperately seeking work in the nightclubs of Paris. Serge had taken the statuesque German blonde into the studio to record the theme song, but he didn't like her sombre, death's-head voice and binned the tape. It would be another two years before Paffgen moved to New York, where she was taken up by Andy Warhol and introduced into The Velvet Underground under her better-known name, Nico.

The song was recut by Gréco, but not without some difficulty; the singer spoke of her dread at having to try to sidestep Serge's latest conquest, the beautiful, but highly possessive, Béatrice. Françoise Antoinette Pancrazzi, the name Béatrice was born with, was 32 years old, three years younger than Serge, when they married in 1964 (the same month that The Beatles played the Olympia in Paris, sharing the bill with Sylvie Vartan, Johnny Hallyday's wife). Though, like his first wife Elisabeth, Béatrice came from a well-to-do family, there the resemblance ended. Elisabeth had favoured a bohemian existence, whereas Béatrice promised the good life – a fine apartment in a great address behind the Madeleine for starters and a slew of expensive gifts. On one occasion she bought Serge a gold watch from Tiffany's – then threw it out of the window when Serge, as he often did, came home drunk. When the couple made up she went back to Tiffany's and bought him the same watch upgraded to platinum.

Serge knew his new partner was jealous – he probably enjoyed it to a certain extent, as a lot of insecure men do – but as early as his wedding day he realised, he said later, that he had made a mistake. As they left the ceremony, Serge was approached by a female fan. His new wife hit the roof.

Negotiating a path that allowed him to meet up with his predominantly female clientele and keep his marriage going was proving a tough order, but Serge made it to the first anniversary, which Béatrice celebrated in typically extravagant fashion by presenting him with a Steinway grand. In fact it was a shrewd move on her part. As a means of escaping from her, for the odd night at least, he had told her he was going to his parents' apartment on Avenue Bugeaud to write songs at Joseph's piano. With a Steinway at home he now had no excuse to leave. So he threw himself into his work, and 1964 saw two albums, two EPs (one of them another film soundtrack), two singles and a number of songs for other artists to sing.

Gainsbourg Confidentiel – his first 12-inch album – was spare, sophisticated jazz with a rock-swing element, on which he was joined by two jazz musicians he'd seen performing in Bud Powell's band in a Paris club, Elek Bacsik and Michel Gaudry. The contents of the *Chez Les Yé-Yé* EP were joined by eight new tracks, several of them with Anglo(ish) titles – 'Le Talkie-Walkie', 'No, No Thanks No', 'Negative Blues' – plus the fine 'La Fille Au Rasoir' (The Girl With The Razor) and 'Sait-On Jamais Où Va Une Femme Quand Elle Vous Quitte' (Do You Ever Know Where A Woman Goes When She Walks Out On You). A quick album to make – it took just a couple of days to record, with Guadry and Bacsik given a lot of room to manouevre and a lot made up as they went along – it also brought him some of his best reviews so far, with the important French newspaper *Le Figaro* praising his "nonchalance, keen eye, sombre voice and icy irony". Serge enjoyed working with the electric guitar player and acoustic bassist so much that he kept them around to do his next film soundtrack, *Comment Trouvez-Vous Ma Soeur?* (How Do You Find My Sister?), which featured 'Rocking Horse', 'No Love For Daddy', 'Marshmallow Man' and the wonderfully-named 'Éroiticotico'. Sex songs, then.

At the same time he was working on a new album, the significant *Gainsbourg Percussions*. Lively, Afro-Latin jazz-rock, Serge was accompanied on his first foray into world music solely by percussion instruments and twelve female backing singers – French women told to sing like Africans, since the real thing wasn't so easily available. Turning the usual French studio hours on their head, they recorded from 9pm to 5am and emerged with an exotic, rhythmic, experimental yet still highly listenable record. In later interviews, Serge would say it had been his attempt at updating stale French music without going the yé-yé route and copying styles already established as successful by the Anglo-Saxons. He had listened to a lot of African music, he said, including Miriam Makeba records and a real Watusi war chant – listened so closely to some that posthumously he is still being sued, by a U.S. based African musician, Olatunji, who alleged marked similarities to three songs on his record *Drums Of Passion*. He then hit on his theory that what French pop music needed to rescue it from its torpor was percussion, its sound jarring wonderfully with the smooth sounds and harmonies of French pop. The African rhythms added a touch of Gauguin-esque exoticism, while percussion, he said, was the musical equivalent of abstract art's take-over of figurative painting.

The album's memorable characters included Joanna, the corpulent dancer from New Orleans, and Jeremie, who had let his lover tattoo him all over and doesn't know what to do now he doesn't love her any more. That laugh you can hear on 'Pauvre Lola', incidentally, was supplied by a French popette by the name of France Gall.

The critics could have been kinder, but their relative lack of enthusiasm was understandable at a time when The Beatles' 'She Loves You' was topping the charts. And *Percussions* was ahead of its time. But nevertheless, Serge was happy. Milord L'Arsouille, the club were he had worked as a journeyman piano player, had invited him back for a one-month residency as headliner. And his wife Béatrice had made him a first-time father of a baby girl he named Natacha.

Chapter 5
BABY POP

In February 1965, Serge received a request from Barbara, *"la Grande Dame de la Chanson"*, to open up for her on tour. They called Barbara the "Lady In Black", the dramatic, glamorous Left Bank *chanteuse* who, along with Gréco, was one of the very few females to gain entry into the ultra-private, intellectual, Brel-Brassens club. The Anti-Yé-yé, in other words. In spite of the paralysing stage-fright which still afflicted him, and the fact that his last live shows had not been well received, he said yes. Perhaps life with Béatrice and a baby was already becoming too claustrophobic; or maybe he simply liked the idea of playing to audiences who knew him from his old days as a nightclub performer (which is where he had met Barbara) and who would appreciate him for the sophisticate he was instead of deriding him for the popstar he wasn't.

It must have been doubly mortifying for Serge, then, when those very same people booed him. Total public humiliation – like being mocked by the whores in Barbès but, under a stage spotlight, magnified a hundredfold. Admittedly, at that time – when he still had the singing voice that Jane said he later couldn't stand to hear – he was not the most confident of live performers. Barbara told biographer Gilles Verlant of seeing Serge shaking with nerves backstage before going out to perform. After a particularly bad reaction from the audience mid-way through the tour, he sat up talking with her half the night, finally telling her he wanted to leave. He did. And didn't set foot on a stage again for another 13 years.

Back in Paris, stuck between the proverbial rock and a hard place – the yé-yé crowd didn't like him because he was too old-school; the old-school, it appeared, just didn't like him – Serge was disconsolate. Although there were still plenty of artists covering his songs (even the bespectacled and virtuous Nana Mouskouri), his own versions had got him nowhere; and with the pop charts in 1965 almost completely taken over by British and American artists (even the biggest French copyists with their Franglais translations were being nudged out of the picture by the originals, The Beatles, Bob Dylan and the rest) his hopes, at the age of 37, of becoming a popstar were getting dimmer by the minute. "I want to be a star in '65," he announced to an interviewer. "I've waited six years; that's enough." How he planned to do it, he said, was by "throwing myself into rock – real rock." He would write, he declared, a dozen hit rock songs that year.

And then he won the Eurovision Song Contest.

The annual competition, these days a byword for kitsch and unspeakable pop cliché, was launched in 1956 by the canny continental music industry as a means of bringing non-Anglo Saxon Europop music to the attention of a wider audience – although the U.K., with its usual hesitant attitude towards all things European, refused to have anything to do with it until it looked like it might be successful and joined in the following year. Serge's song 'Poupée De Cire, Poupée De Son' ('A Lonely Singing Doll' was the English title it was later released under by Twinkle) was sung by France Gall, one of those barely pubescent popettes the French are still so fond of. A sweet 16-year-old yé-yé star with an innocent moon-face and a Beatley mop of blonde hair. 'Poupée...' was catchy, and on the surface pretty annoying – perfect Eurovision fodder in other words – but closer examination revealed perspicacious lyrics about the ironies and incongruities inherent in baby-pop: young people setting off to discover life and, particularly love to the accompaniment of songs sung by a young person too inexperienced to know what they're singing about and, in addition, condemned by their celebrity status to being the kind of outsider who would not quickly learn. "Alone sometimes I sigh, I ask myself what good it does to sing about love without ever having known... the warmth of a boy," sang little France (though in French, of course) before concluding hopefully, "But one day I will live my songs."

It easily trounced the competition (including British entry Kathy Kirby's not entirely memorable 'I Belong') to take first prize – for Luxembourg. France hadn't wanted it. One would have to suspect sour grapes on their part to discover they were the only country that failed to award 'Poupée...' the highest points.

Serge's introduction to the world of baby-pop had come the previous year. Philips, had signed up the young France Gall, and Denis Bourgeois – the man who had not only set up Serge's record deal but his publishing company – thought it would be highly advantageous to the latter if the two new labelmates got together. A meeting was set up between Serge, Gall and her omnipresent father and producer. He played them a new song he had written, 'N'Écoute Pas Les Idoles' (Don't Listen To Idols) and she liked it; the words reflected her ambiguity towards her new-found fame. Alain Goraguer spent the morning arranging it for a four-piece pop band; in the afternoon they went into the studio and recorded it and, almost as quickly, it was a hit. Ironically, the yé-yé that had almost made Serge give up music brought him his first big chart success. And unlike poor young France Gall, it didn't trouble him in the least.

The press called Serge's little singing doll a "breath of fresh air" and wrote of her "gaiety and enthusiasm". The teen magazines in particular descended on the dazed Eurovision prize-winner, bombarding her with the usual pertinent interview questions. Was Serge her ideal guy, they asked? No, she said, she preferred blond-haired blue-eyed boys but she liked Serge because he was "odd". Did they plan to get married? No, but she would continue to sing his songs because he managed to capture her very essence in his words. She was still too naive to understand that the essence of her that Serge had captured in two subsquent songs he wrote for her, 'Baby Pop' and 'Les Sucettes' wasn't quite the one that she had in mind.

Concealed among the words of 'Baby Pop', with its portentous refrain – in translation: "Sing, dance, Baby Pop, as if tomorrow, Baby Pop, might never come; Sing, dance, Baby Pop, as if tomorrow, Baby Pop, in the early hours of morning, Baby Pop, you must die" – was a fatalist pushing forty, an ironist rather than a reckless teenager abandoning herself to pop. And to all but the most innocent, 'Les Sucettes' (Lollipops), about a little girl called Annie who loves to suck on lollipops until the *anis* (that aniseed flavour that the French so love in their drinks, Serge – a great fan of Pastis 51 included) runs down her throat – evinced a middle-aged male defilement fantasy more than it did an adolescent girl's sugar cravings. Sadly, France Gall *was* the most innocent. When, after it became another hit, its meaning was pointed out to her, she was mortified, hiding herself away for weeks, refusing to face anyone. When she did finally comment, she attested that she had sung Serge's songs "with an innocence of which I'm proud. I was pained to then learn that he had turned the situation to his advantage, mocking me"[1]. Serge was unrepentant. "It's the most daring song of the century,"[2] he said in an interview with *Rock & Folk*. Double irony was that a cosmetics company approached his publishers for permission to launch a range of Baby Pop beauty products, aimed at just such little girls.

Some years later Serge would say, "it was France Gall who saved my life," because until she sang his songs, "when it came to young people I was totally out. I don't regret that part of my life at all. Suddenly I still existed."[3] His popularity as a hit songwriter had soared; his name seemed to be on the credits of half of the singles released by female singers in the mid 1960s in France. There was Petula Clark with 'O O Sherrif' and 'Les Incorruptibles'; nightclub singer Régine, (aka 'Queen of the Night') with 'Les Petits Papiers'; actress and pin-up Valérie Lagrange (the first woman to pose naked for *Lui*, France's then-equivalent of *Playboy*) with 'La Guérilla'; Brigitte Bardot with the delicious 'Bubble Gum'. Serge's wife Béatrice, by all accounts, was even unhappier at this new breed of women he had been working with since breaking into the yé-yé market than she had been when her path crossed with the magnificent Juliette Gréco.

At least his part-time acting career seemed to offer the opportunity of some room to breathe, so after an almost two-year absence Serge took a role in the TV series *Les Cinq Dernières Minutes* (Last Five Minutes), playing a tramp suspected of murder who is finally cleared and set free. According to legend, once again – as with *The Slaves' Revolt* – his acting skills were such that strangers came up to him in the street after it was aired and congratulated him on his release from jail. He followed it up with a part in *L'Inconnue De Shandigor* (The Unknown Of Shandigor) which – praise the heavens – would necessitate spending a fair bit of time in Switzerland. In the end though, he gave in to pressure and took Béatrice with him. But once the film was over and they were back in Paris, he packed some clothes and left. A succession of Parisian hotel rooms followed, Serge switching location each time his wife tracked him down. After finally discovering how she always managed to find him – friends in high places had the police run checks on all the hotel registers – he moved into Swiss director Pierre Koralnik's apartment.

Finding peace and quiet at last, Serge worked on songs for his own next record which had been due in the summer but which he had failed to release. And the end of 1965 found him back in England, recording a four-track EP with Arthur Greenslade and his "extrêmement pop" orchestra. *Qui Est In, Qui Est Out* (Who's In, Who's Out) – released in early 1966 – also featured 'Shu Ba Du Ba Loo Ba', influenced by some music he heard in a Soho nightclub, the enduring 'Marilu', and the classic 'Docteur Jekyll Et Monsieur Hyde'.

But the rock stardom he had hoped for failed to materialise. Instead he set himself up as a one-man songwriting factory, churning out songs over the next two years for clients from the sublime to the ridiculous. He answered his critics – among them his flatmate Koralnik who accused him of "casting pearls before swine" by tossing off song after song for lesser talents – by declaring that he was "incapable of mediocrity. I'm quite capable of coming up with a number of farces like 'Les Sucettes'. But to write mediocrities, even for a lot of money, is something I could not do."[4]

There were songs for, among others, Sacha Distel, Dominique Walter (Michèle Arnaud's wannabee-popstar son), and the Egyptian singer Dalida (a kind of exotic Cher, who would go on to be a big gay disco icon in the '70s), for whom he wrote 'Je Préfère Naturellement' (Naturally, I Prefer), an 'All I Want For Christmas Is A Beatle'-esque throwaway, about a woman loving four pretty Englishmen with their long hair and clergymen's boots and lace collars like little English lords (*"comme tous les Anglais"*!). He also wrote two more for France Gall – 'Nous Ne Sommes Pas Des Anges' (We Are Not Angels) and 'Teenie Weenie Boppie', which, taking account of the burgeoning psychedelic scene, was about a little sweetie putting acid on her sugar lump and blowing her mind. Serge even took a shot at writing a second Eurovision winner – for Monaco this time, 'Boum Badaboum' sung by one Minouche Barelli – only to be thwarted by the British who won their first Eurogong with Sandie Shaw singing 'Puppet On A String' (its title echoing the song he had written for France Gall).

The reason for this seemingly indiscriminate productivity had been to "take people who were in fashion, work for them then get myself out smartly without having really compromised myself," he said. "It opened up the record market for me and allowed me to then put out whatever I liked."[5] But hadn't he always put out whatever he had wanted? And this failed to explain why he had agreed to a request from the Israeli embassy to write an inspirational march for the use of their army during the Six Day War...

But there *were* mid-60s Gainsbourg gems. Like 'Les Papillons Noirs' (The Black Butterflies), written for Michèle Arnaud's comeback record. And, more importantly, the soundtrack to Koralnik's TV musical *Anna*.

✳ ✳ ✳ ✳ ✳

In the years that had passed since she first championed Serge at at Milord L'Arsouille, Michèle Arnaud had given up singing to become one of the most powerful TV producers in France. It was she who had introduced Serge to Koralnik and was backing *Anna*, his tale of a young man who works in an ad agency who becomes obsessed with the girl he comes across in a photograph, searching Paris high and low for her like Cinderella's Prince Charming, before noticing – when his loyal assistant Anna finally takes off her glasses – that she'd been there under his nose all along. For the leading role Koralnik pictured a wild, beautiful foreign woman – someone like Serge's friend Marianne Faithfull. In the end the part went to Anna Karina, the 26-year-old Danish former model and actress married to (and appearing in the early films of) Jean-Luc Godard.

Sandwiched between the slinky instrumental opener 'Sous Le Soleil Exactement'

(Under The Sky Precisely) and bold, contemporary orchestral-rock closer 'Je N'Avais Qu'Un Seul Mot À Lui Dire' (I Have Just One Word To Say To Him) was some splendid music – like the rock-meets-Country & Western 'Pistolet Jo' (Pistol Jo) and 'Un Poison Violent, C'Est Ça L'Amour' (A Violent Poison, That's What Love Is) which namechecks Serge's future friend and associate, Princess Margaret's husband, Anthony Armstrong-Jones. Some are half-sung, half-spoken by Serge or *Anna*'s co-star Jean-Claude Brialy, and the rest are topped by Karina's small, coy, breathy voice – it was the first time the actress had ever sung. The smart, atmospheric, sound-effects stuffed arrangements were down to Michel Colombier, Alain Goraguer's replacement.

"French rock before there *was* French rock," declared Serge. "An attempt," said the critics, "to fuse intelligent words to *un rhythme de jerk*." The dance, not the pastime. Meanwhile, 'Hier Ou Demain' (Yesterday Or Tomorrow) – a song written for the musical but not on the album – was recorded and released on a separate EP by Koralnik's *Anna* of choice, Marianne Faithfull.

"When I was 17," said Marianne, "and a big hit in France, I was in Paris a lot and I got to know Serge very well. He was a poet, a genius, an egotist, and I suppose in today's terms extremely arrogant. Humble wasn't in Serge's book, none of that nonsense; he knew exactly who and what he was. Exactly the sort of person I have always got on with. Plus he was an incredible Anglophile – that's one of the reasons he got into Jane and me – and we became very good friends."

Friends, not lovers. "We never had a relationship based on any kind of sex thing. Sex was one way of relating with Serge – probably his favourite way with a woman. But all I did know was that for me to go the Jane route, to fall in love with him, have sex with him, marry and have children, would have been a disaster – partly because having children is not my thing; I'm just not a nurturing kind of person. We had a philosophical affinity, a serious platonic friendship based on surrealism, poetry and Oscar Wilde. I was a fan of his from the very beginning – even before he was a singer, when he was a poet – so of course I wanted to be included. And naturally he wanted me to be in *Anna* and he wrote this song for me called 'Hier Ou Demain'. It was all so natural; the next step after that little TV film would have been for us to write together." The fact that Marianne was neither in *Anna*, nor wrote with Serge was, she said, "just one of those things; you're into your own vision at the time and you put things on the back-burner and don't do them right away, and then it's too late."

After *Anna* was broadcast in early 1967, Serge moved out of Koralnik's apartment and into a place of his own – a tiny flat in the Cité Internationale Des Arts Et Lettres, a kind of centrally located low-rent, Peabody Building, established by the novelist and art historian André Malraux to provide short-term housing for artists of all media and nationalities. He stayed there for two happy years and might have stayed even longer if he hadn't already long over-run the maximum one-year tenure. Recently divorced from Béatrice, he appeared to be making the most of his new 'Salut Les Copains' – approved eligibility status (he had finally been featured in the yé-yé bible, alongside the likes of Johnny Hallyday, Eddy Mitchell, Françoise Hardy and France Gall) and was leading a full social life. However he still found the energy to write an astounding number of songs for other artists and to go to London to

record his own next EP.

Comic Strip – with its cut-out letters cover, a decade ahead of The Sex Pistols' *Never Mind the Bollocks* – was recorded with David Whitaker and producer Giorgio Gomelsky (who, a fine example of the *entente cordiale*, had worked with both The Yardbirds and Johnny Hallyday). Its all-Anglo titles – 'Comic Strip', 'Hold-Up', 'Torrey Canyon,' 'Chatterton' – encompassed comic books, robbery, an oil tanker disaster and the death of a poet, set to a quasi-Booker T. riff. Serge was on fine form.

And the music just kept on coming. Three other EPs in 1967 featured selections from soundtracks he'd written to two films – *L'Horizon* and *Toutes Folles De Lui* (All Crazy For Him), the latter boasting titles like 'Goering Connais Pas' (I Don't Know Goering), 'Le Siffleur Et Son One Two Two' (The Whistler and Sound One Two Two) and 'Woom Woom Woom' (er, Woom Woom Woom), and a TV show, *Vidocq*. He also turned out music for the James Bond-esque film *Carré De Dames Pour Un As* (Four Queens For An Ace), *L'Espion* which starred Montgomery Clift, and *Les Coeurs Verts* (Green Hearts).

After scoring and acting in *Le Jardinier D'Argenteuil* (The Gardener of Argenteuil), Serge took a role opposite Jean Seberg in *Estouffade À La Caraibe* which, contrary to the title, was shot not in the Caribbean but in South America. And memorable only for Serge spending 13 hours in a Colombian jail – nothing to do with the local prositute he'd brought to the set to watch him play his part from the folding canvas chair marked 'Gainsbourg', but for the crime of reckless smoking. After lighting one of his 60 daily Gitanes in a flimsy, bamboo-clad restaurant, he tossed the match over his shoulder and accidentally set the place on fire. The toughest part of the experience, he would always say, was that he had to spend his entire time behind bars without a cigarette – since his defence to the cops who took him away had been that he didn't smoke.

In July 1967, while shooting another film, *Ce Sacré Grand-Pere* (That Darned Granddad), Beatrice turned up on the set to announce that she was pregnant with his second child. His ex-wife had been one of the women he had been squiring during his time at the Cité Internationale, a temporary reunion which had come about on a visit to see his daughter Natacha. Shortly to be joined by a little brother, Paul. But when Serge moved out of the artists' dwellings he didn't move back in with Béatrice and the children. Once again, Joseph and Olia got their son's room ready for him on Avenue Bugeaud. Any thoughts his ex-wife had that he might change his mind and return to his other family must have been dashed when, in October 1967, Serge went on Sacha Distel's TV programme *The Sacha Show*, and renewed his acquaintance with Brigitte Bardot.

Chapter 6
INITIALS B.B.

"There's a trilogy in my life," said Serge in *Mort Ou Vices*, "an equilateral triangle, shall we say, of Gitanes, alcoholism and girls – and I didn't say isosceles, I said equilateral. But it all comes from the background of a man whose initiation in beauty was art."[1] Brigitte Bardot – or 'B.B.', as the French call her; pronounced *bébé*, translation 'baby' – was the actress for whom the term 'sex-kitten' was invented. Playful, unselfconsciously sensual and dangerously beautiful, Bardot, since her 1952 screen debut in *Girl In A Bikini*, had become an international superstar – though more as a result of her appearance in her husband Roger Vadim's 1957 film *And God Created Woman* than for her recording career. Bardot had been signed by Serge's record company Philips in 1962 and she had already released two singles that her labelmate had written – 'L'Appareil À Sous' (Slot Machine) and 'Bubble Gum', her oddly-detached vocal making Serge's soon-to-be patented ennui sound positively over-excited – before they both found themselves booked to appear on Sacha 'Raindrops Keep Falling On My Head' Distel's prime-time Saturday night TV show. It was 1967, barely two months after the so-called Summer of Love, and Serge fell for B.B. mightily. She was, Sacha told Verlant, "the dream of Serge's life."

It must have seemed like a dream come true to find that Bardot was attracted to him too, and that their latest rendezvous should happen at the exact same time that her second marriage – to Gunther Sachs, the much-photographed, medallion-wearing, millionaire international playboy – was on the rocks. She invited him to appear on her *Le Bardot Show*, and what started as a working relationship soon developed into a love affair.

A discreet one to start with; unlike Serge, Bardot had a horror of press attention. They would meet furtively at friends' apartments, before caution was thrown to the wind and the paparazzi would regularly snap them at all the top niteries or in Bardot's convertible Triumph Spitfire (Brigitte at the wheel; Serge couldn't drive), gliding through a Paris plastered with photos of B.B. in thigh-high boots and black leather mini-skirt straddling a motorbike – an advertisement for her latest Serge-penned single, 'Harley Davidson'. On her show – whose video-clip approach was years ahead of its time for France – the stream of Gainsbourg classics inspired by his new love or demanded by her producers were performed by the pair of them in a veritable *Cher Show* of costume changes and with various outlandish backdrops of the cod-psychedelic variety that you only ever saw on '60s TV shows. For 'Comic Strip', for instance, Bardot was made up as a black-wigged Barbarella character, surrounded by bright 'comic-book' balloons bearing the sound-effects 'Zip!', 'Pow!', 'Wiz!' etc. For 'Bonnie & Clyde' – not to be confused with Georgie Fame's far less noir UK hit of the same name – Serge played the part of Clyde in shirt sleeves, shoulder-holster and cigarette, while B.B. in a long skirt, short wig and beret was his loyal moll.

It was an intense relationship, very sexual, as Serge's arranger Michel Colombier testified to Verlant. He and Serge were scheduled to work together one day and the singer didn't show; when Colombier phoned him he apologised, saying that he was running a little late. By evening Serge had still not arrived. Colombier phoned a second time. It wasn't his fault, Serge told him. "Every time I put my shirt back on, she takes it off again." Her nickname for Serge, apparently, was *"gueule d'amour"* – 'love face'. But the women's magazines and scandal papers of France had a quiet different take on his appearance and the debate that had begun when he was seeing Juliette Gréco was resurrected. Column inch after column inch deliberated on why such a celebrated beauty should pick such an "ugly" man. Bi-linguists might ponder on the fact that the French word for 'ugly' is *'laid'*.

"Ugly-beautiful is what it's called, I believe," said Marianne Faithfull. "Serge was incredibly attractive, in a Mick Jagger kind of way. He was also very sexual. This is a man that you know – *I* always knew – that if you did go to bed with him you would come out of that room well-pleased. *Seriously* well-pleased."

Years later, asked by inteviewer Bayon to analyse his attraction for women, Serge came up with "a cocktail of nonchalance in my gestures, and the aura of celebrity of course, plus a sense of movement in space, a sort of – I would say – *class*."[2] At the time, though, he simply gave a Gallic shrug; after all, he was going out with the most beautiful woman in the world and they weren't. And he was in love. His liner-notes to their joint 1968 album *Bonnie And Clyde* declared, "These songs of Brigitte's and mine are, above all, love songs – combat love, passionate love, physical love, fictional love. Amoral or immoral, it doesn't matter, they are all totally and utterly sincere."[3]

The title track was one of two songs that Serge had written in the space of a night following a disastrous early date with Bardot. Either struck dumb with nerves, or alcohol, depending on whose story one believes, his usual wit deserted him, the evening was a flop and he thought he had blown it for good. But she phoned the next day and demanded as a penance he write her "the most beautiful love song you can imagine". 'Bonnie And Clyde' was one of them. The other was 'Je T'Aime, Moi Non Plus'.

* * * * *

Late one night in the winter of 1967, Serge and Bardot went into a dimly lit Barclay studio in Paris and recorded Michel Colombier's arrangement of 'Je T'Aime, Moi Non Plus' in an intimate two-hour session, the two singers squashed into the same small, steamy glass booth. Very intimate, apparently; what engineer William Flageollet described to Verlant as "heavy petting". Word leaked to the press that it was an *audio verité* recording, with Sunday newspaper *France-Dimanche* reporting that the four minutes 35 seconds of "groans, sighs, and Bardot's little cries of pleas-ure" set to almost church-like organ music gave "the impression you're listening to two people making love." Being journalists, of course, the next thing they did was call up Bardot's husband and ask him what he thought of it. His reply made the next day's headlines: Furious Gunter Sachs Demands The Single Be Withdrawn – something which Bardot's agent was adding her voice to less publicly, behind the scenes. Bardot was about to star with Sean Connery in an international film and it was not a good time for a scandal. And, apart from that, Bardot hated scandals. She wrote Serge a letter pleading with him not to release it.

Serge protested: "The music is very pure. For the first time in my life I write a love song and it's taken badly." But he had witnessed the thin line between love and hate that the press and public so evidently had for her and put the tapes away in a drawer. They would stay there until 1986 when, six years after her last record release, 'Toutes Les Betes Sont À Aimer (All Animals Are For Being Loved), recorded to raise money for the French equivalent of the RSPCA, she finally gave permission for their "sublime" version of 'Je T'Aime…', as Serge described it, to come out.

"Well we all know Bardot is an idiot," grunted Marianne Faithfull of the original decision to proscribe the song. "Of course when Serge had her she was in peak condition, tip-top form – but always very conformist." Serge had later asked Marianne to do the song with him. "Hah! He asked *everybody*," – including actress-singers Valérie Lagrange (the former pin-up) and the beautiful Mireille Darc (Alain Delon's ex-wife), the latter very nearly coming to fruition.

"I don't know why I turned him down," mused Marianne. "I would say, to my shame, that I was wrapped up in the beginning of my affair with Mick Jagger and *he* wouldn't have liked it either. Maybe I was too young, maybe I was just embarrassed. I'm sexual, but in a very different way. I would accept now, but at the time being the 'angel' I was… Actually that would have made it even funnier. I wish I'd done it, actually." But Serge, quite frankly, had other things on his mind, chief among them trying desperately to hold onto Bardot, who was physically away in Spain making a movie and emotionally drifting back to Gunther Sachs. During their brief separation, while Serge stayed in Paris writing the album he had promised to actress Jeanne Moreau, she decided to give her marriage another chance. The love affair was over.

Serge was desolate. He had always "believed deeply and absolutely in an ideal love" he told Bayon. "And I searched for it." This third time he thought he had found it but she had abandoned him. Not only that, she had taken with her his opportunity to have a big hit record with his name blazoned across the top. Being a Frenchman there were two options open to him – throw himself in the Seine, which he announced to everyone that he would do, or be seen out with as many beautiful women as he could find. He opted for plan B. Thanks to the tabloid attention that came courtesy of B.B., he was not only one of France's most popular songwriters but one its best known *séducteurs* as well. ("I have known many women horizontally," said Serge, adding gallantly, "but I cannot tell who they are.")[4]

While the *Bardot Show* was broadcast in the States (a promo album was pressed in its honour, *Special Bardot*, featuring duets on English language versions of 'Bonnie And Clyde' and 'Comic Strip') Serge was in London, where only a single, 'Harley Davidson', was released, to make the album homage to his lost love, *Initials B.B.*

Scribbling furiously on the ferry-ride to England, to finish the songs, Serge recorded four new numbers with Arthur Greenslade and his orchestra (plus heavenly choir) to add to familiar tracks like 'Torrey Canyon', 'Shu Ba Du Ba Loo Ba' and 'Docteur Jekyll Et Monsieur Hyde'. The resulting album was a mix of bright, brittle pop-art pop, rich orchestral-pop and soulful rock.

Back in Paris, he resumed the frenetic working pace that had marked his post-Eurovision career; at one point in 1968 he had two studios on the go at the same time, a different female singer in each of them, while he ran back and forth between the two. He had songs in the shops sung by old-school nightclub singers – like Régine and *revue* star Zizi Jeanmaire (a kind of French Liza Minelli with more sequins and feathers) – and by more contemporary artistes like Françoise Hardy, who sang his lovely 'Comment Te Dire Adieu/It Hurts To Say Goodbye', a song one might have thought to have been inspired by the Bardot affair, but which Françoise Hardy said was written for her. "It was an American instrumental I stumbled upon by chance and which I liked a lot. It was my manager's idea to ask Serge to write lyrics for it. I thought he would refuse, since he only wrote words for his own songs, but he accepted and telephoned me with the lyrics at the Savoy Hotel, where I was staying in London." Serge also composed three more film soundtracks: *Le Pacha*, *Manon 70* (starring Catherine Deneuve and containing 'Manon', the song he once claimed was one of the best he'd ever written) and *Mister Freedom*, a satirical super-hero film in which he played the part of Mr Drugstore.

Now aged 40, he was still living at his parents' home. His father was doing his best to change this situation. Ever since Serge had moved out of the artists' dwellings, Joseph had been following his instructions to look for a place for him as Serge didn't have time to do it himself. But, since his son was as particular in his domicile requirements as he was in just about everything else, it wasn't proving an easy task.

"Serge was very snobbish," said Jane. "He wanted nowhere else but the Rue de Verneuil, so he had his father look in the *Figaro* every day." He finally found a "sweet tiny house". Serge agreed to take it right away and a team of leading decorators and designers were hired to turn the interior of the former stables on the narrow street in Saint-Germain into a masterpiece.

Serge, meanwhile, had his time taken up working through the list of films that demanded his acting and compositional skills: *Érotissimo*, *Paris N'Existe Pas* (Paris Doesn't Exist) and his latest, *Slogan*. Director Pierre Grimblat's semi-autobiographical film had Serge in the starring role, as a director of commercials, who meets a woman at a film festival, falls in love and leaves his pregnant wife for her, only for his new love to find another man and abandon him in turn. Grimblat had initially favoured the elegant actress Marisa Berenson for the part of the love interest – a choice that appealed to Serge considerably, since it held out the possibility of an off-screen relationship as well. But at the last minute Grimblat changed his mind and decided that he wanted an English girl. A casting trip across the channel threw up the perfect candidate – a young actress with that perfect '60s Swinging London look: long, ironed hair, big eyes and coltish body shoehorned into a belt-sized mini-skirt. Her name was Jane Birkin.

Chapter 7
INITIALS J.B.

"When I heard here was a film test going on in the Kings Road and they were look-ing for a girl to be in a French film," said Jane Birkin, "I went along with the Charlotte Ramplings and the Jacqueline Bissets and everybody else, and apparently someone told Pierre Grimblat, 'That girl you are looking for is upstairs'." The direc-tor had seen Jane in *Blow Up*, Italian director Michelangelo Antonioni's seminal 1966 film set in England; hard to miss her really when, still a teenager, she was the first full-frontal nude to appear on a U.K. cinema screen.

Jane had been a stage actress since the age of 17, as had her mother before her (Judy Campbell, who also laid claim to being the first to sing 'A Nightingale Sang In Berkeley Square'). Taken up by photographer David Bailey, whose penchant for doe-eyed, mini-skirted, colt-like girls was legendary, she landed a role in Beatles director Richard Lester's *The Knack* and in *Wonderwall*, the film featuring music by George Harrison – a cinematic C.V. that as good as stood for '60s Swinging London. At 17 she had also got married – to John Barry, the celebrated film composer associated with the James Bond theme. He was 13 years older than her, "and with a reputation for being mad, bad and dangerous to know. And of course three years later he left me." With a baby daughter, Kate. "That's why I so readily accepted to do a film test in France – to get away and do anything to make some money, since he had gone off leaving one with nothing – and try to make a life for Kate and me."

Two days after the audition, Jane was in a Paris taxi, heading for her first French screen-test. "I couldn't speak French – I had about two hours to learn it with Grimblat's Chinese valet – and I remember on the taxi-ride to the studio thinking, if I could just have a tiny accident, break a leg or finger or something, just something so that I wouldn't have to go through this film test in a language I didn't understand. And while I was waiting for my turn, I heard another girl saying all the lines absolutely beautifully and I thought, 'She's perfect'. It was Marisa Berenson. But Pierre Grimblat wanted me for the part."

Her first meeting with her co-star Serge was not auspicious. "Marisa Berenson was beautiful and aristocratic so of course Serge, being very snobbish, wanted her, and when I turned up, gawky and awkward wearing, I think, my sister's dress, all he saw was a girl who'd turned up from England with her big teeth and short dress and not knowing a word of French. And he was so arrogant and sarcastic and snobbish! I think I said something stupid like 'Why don't you ask how I am?' and he said *'Parce que ça m'est égal'* – 'because I really couldn't care' – which at least was more elegant than *'je m'en fous'* ('I don't give a fuck'), so he was a gentleman. And then I started to cry, because I mixed up my private life and the movie script. He had to admit that I could cry rather well, but he was also vaguely disgusted – and yet he didn't sabotage the fact that Pierre Grimblat wanted me, although he probably did have a veto. After all, he was infinitely well-known." In France, anyway. Jane, being

British, naturally had never heard of the celebrated Gainsbourg, "and he was rather put out when I called him Serge Bourguignon. I suppose it was the only French name I knew, from French cooking." Not a great start.

And so things went on, until the Paris street riots of May 1968. The celebrated student revolution, which helped change French social and cultural attitudes – as well as pushing disposable pop music aside to make way for the new progressive rock and ponderous singer-songwriters – also put a temporary halt to the filming of *Slogan*.

"When Grimblat's Porsche was blown up on the Boulevard Saint-Germain, I had to go back home. Finally, after about three or four weeks they let me come back to France." During her absence, Jane had been doing her homework, reading – with the help of an enormous dictionary – a book of Gainsbourg lyrics that she'd bought before leaving Paris. "They were wonderful; extremely witty and clever, but very cruel and cynical." She started to thaw towards him.

But when she met him the next time, conducting a press interview at his parents' apartment on Avenue Bugeaud (work to achieve decor perfection was still going on at 5 Rue De Verneuil), he, evidently hadn't. "The whole walls of his room, I remember, were covered in enormous pictures of Brigitte Bardot. Serge – who was wearing a mauve shirt, a complete dandy – was playing them 'Je T'Aime, Moi Non Plus', which made me feel slightly awkward, because I got the point. And I got my hand stuck in a tin of Chinese biscuits and I was bleeding somewhat, to which he paid no attention whatsoever, he went on with his interview."

On the set, things went from bad to worse.

"We started off a scene in the film where I had to be naked, sitting on the edge of the bath. Serge, somewhat satisfactorily, was in the bath and allowed to wear an immense pair of red, white and blue-striped swimming trunks; I remember thinking, gosh, men are lucky, and where he's looking up from I hate to think what he can see. And I felt extremely awkward under the circumstances, because it seemed to me that he had no pleasant feelings towards me whatsover, and by this point in the film one was supposed to be madly in love. So I said to Grimblat, 'Could you fix a dinner where we could just talk about it? Because if he would rather have had Marisa Berenson or somebody else, I quite understand, but it's very difficult to do scenes with someone who seems to find you so positively unattractive'."

So an evening for three was arranged at Régine's, from which Grimblat discreetly absented himself to leave them alone. "We were there for a long time," recalls Jane, "and I asked Serge to dance." (Serge had actually been waiting for 'un slow' so that he could ask Jane the exact same thing). "And he stepped on my feet! I was so surprised. I thought, 'So this sophisticated, arrogant, seemingly confident man doesn't know how to dance' – and I realised it was because he's in fact shy. He seemed so worldly-wise but at the same time he was very childlike.

"From there he took me to another nightclub – to every nightclub in Paris until six o' clock in the morning. We went to Madame Arthur, where his father used to play the piano for the transvestites, who all came up kissing Serge and saying '*Ooh chéri*, how are you?' And he took me to the Russian nightclubs where the Russian violin players played until we got into the taxi on the street and Serge stuffed 100F notes into their violins – he loved them and they loved him – and he told them *'Nous sommes des putes'* – 'we're all prostitutes' – and asked them to play the 'Valse Triste', that terribly melancholic slow waltz of Sibelius, which they played right up to the taxi, and which ever since he always called 'Jane's song'. Afterwards, I thought he was going to take me to his parents' house, like all good boys do, but no, he took me straight to the Hilton – where they asked him if he wanted his usual room!"

Jane was horrified. What had started out, quite successfully all things considered, as a quest for an *entente cordiale* was heading towards becoming another notch on his rented bedpost.

"In the lift as we were going up, I was pulling faces to myself thinking, gosh, how could I have got myself into such a mess. I had only known John Barry in all my life; I hadn't known anybody else ever and suddenly here I was with someone who had only taken me out for one night."

Once in his room she pleaded necessity to use the bathroom, where she hid out as long as she could "and tried to tidy myself up and try to look as if I was used to this sort of thing. By the time I got back into the bedroom he was asleep. There he was, he'd drunk so much that he was out cold. And I was so relieved! It meant I could nip out to the drug store and pick up a little 45 record of this song we had been listening to all evening which was 'Yummy yummy yummy I've got love in my tummy' by God knows who," – The Ohio Express, actually – "and I stuck it between his toes. Still he didn't move – and I went back to my hotel with Kate and her nappies – which were flying in the wind outside so that the hotel looked like the outskirts of Naples – and my honour was saved." As, to Grimblat's relief, was the film.

✱ ✱ ✱ ✱ ✱

After that night, Serge and Jane were inseparable. "We went off to Venice together and I wrote to my best friend Gabrielle, he's just perfect and funny and completely original and the first man I've ever met who actually cared about whether things were nice for me. He cared a terrible lot about whether you liked this or that, and whether you felt good when he would fill a room full of white flowers.

"When we got back to Paris – we were staying at L'Hôtel Des Beaux-Arts, in Oscar Wilde's bedroom – I said, 'I've got to leave and go back to London. I can't stay on – because it will happen like it happened with John Barry; I will become a clinging person, and then slowly they'll become disgusted and I'll become –' I think I said something stupid like 'a cauliflower'.

"After having waited for John Barry to come home and run his bath and cook his turtle soup and be – as a journalist from *Newsweek* put it so well – 'John Barry and his E-Type Jaguar and his E-type wife', which is exactly what I was, I never wanted to be in that situation again. And Serge, sat in front of the window all night long with a candle, crying. It was most melodramatic and very Russian, very Jewish."

Pierre Grimblat once again saved the day. As a glum Serge and Jane were having their last supper before she returned to England, he showed up at the restaurant with another director, Jacques Deray, in tow. Deray handed Jane a note, asking if the next day she could fly to the South of France where he was shooting *La Piscine* (The Swimming Pool) with Alain Delon and Romy Scheider in St. Tropez. An ecstatic Serge came too.

"Whereupon Serge hired the most enormous limousine. He was rather reluctant to tie the baby's pram and all the nappies onto the roof because it degraded the car into a vehicle of a different sort and anyway, in St. Tropez, you couldn't go down any of the streets in it, they were so tiny." But it was an Alpha male thing – he was intensely jealous of Jane's handsome co-star. "My mother said that he was panic-struck that I was going to go off with Alain Delon."

Jane had a similar moment when they were sitting in a St. Tropez restaurant and one of its best-known residents walked in. "I saw his face go white: papier-mâché. It was Bardot. So I realised it was difficult for him.

"Similarly when we were in London and John Barry turned up to take Kate off for a walk and, watching at the window that impeccably elegant man take her by the hand and go off down the street, I started to cry. Whereupon Serge leapt to the piano and started playing the James Bond theme in a furious way. But some things take a long time to get over. It's like one of those children's slate things where you can pull the paper down and make the picture disappear, but if it's been written too strongly you can still see the shadow until over time it's transformed into something quite different, until the original drawing is forgotten. And that's how it was with us. It wasn't at all the banal thing that people always want to see it as – the Pygamalion who picks you up because you're young and pretty. Because A, he wasn't interested in me at all in the beginning. B, there was only 20 years difference between us. And C, we were both totally miserable people trying to get over what seemed to be the love of our lives. But, little by little, we rubbed the other people out and became the principal characters in quite another story."

The day he left for Paris – Jane begging a very churlish Alain Delon to drive her to the station to say goodbye, then running along the platform like a little girl as the train pulled away – she found that Serge had covered their bathroom mirror with lipstick messages: "All over it were hearts and the words 'je t'aime, je t'aime, je t'aime, je t'aime, je t'aime'. My mother said to my father: 'I think this is it'."

The theme tune to the successful *Slogan* was released as a single in 1969. It featured Jane's singing debut, her heavily-accented "choirgirl's voice", as Serge called it – as with other women he recorded, he urged her to sing higher than her natural register to achieve the cracked fragility he liked – duetting with his breathy mumblings over big orchestral arrangements by Jean-Claude Vannier (whom Serge had met on *Paris N'Existe Pas*). "He liked working with actresses," said Jane, "because he could tell them what to do – make them sing like he sang, very close to the microphone and whisper sensually. He found it far more interesting to make beautiful actresses sing than singers with beautiful voices."

And he asked Jane to record another duet with him – the song he had written for Bardot, 'Je T'Aime, Moi Non Plus.'

"When Serge first asked me to do a new version of 'Je T'Aime, Moi Non Plus' with him I said no," said Jane. "I'd heard the Bardot version and it was just too impressive, and I was jealous when I thought of him shut away in a tiny studio with this exquisitely beautiful girl."

"I don't know how he got Jane to do it because she was such a lovely English upper-class schoolgirl," said Marianne Faithfull. "But of course, he would have got her to do it by fucking her brains out! And 'Je T'Aime, Moi Non Plus' was perfect for Jane. She was born for it."

Chapter 8
I LOVE YOU, ME NEITHER

When, in 1991, Serge secured a place in the renowned French encyclopaedia *Larousse*, slotted betweeen the painter Thomas Gainsborough and Nietzsche's poetic opus 'Gai Savoir', the song the compilers selected as representative of his oeuvre was 'Je T'Aime, Moi Non Plus', his duet with Jane Birkin. A song whose release as a single in 1969 caused outrage in several languages, at least one excommunication, incalculable unplanned pregnancies and sales in excess of six million singles world-wide.

While its vaporous, quasi-classical melody had its roots in an instrumental that Serge had written for the 1967 film *Les Coeurs Verts*, its title, he claimed, had been inspired by something that Salvador Dali once said: "Picasso is Spanish – me too. Picasso is a genius – me too. Picasso is a communist – me neither (*moi non plus*)."[1]

Although there are several Gainsbourgologists who claim that this was a later press invention on Serge's part – and its neat way of bringing the conversation around to his own artiness, anti-communism and genius would certainly have been the kind of shrewd device he liked – it must be said that he did have a lifelong habit of coming across a catchphrase or a slogan and twisting it into a title which would serve as the inspiration for a song. And it might also be worth remembering that Serge – who never hid his admiration and affection for Dali, from buying his paintings and borrowing his home decor ideas to accompanying him on porn-watching sessions – had one of his seminal sexual experiences (which had long since become a favourite anecdote) with a woman he no longer loved, on the surrealist's living-room floor.

Certainly 'Je T'Aime, Moi Non Plus's' languid, almost over-pretty, chocolate-box melody contained some surreal images for a love song – *"je vais et je viens, entre tes reins"*, translation: "I come and go between your kidneys". But then, as the title indicated, this was a love song that denied it was a love song; or was too cynical or insecure to own up to what it really was.

Something that Serge told Bayon in his 'Mort Ou Vices' interview comes to mind: All the key women in his life, he said, had told him that they loved him, "But me? Never. I feel it, but I don't know how to say it – although I love to hear it said."[2]

"I was shocked," Dominique Blanc-Francard (who years later would go on to become Serge's engineer) recalled the first time he heard the song on the radio as a teenager in France. "But at the same time I was excited. It was great – and it was amazing that someone had dared to do that. No-one else I know of in France had ever gone that far on a record, and certainly not with the talent that the record showed. I think that was what was so special about it – to have managed to be so provocative and at the same time to make such a beautiful piece of music. There are a lot of Anglo-Saxon artists who have been just provocative – Bowie, Lou Reed –

but never in France, and never with such a beautiful, and such a *chaste* melody."

But the lyrical subtleties were lost on late '60s Brits (a repressed, quite puritanical bunch, in spite of the efforts of Swinging London and "free-love" hippiedom); these, after all, were people who believed that "French" was a sexual position. What they heard on 'Je T'Aime, Moi Non Plus' was a slippery, expertly-stroked organ; a man and a woman's orgasmic groans; and a vaporous, soft-focus melody, the musical equivalent of a Vaseline-smeared *Emmanuelle* movie. Here it was known as "that dirty record" – confirmation that life across the Channel was one of unchecked lubriciousness, and as essential a part of any successful seduction as a nice chilled bottle of Blue Nun.

The press, of course, speculated – as they had with the Bardot version – that Serge and Jane had recorded a live sex session on a tape-recorder hidden under the bed. "To which Serge, said, 'Thank goodness it wasn't, otherwise I hope it would have been a long-playing record'. We made it," said Jane, "very boringly in the studio in Marble Arch, both of us in sort of telephone cabins. When you recorded in the old days you only had two takes anyway. He also put his hand up – because he was very afraid I was going to go on with the heavy breathing two seconds longer than I should and miss the high note – which was very, very high, an octave higher than the Bardot recording, because Serge thought that was more perverse, like a little choirboy – so he was waving at me like a madman from his cabin."

All in all it was a better version, Serge said, than his original recording with Bardot. That one was "sublime", he told Bayon, but at the same time "it was too... hot, whereas with Jane and me it was total technique. It's like fucking: if you fuck hot, you fuck badly, if you fuck *technique*, you fuck better." With Bardot he said "It was a horrifying kind of copulation, which was, I believe, *too much*."[3]

As soon as they had finished recording the song, Serge and Jane rushed back with it to Paris. "The hotel where we were living at the time – where Oscar Wilde died; Serge liked it because of that anecdote – had a restaurant in the wine-cellar where people could sit in the little compartments and have dinner. There was a man that used to play rather slow and discreet records for background music. Serge couldn't resist popping on 'Je T'Aime, Moi Non Plus'," said Jane. As they sat back and watched, "Everybody's knives and forks were in the air, suspended. Nobody went on eating. Serge said 'I think we've got a hit'."

So did the record company chief. "He already knew the song because he'd heard the Bardot version, but he listened to it and said, 'Well Serge, I'm willing to go to prison but I'd rather go for a long-playing record, so go back to London and make another 10 songs, and I'll bring it out under a plain cover'. So we went back to England – Serge made up a couple of new songs on the ferry boat and we resung a few others so we could put out an L.P. And they put 'Je T'Aime, Moi Non Plus' out in a plastic cover on which they wrote *'Interdit aux moins de 21 ans'*." Over 21s only. Which of course guaranteed that sales soared.

Meanwhile, in Italy, 'Je T'Aime, Moi Non Plus' was banned after being denounced as "obscenity" in the Vatican newspaper, *L'Osservatore Romano*. "The head of Phonogram in Italy was sent to prison and excommunicated," said Jane – actually a two-month suspended sentence and a fine for the distributor. "Serge said it was the biggest PR he could ever get. Then they heard about the record in South America through this Vatican newspaper and it got slipped back into Italy under the camouflage of Maria Callas record covers. So the whole thing from then on was extremely stimulating and exciting, because no-one had ever done anything like it before." Bans followed in Spain and Sweden. In the U.S., with very limited airplay, it hit an implausibly perfect *soixante-neuf* in the singles charts; the song seemed to take on a life and an inbuilt publicity campaign of its own.

In Britain, soon after its summer '69 release, the BBC predictably banned it, announcing that the song was "not considered suitable for play". Equally pre-dictably, the statement ensured that the record would be a hit. On August 2 the song made it to number two in the charts – and would have gone to the top if Philips' U.K. arm, Fontana, had not bowed to pressure from its international H.Q. They too issued a statement, which announced: "Certain sections of the press and general public have seen fit to make a controversy over the contents of this recording. And as Philips does not intend to allow any of their products to be the subject of controver-sial matters, the record is being withdrawn from our catalogue."

"Philips," said Gilles Verlant, "was partly owned by the reigning Dutch queen Juliana. When she heard of the scandal, the story goes, she told the board of direc-tors she was displeased and asked for the song to be dropped immediately."

At which point British keyboard player Tim Mycroft, operating under the group name Sounds Nice, took the opportunity to step in with an instrumental version, renamed 'Love At First Sight'. His reasoning made sense: since the BBC's ban (which, with their near-monopoly of the airwaves at the time, effectively meant zero airplay, outside of a couple of pirate stations and discotheques) had been based on the song's lyrical content (although, since the lyrics were in French, no-one could precisely say what they were about) there could be no possible objection once the words were removed. Profiting from the song's new infamy, Mycroft's rendition charted too, reaching number 18 on September 6.

Then suddenly Serge and Jane's version was back in the shops again – resusci-tated by an independent record label Major-Minor. On 11 October 1969 it made it to number one. 'Je T'Aime, Moi Non Plus', the first foreign-language single to take the pole position, spent a total of 34 weeks on the U.K. chart.

Over the years it would continue to make the odd – sometimes very odd – reap-pearance. First, as expected, came the spoof version: *Up Pompeii*'s Frankie Howerd duetting with June Whitfield in 1971 on 'Up Je T'Aime'. Upholding the fine repu-tation of British sexuality, it featured June trying to stir the snoring Frankie by whis-pering French words of love in his ear, only to be met by protests: "Not again! Do you know what time it is? What on earth's got into you? It's not Friday, is it? Speak English, woman!" and so on. In 1974, the Jane and Serge original was reissued with a sexy picture-sleeve, bringing it back in the charts for a third time, this time reach-ing number 31. The following year, Judge Dread's interpretation of the song made it into the top 10.

Even into the '80s, the song could still shift copies. A quite dreadful cover by actors Gordon Kaye and Vicki Michelle from the TV series *'Allo, 'Allo*, singing in their characters of René and Yvette, managed to squeeze into the Top 60. The '90s in their turn brought a bagpipe version by The Lothian & Borders Police Band. The song made its last, and possibly least appropriate British appearance of the millennium as the theme music to a British TV commercial – the not entirely erotic John Smith's Bitter beer.

In the U.S. 'Je T'Aime, Moi Non Plus' was tugged into a 16-minute epic in 1978 by disco queen Donna Summer and tackled by Cibo Matto and Sean Lennon on jazzman John Zorn's tribute album to Serge. As this book went to press, Madonna had sought and been granted permission to record her own version of the song and, since her original plan – a reputed duet with Britney Spears – sadly (or not) fell through due to their "divergent schedules", she was last reported to have approached David Bowie to be her new singing partner.

In Australia the song was translated into English by Mick Harvey of The Bad Seeds and sung by Nick Cave and Anita Lane. But it was the U.K. that truly embraced the song – for which Serge had a theory. He shared it with French magazine *Rock & Folk* in 1971: "I know certain people close to Princess Margaret who think it's about sodomy. A fact which made them very happy. Perhaps that's the reason why I got to number one in England."[4]

The source "close to Princess Margaret" one assumes, was Lord Snowdon – alias Anthony Armstrong-Jones, the man namechecked in 'Un Poison Violent, C'Est Ça L'Amour' on *Anna*, and Serge's future album-sleeve photographer. Snowdon also told him, to Serge's utter delight, that on one of his trips with the wife to the Caribbean, the brass band dispatched to the airport to give the distinguished visitors their official greeting played the only two "British" tunes they knew – the U.K. National Anthem, and 'Je T'Aime, Moi Non Plus'.

"Even now, when I go to England," said Jane, "taxi drivers screech to a halt when I can't resist saying I was the girl who sang 'Je T'Aime, Moi Non Plus'. One of them turned round and said, 'I had three fucking children to that record!' He had it at home and I went there and signed it. It's a historical record – but it's also a criminal record; you're reminded of it constantly. All I got from the British press for the last 30 years, was 'what dirty records have you made, Jane?' which was a bit demoralising. But actually, if you're going to be well-known for something until you die, why not that?"

In a sober moment, Serge claimed that his hymn to sexual liberation was, in fact, an "anti-fuck" song, about the desperation and innate impossibility of physical love. If the Vatican had not approved of its "almost liturgical" melody, they could at least have commended him for lyrics in which he did not allow himself to come. Anyway, he joked, the record was too short: "As for reaching a climax, it would have had to have been a 12-inch record for that."[5]

Whatever, at the age of 41 and after 11 years in the business, Serge finally had his hit. An enormous hit. One that deserved a mark of recognition. Since nobody had awarded him one, he took himself off to Cartier the jewellers and ordered himself a star – a Jewish star, in platinum. A first step towards exorcising the rejection and humiliation of his teenage "sheriff's badge" years.

In the wake of the success of the single, the record company rushed an album into the shops: *Jane Birkin, Serge Gainsbourg*. Jane's name first. "He wanted me to be a star; that's what he did to people he loved," said Jane. Due to the time pressure, several old songs had been resurrected, including 'L'Anamour', which he had originally written for Françoise Hardy, and 'Les Sucettes', the song which so upset the young France Gall. Among the new ones was the less than essential 'Orang-outan', inspired by Jane's stuffed toy monkey, her lucky mascot. Better were 'Jane B', set to a slinky, orchestral version of Chopin's Prelude No. 4, Opus 28 (which, in deference to the composer, he kept in its original key) and '69 Année Érotique' (69, Erotic Year), which became their next single – their dare one say tongue-in-cheek equivalent of 'The Ballad Of John & Yoko'.

Like their Anglo-Japanese counterparts, the *couple à scandale* were everywhere. *Slogan*, their first film together, was released in the summer of '69 – a big success with the critics, the public, and the paparazzi who supplied the rapacious tabloids with photos of the pair at the premiere, Serge looking like he had just got out of bed and Jane dressed in a small pair of black panties topped by a see-through mini-dress.

"I'm Not Ashamed To Show My Wife Off Naked",[6] read the headline in the Sunday newspaper *France Dimanche* – something Serge would back up less than three months later when he photographed Jane nude for the cover of *Lui* magazine. In the text he wrote to accompany the pictures, he referred to Jane as his "little hermaphrodite", proclaiming, "They're going to love you, them neither" and that she was guaranteed "to ruin their health."[7]

Said Jane, "Serge would go to buy the newspapers every day just to see if we were in them. We were in them constantly. He *adored* it. He used to say, *'Nous sommes mythiques'* – we're mythological – therefore what people say about you, what they get right or wrong, doesn't really matter as long as you're there, and the lies are probably better than the truth half the time. But this is somebody who would ring up *sobbing* because somebody had written something nasty about him."

Meanwhile, leaving the tabloids behind them, Serge and Jane headed for Nepal where, this being the hippie era, they were appearing together in a movie called *Les*

Chemins De Katmandou (Paths Of Katmandou). They followed the hippie trail to India for a short holiday, before co-starring in *Cannabis*. Serge's soundtrack – released in 1970 on an album dedicated to Bartok and Jimi Hendrix – was nicely summed up by Peter Doggett of *Record Collector* as "a Leonard Cohen concept realised over music borrowed from The Move's *Brontosaurus*. Linking erotic obsession and death, it was an eerie, compelling piece which established the core Gainsbourg sound of the next few years". With the exception, that is, of Serge's second soundtrack of 1970 *Un Petit Garçon Nommé Charlie Brown* (A Little Boy Named Charlie Brown), a French adaptation of a Rod McKuen song for the *Peanuts* film. If there was one thing Serge really did not like, it was people thinking they had got him pegged.

The worldwide travelling continued – to Casablanca to visit Serge's twin sister Liliane, to the Isle of Wight for Christmas with Jane's family (an outing which would become an annual event), to New York to promote 'Je T'Aime, Moi Non Plus' and to Yugoslavia to make two films: the big-budget *Romance Of A Horse Thief* with Yul Brynner and Eli Wallach, and a small local production, *Le Traître* (The Traitor), where Serge and Jane played members of the French wartime resistance. Other than Serge's genetic nervousness at being so close to Russia, two incidents from the Yugoslavia experience would have some future significance. First: in the process of illustrating a point during a heated debate in a restaurant, Serge took a Yugoslavian bank-note out of his wallet and set fire to it. Highly illegal; he was charged with being a capitalist provocateur and given 48 hours to leave the country. Since the second film was still being made, the producers persuaded the authorities to let him stay another fortnight to finish it. Two weeks later on the dot, the Yugoslav police were on the set, waiting to escort him to the airport.

Second: "In Yugoslavia," said Jane, "he got paid in cash, and when he got back to Paris he used it to buy an old Rolls Royce, because it tickled him pink to pay for it with communist money, and he used it as an ashtray because he didn't have his driving licence." Serge's Silver Ghost – in his view "the most aesthetic in the domain of the automobile"[8] – would spark an idea for another album.

His record company, as record companies do, had expected, and asked for, a remake of his hit. But Serge shrugged. The success of 'Je T'Aime, Moi Non Plus', he said, had changed him. "Having millions of listeners is quite impressive. I've got money – so let's move onto something serious."[9] His next release was going to be the first – and finest – French concept album. The *Histoire De Melody Nelson*.

Chapter 9
SPIRIT OF ECSTASY

Histoire De Melody Nelson is Serge's beautifully strange and brooding concept album about the love affair between a middle-aged Frenchman and an under-age English girl, set to music that sounds like a late '60s jukebox landed on an orchestra accompanying a reading by Samuel Taylor Coleridge. Staccato electric guitar, piano rolls, a quasi-psychedelic rock combo, strings, a 70-piece choir and an omnipresent thick, rubbery, doom-laden bass, that rumbles through the 28-minute, seven-track album like the wheels of a big, old car propelling the story to its fateful conclusion.

Muttering close to the microphone, Serge tells his story of sex, aesthetics, death, obsession and the impossible ideal of purity in a haunted, deadpan voice, like a French Ancient Mariner compelled to prop up another bar and recount the tale over again to yet another indifferent stranger. The opening track, 'Melody', finds Serge behind the wheel of his 1910 Rolls Royce, suddenly aware that the Spirit of Ecstasy – literally and figuratively – has led him to a dangerous, isolated spot in an unsalubrious Paris suburb. Losing control – of the car and himself – he runs into a girl on a bicycle, watches her tumble into the road like a doll, her skirt flying over her head to reveal her innocent white knickers. Her name was Melody, an English girl, barely 15 years old, with red hair – "her natural colour" – he adds with a mix of poignancy and regret.[1] The stage is set for danger and sex. But first the music glides into an innocent, acoustic 'Ballade De Melody Nelson', as the driver finds out more about the *"déliceuse enfant"*. Only after the lush, old-time-romantic 'Valse De Melody' and the trumpet-laden declaration of love, 'Ah! Melody', does he take us off to the funky 'Hôtel Particulier' – one of those places where you rent rooms by the hour –

where, reflected in the mirror above the rococo bed, we watch him deflower her. (Unlike 'Je T'Aime, Moi Non Plus' this time, Jane said, there *was* a tape recorder under the bed – the horsey laugh on this track is the sound of her being tickled in a hotel room).

But young Melody gets homesick – for Sunderland! – and she flies back home – an act which forces her desperate lover to invoke the little-known 'Cargo Culte' to bring the plane and its precious cargo back to him. (This bizarre cult, Serge claimed, had begun during the Second World War after a New Guinea tribe, seeing planes flying overhead for the first time, prayed to their gods to bring them to earth to deliver up their riches. The high number of planes downed during wartime, apparently, gave the cult a certain credibility.) But the plane crashes, leaving a tormented, broken middle-aged man face-to-face with his own solitude, and with "nothing to lose and no God to believe in".[2] Jean-Claude Vannier's arrangements in the finale make the hairs stand up on the back of your neck. But the tragedy, of course, was inevitable. Once she had lost her virginity, the underage redhead had to die, in order to keep the ideal of beauty, youth and purity alive in his imagination. (As he once told *Actuel* magazine, showing the journalist around his house with its framed pictures of Marilyn Monroe on the walls, his fixation with the actress had come about "because she is dead"[3] and thus could never be corrupted or spoiled.) And, apart from that, it was a love story, he said, and "all love stories end badly."[4]

This particular love story – somewhat pessimistically perhaps – was clearly inspired by Jane and himself. "Melody *is* Jane," he said. "Without Jane there wouldn't have been any record."[5]

"Though he never ran over me on a bike, nor was I a minor – although I was 20 years younger than him, so it was the general idea – it was was the first thing that he said he would write for me. He was rather put out when I first met him that I thought he was called Serge Bourguignon, so he slipped me a rather nice little leather-

covered book," said Jane, fetching it down from the bookshelf in her Paris apartment. "Here it is: *Chansons Cruelles*. People would always say to me, 'Ah, but he's so very cruel', because all his songs then *were*, like 'En Relisant Ta Lettre'; he said it was his period of misogyny and also misanthropy, and it showed in his songs. In the front of the book he wrote a dedication, in a very consciously artistic way in half-red, half-black ink: *To Jane Mallory* – which is my second name – *for whom I shall write the story of Mallory, or the story of Melody Nelson, Je T'Aime*, and on the next page he wrote *Moi non plus*. Therefore he had already got the idea in 1968 when he met me that he was going to write a song about a girl who came, like my father did, from the North of England."

Somewhere along the way, the story became fused with another idea he had of writing a musical based around one of his favourite novels, *Lolita*. "I even asked Nabokov if I could put his words to music," he told *Rock & Folk*, "but he refused, because they were in the process of making the film of his book."[6]

Serge had said that *Histoire De Melody Nelson* took him two years to plan – and eight hours to write. Said Jane, "He did take time on *Melody Nelson*. Normally he was terrifically lazy and wouldn't write anything unless he was really pushed, which meant once the studios had been fixed and he couldn't actually put it off he would start writing, sitting up at the piano all night through with black coffee and cigarettes. But he wrote *Melody Nelson* when I was doing another of those funny films (in Oxford this time), and he was bored because he had to wait for me to come back. His songs were so very much more sophisticated than the stuff that I was turning out in movies.

"The actual recording of it in the studio in Marble Arch was one of the most exciting things. As for the ending, we'd never heard anything like it. We were ecstatic. My brother Andrew was so enthusiastic about it that he got a demo and ran to every single English disc jockey he knew to have it played – he was absolutely convinced that it was going to be an overnight hit in England. But no-one wanted to play it. Even in France it wasn't a number one. Although it's a gold record now, and for most people it's their favourite." Among them Isabelle Adjani, who called it "musical literature", and Françoise Hardy – who nominated it as her favourite album of all time along with Stan Getz's *Focus*, finding it "a completely new and utterly, inimitably original work."

It spawned an excellent half-hour French TV special that was broadcast at Christmas 1971. Shot on video – at that time a rarity – by avant-garde director Jean-Cristophe Averty, the ghost of Melody was evoked through vaporous, superimposed images, while the Spirit of Ecstasy insignia morphed into a winged go-go dancer and frugged away against the backdrop of blobby, psychedelic lights. And fifteen years later it spawned a comic book, *Où Est-Tu Melody?* (Melody, Where Are You?) by the relatively unknown cartoonist Iusse.

Despite selling little more than 15,000 copies on its release, it was a highly influential album. Thirty years on, it still is. Among its leading French disciples are two that have achieved the cross-over to British audiences that Serge had always craved: nu-disco star and Madonna producer Mirwais, who sampled a chunk of 'Cargo Culte', and instrumental dance band Air. "There are so many things about

Melody Nelson," said Air's Nicolas Godin, "the sound, the composition, the sobriety. It's a very sober record; there's only one bass, one guitar, one drum and some strings, that's all. And the lyrics are superb. The words are an important consideration with Gainsbourg. Anglo Saxons only listen to the music, but the lyrics of Serge Gainsbourg are pure poetry. His influence has been an unconscious one but very powerful."

"You put on Air," said Nick Currie of Momus, one of the growing legion of British Gainsbourg devotees," and you say 'Where are the vocals?' because it's just Gainsbourg backing tracks really. I wonder what Gainsbourg would have made of *Moon Safari*? Would he have sued them? He probably would have collaborated and brought in a young girl singer! For a long while, Gainsbourg was still considered kitsch by a lot of (British) people, something you sniggered about. I don't think people realised at that point just how experimental it is, how beautiful the arrangements are and how important that Gainsbourg sound – especially on the early '70s albums like *Melody Nelson* – was going to be for pop music."

"The first thing that turned me onto Gainsbourg was *Melody Nelson*," said British DJ and composer David Holmes, who sampled it on his hit album *Let's Get Killed*. "I was knocked out by everything about it – the funk, the epic strings. I'd never heard anything like it in my life. It was one of those things that you wanted everyone to hear. As regards sampling it, everyone was doing these collaborations, and I thought it would be top to get Eric Cantona to do *Melody Nelson*. That album just blew my mind."

It had a similar effect on American artist Beck: "There's an ambition, a conceptual depth to *Melody Nelson* that's incredibly hard to pull off but which Gainsbourg does completely. It's very cool and its dynamic is genius. There's this band that's completely rocking on this almost acid tangent, but they're buried in the mix with him whispering on top, and he's the loudest thing on it. It's one of the greatest marriages of rock band and orchestra that I've ever heard."

"It can be seen now," wrote Alan Clayson in his Gainsbourg biography *View From The Exterior*, "as bridging a gap between the late 1960s magnum opi contemporaneous with *SF Sorrow* by The Pretty Things – the first rock opera – and *Sgt Pepper* and, with *Tubular Bells*, setting the syncretic and expensive standard, for the 'works' of the mid 1970s albums, with interlocking themes, leitmotivs, segues." The French rock press, adopting a respectful stance that was new for Serge, hailed it as a "symphonic poem of the pop age."[1]

So, being Serge, he followed it with his dance invention 'La Décadanse': grab partner's breasts from behind, grind groin in her butt and wiggle about.

The photo across the centre pages of *Histoire De Melody Nelson*'s lyric booklet debuted Serge's new look: dishevelled hair falling over his casually unbuttoned collar and several days worth of stubble on his downturned face. The rest of the package (not visible in the photo, shot from the waist up and in shirt-sleeves) consisted of a double-breasted jacket, American jeans and soft white dancers' shoes worn without socks. Jane's idea.

"The long hair I told him made him look like a Russian poet. And the stubbly look – I think he liked having a little bit of beard because he had waited until he was about 25 for his beard to grow, and he'd suffered from that, being mocked by prostitutes because he looked so young. He had no hair on his chest at all, which I thought was extremely sophisticated – impeccable! – and a rather smooth face which I told him once made him look like a Tartar. But he had a beautiful growth of beard, because it didn't just grow all over the place like some people, just a tiny bit here and there, which made his face look thinner.

"We bought his little jacket at the antique market in the King's Road – it was a girl's jacket; if you look at the front of it it has two seams for bosoms – and he wore it with a pair of jeans for the first time. I bought the shoes for him – he loved Roland Petit and Roland's mother had a place for ballet shoes and clothes, so I went there and there was a basket of things on sale. He had always complained that shoes hurt him too much, he'd like to find a pair that were like a pair of gloves, and that's what they were."

As for Jane, she was on the album's cover, wearing a short red wig and pair of patched bell-bottom jeans, a stuffed toy hiding her naked chest. "By the time he had the cover done, he'd decided that he wanted Melody to have red hair, so they bunged

a wig on my head and put on a lot of freckles. I'm holding my monkey – which I buried with Serge because he always wanted it – in front of my jeans. I had to have them open, because I was four months pregnant with Charlotte." A third significant aftermath of that Yugoslavia trip.

Six months after the release of *Histoire De Melody Nelson*, in the early hours of the morning of 21 July 1971, Jane gave birth to Charlotte Lucy in a hospital on the outskirts of London. "Serge wanted her to be born in England," said Jane, "and so did I." The new father was ecstatic. His only sadness was that his own father wasn't around to share his happiness – Joseph had died three months earlier, at the age of 75.

When they returned to Paris it was to the former stables on the Rue de Verneuil that Joseph had found for his son, and which were still being done up to Serge's singular aesthetic requirements.

"We had been living in the Hôtel Des Beaux-Arts for a year," said Jane, "and finally I said to him, 'You're ruining yourself in this lovely hotel. Let's go to Rue de Verneuil, even if we're just on camp beds, and then we can we be with Kate too – because Kate was in a different room and I didn't want her to be miserable." Nor did Serge, who adored Jane's daughter by John Barry and was bringing her up as his own.

The interior of 5 Rue de Verneuil had been so transformed as to be unrecognisable. About as far from the average rockstar residence as a place could get, almost the entire interior was black – black walls, black ceiling, black marble floors, a big black fireplace in the black living room, a black sofa and black Steinway babygrand. The black corridor led to the master bedroom and the bathroom – both black – and the black front door was opened by a uniformed valet by the name of Mamadou – black. "For me," said Serge, drawing on his artist's training, "black is not a colour, it's a value, a no man's land."[7] It was neutral territory, a place of perfect calm. Mamadou, a friend of Yul Brynner's retainer, was there to help maintain the order that Serge told Jane he needed in his "impeccable" home. "He said that he had such a mess in his head that he couldn't tolerate mess in front of him. It would have driven him mad. There was such *'un désordre dans la tete'* – a disorder in his head – he said that he needed to have order in his life. Even if his *ordre* was complicated for other people, because it was just so, he had to have it."

The black walls had been inspired by the night he spent with his first wife Elisabeth in Salvador Dali's apartment. "He noticed that the walls had been done in astrakhan," said Jane. "Extraordinary! So he had his walls done in black, but black *felt* – the material they used to make army trousers." An homage perhaps to his military service days. "He was," Jane mused, "rather fond of uniforms..."

Dali's bathroom had also caught the young interloper's eye. "He saw that Dali's bath had a silk sheet draped over it in a very artistic and lovely way – this extravagant man would run the water over the sheet, bathe on it, then let the water run out, and fold the sheet and put it in the laundry basket. How chic can you get? So Serge got a very low bath, inspired by Dali's, and a loo that came from Venice that was hundreds of years old. But he never had a bath, because he hated being submerged in water – absolutely terrified of it. He used to wash every particle of his body, little by little – a cleaner man you couldn't wish to find; perfumed feet and everything. He used to say that I was a fish because I used to spend my time in the bath" – anxious the whole time in case the cut-glass lamp above the tub fell on her, like a scene out of *The Phantom Of The Opera*, while she soaked.

"Serge said perhaps we should watch the children while they're bathing, but he didn't take it out – he just had a second piece of glass added to be absolutely sure. Because his eye was artistic to such a degree."

He had even had all the glass removed from the windows and replaced with tiny panes of bubbled crystal in different colours that let no light in on the blackness at all. "Instead he had these incredibly modern lights; his Dali and Klee paintings, some very old paintings he had and the oriental things that I'd bought him, were lit just so. When I gave him an anatomy angel, opened up at the back, with a Victorian face, he had it lit from underneath the chimney. If he didn't like the presents, they would disappear, and if he did like them he would display them, with this extraordinary sense of lighting. He didn't like daylight, because he couldn't *organise* daylight. He always used to say to me, 'I want to order everything'. He wanted to control life."

As big an influence as Dali on Serge's sense of style was the *fin de siècle* novelist and art critic J.K. Huysmans, a leading light of the Decadent movement. When Serge first met Jane's brother Andrew, he sent him off to get the English translation of Huysmans' *À Rebours* (Against Nature). It tells of an aristocrat so heavily steeped in the Baudelarian cult of artificiality and an aesthetic dislike and mistrust of uncontrollable nature, that he withdraws from the real world into his own private universe where everything is geared to his perverse sensibilities. Number 5 Rue de Verneuil, said Serge, was "the museum of my memories". But Jane did have a small refuge of her own inside the black museum. "I had my own little room – he used to come in and inspect it to see if it was tidy and say, 'How can a human being live in such disorder?' but I used to scream and shut the door. Because it was my only spot where I could leave everything in *la merde*."

That a man who was such a stickler for neatness should have been persuaded to let his hair grow, unbutton his collar and leave his face unshaven for days is quite remarkable; and though it was initially achieved through an appeal to his vanity – "I told him it was much more attractive" – it would quickly become just another aesthetic thing he could control. "He bought himself an electric razor and one of those hairdresser clippers," said Jane, "and he got the stubbly look down to a fine art."

Decor aside, Serge and his "little harem" of Jane, Kate and Charlotte, were leading a happy, and really quite normal life for a family the press dubbed "the champions of anti-conformism". Serge and Jane hadn't married – they'd meant to; Serge had proposed and Jane had announced that they would wed when Charlotte was six months old – but, after balking at Serge's idea of making it a big media circus, Jane put it off. Depending on whom you believe, they either married secretly some months later with just close family members as witnesses, or they didn't get around to it. Since it's something they never talked about, and since penetrating the bureaucracy of the country that invented the word, would take most of a lifetime, in the interests of making the publication deadline I must sadly leave this area of their lives a neutral black.

Meanwhile, Jane's film career was going from strength to strength. Serge, devoted as ever, accompanied her on all her shoots, occasionally taking lesser roles in her films – like *Sérieux Comme Le Plaisir* (Serious Like Pleasure) for instance, and *Trop Jolies Pour Etre Honnêtes* (Too Pretty To Be Honest) – as well as turning his hand to several soundtracks.

"He followed me on everything," said Jane. "We weren't separated for a week. He would sometimes write while he was on the very bad films I was making – he would say he felt so comfortable in his little room in the Rue de Verneuil that he could never really write there."

There were songs for Françoise Hardy and her husband Jacques Dutronc, for old friends Juliette Gréco, Régine and France Gall, and another *revue* for Zizi Jeanmaire, this time staged (and recorded for an album) at the Casino de Paris. There had been rumours of a collaboration with Dali on a dance, but if that came to nothing, at least Serge's much-maligned disco single 'La Décadanse' was given a second wind. Actor-director Claude Berri asked to use it in his new film *Sex Shop* – made in 1972, the year that France liberalised its pornography laws. It starred Berri as a book-seller advised to open a sex shop when his business failed and who discovered, that as his new enterprise became ever more successful, his marriage was falling apart, as his customers and merchandise tempted him into sexual experimentation. Serge wrote two more pieces for it, which were released as a single: 'Sex-Shop' b/w 'Quand Le Sexe Te Choppe' (When Sex Nabs You). That and a second soundtrack single taken from his soundtrack to *Trop Jolies Pour Etre Honnêtes* – 'Moogy Woogy' b/w 'Close Combat' – were Serge's only releases in 1972.

Jane's film success had led to demands from the record company for an album, and Serge spent the last weeks of the year writing songs – several of them with *Histoire De Melody Nelson* arranger Jean-Claude Vannier – for her solo debut *Di Doo Dah*. They recorded it in England. "He said I should always have the *'caractère anglaise'*," said Jane. Interestingly though, the lyrics he wrote for were almost exclusively French – hardly a touch of Franglais, with its only English words in the title of 'Help Camionneur' (Help, Lorry Driver), about a female hitch-hiker with fantasies of being fucked by a heavyweight trucker in his refrigerated lorry, and the gazetteer of street names in 'La Baigneuse De Brighton' (The Brighton Bather), a poignant track about a girl reading a postcard from her lover which closes with the punchline, "Hi, poor little idiot; goodbye, it's over."[9] Naturally there were songs about sex – like 'Mon Amour Baiser' (My Love Kiss) which lists 21 different ways to kiss, and 'Leur Plaisir Sans Moi' (Their Pleasure Without Me), a woman's view of male masturbation – but just as many picked up on Jane's tomboy image – the *"garçon manqué"* of the title track. Serge gives her his second ode to a motorcycle to sing, 'Kawasaki', while 'Les Capotes Anglaises' (would you believe, French Letters) finds her inflating 13 condoms and launching them off her balcony. The album – fashionably mellow for the most part, with the odd slash of California steel guitar – was released to a warm reception, though no great commercial success.

All in all, Serge's writing output for the first two years of the seventies had been nowhere near as alarmingly prodigious as it had been in the period pre-Jane. But it was still frenetic enough, evidently. In May 1973 he was rushed to hospital. Serge had suffered his first heart attack.

Chapter 10
A FISTFUL OF GITANES

"Look at this cigarette." Serge pulled another Gitane from the flat, square blue-and-white packet with the gypsy girl dancing in a swirl of smoke, and held it up to the half-light in the living room of 5 Rue de Verneuil for the journalist to examine. "Of course it's eating away at my lungs. But what else could give me that same kind of physiological orgasm, one that renews itself every five seconds, every five minutes? There's the hand-gestures, the click of the lighter, the enjoyment of the tar and nicotine eating away at me." He lit it and took a deep draw. "And these violent pleasures come from soft drugs – like alcohol. How can you give up a minor drug that's such a pleasure?"[1]

Serge had started smoking when he was 13 years old – cheap P4s, the cigarette of choice back then for young French boys who were trying desperately to help their voices break – and had graduated to treacly, unfiltered super-tar Gitanes – a man's cigarette; three to five packs a day depending on whether he was writing or not. "He would work all night with Gitanes and black coffee and come in like a ghost the next day with some new songs," said Jane. It was a habit that had become a superstition, with its own rituals. "It was the only way he could write. Even the way he smoked his cigarettes – when he finished the packet, he wouldn't crumple it up or throw it away, he would always turn the packet over so he would know it was empty." As for the dangers, "he was like a child, he didn't believe anything serious could happen to him."

And the young Jane had come to believe him, to the point where, when he fell to the marble floor clutching his chest, "I couldn't believe he'd had a heart attack. He was so terribly young." Since Serge, though, had something of a superstitious bent, he might well have been expecting it. Years earlier, back when he was still a nightclub pianist, a gypsy had read his palm and predicted that he would travel the world (done), lead a tormented love life (done) and come close to death at 45 years old – his exact age when the ambulance squealed to a halt outside 5 Rue de Verneuil and, blocking the narrow street, unloaded an oxygen tank and stretcher.

First of all Serge wouldn't let them take him on their stretcher. The *Homo Aestheticus* objected to the hospital blanket "which he thought was very a nasty colour. So he whizzed up the stairs – he wasn't even supposed to walk – to get his Hermes rug, which he thought was pretty, and he profited from the occasion by picking up two hundred cigarettes and hiding them under the coverlet so that he could smoke in the hospital. If he didn't smoke in the special care unit it was only because he had a naive idea that oxygen blew up, so he waited until he got into his private room in the hospital to start smoking like a chimney. Unknown to me. Nobody knew. He disguised the smell by spraying the room with eau de toilette. And he used to keep his little medicine bottles, half-fill them with water and extinguish the cigarette ends in them and put them in the drawer by his bed. When he left the hospital, they opened the drawer and found, to their horror, millions of these tiny bottles filled up with nicotine."

After three days in hospital, upset that the press hadn't paid enough attention to his plight, he phoned up *France-Soir* and invited them to send a journalist over for an exclusive bed-side interview. A small matter like a heart attack was not going to stop him working. Neither was it going to keep him from his Gitanes. Taking him, on his release, to convalesce in the small converted presbytery she had bought on the coast of Britanny (though Serge would have preferred "a bunker", said Jane; he didn't want anything to do with "ye olde cottage") she soon discovered that his daily strolls along the beach were less for his health than a way of getting the sea breeze to blow the smell of tobacco off his clothes.

Back in Paris, he continued the ruse by showing a new enthusiasm for taking Nana, their bulldog, for a walk. "But I could smell the Gitanes," said Jane, "and I slapped his face. I couldn't think how he could put himself into such peril after having a heart attack that nearly killed him. But when I told my father he said, 'You're mad. Now Nana won't go out for a walk any more, she'll pee on the balcony, and Serge will just start smoking again.' But I took it as the greatest affront. And so, to be as dramatic as him, I said 'I'll kill myself first if that's what the game is,' and I picked up his packet of Gitanes and I lit the first one and although it made me sick I lit a second one and I didn't stop smoking for the next ten years."

And so, as he always had, Serge lined up his blue and white packets, right side up on the piano, and started writing the songs for his next album, *Vu De L'Extérieur* (Seen From The Outside), returning to the London studio where he had recorded *Di Doo Dah* with Jane to do the instrumentation. Having parted company with Jean-Claude Vannier, he was now working on arrangements with the British composer and session musician Alan Hawkshaw, a one-time member of Cliff Richard's Shadows and future musical director of Olivia Newton-John.

"In the mid to late '60s through the '70s I was what was termed one of the top keyboard players," said Hawkshaw. "To start with, I was just booked to play on a session with Serge. There was only a rhythm section booked, and he walked in. My first impression? Pretty much like it was when I first worked with Demis Roussos – what the heck *is* this guy? Bearing in mind that we were working with such a large, eclectic collection of different people at the time, he was just another guy that came in. But his music. We were used, when we did a session, to being given the parts to play and we'd just play them, but the first session with Serge, he didn't know any parts. He only had a few bars of a piece that he'd got an idea of. So I said look, if we're going to get this done, let me just extend these and you've got a piece of music at the end of the day. And I started to work with him from then on.

"After that I did several of his and Jane's albums – and Isabelle Adjani's and Catherine Deneuve's. I would go over to Paris, take Serge's fragmented songs and pull them into full-length pieces and get the band to play them. Then he would usually go back to Paris and do his spoken-word monologues. I did a lot of composition in a sense, without ever becoming a 'writer', but they paid me well so I was happy enough with that." Unlike Vannier; being hidden in the background for so long had been what led to their falling out.

"He was obviously a controversial character in his own country," said Hawkshaw, "but in England he was more or less on his best behaviour, because nobody really knew him. I think he rather liked that, because he wasn't a 'star', he didn't like people putting him on a pedestal – he was just *different*. He was a lovely guy, Serge – other than the fact that he's blowing Gauloises" (*Gitanes* of course) "in your face all the time. He drank and smoked like you would not believe."

For a good reason: although his doctors had warned him that cigarettes were bad for his heart; others in the medical profession had announced that drinking was good for it; so by upping his intake of one, he figured, he could cancel out the harmful effects of the other.

"He was very difficult to work with sometimes because of the speed which we used to work at – we would book an album over three or four sessions – and because of the language differences. But we could still talk. He was insecure, I'd say, in a lot of ways. And quite nervous, but he was very funny – he had a musician's sense of humour – and he'd break into the session with a joke that took him five minutes to tell what normally would take a minute. But the beauty of it was, because he had limited English, he only told you the words you needed to know instead of flowering it up, and that made it even funnier."

Since Hawkshaw's knowledge of French was even more limited, he had no idea of the subject matter of the songs he was working on. "He often said to me it's a shame I can't understand the words. I only looked at it from a musical point of view, which was the extremes – me doing this heavy rock stuff and funky backing tracks, and him doing this calm, up-front, spoken-word vocal." Most of the songs on *Vu De L'Extérieur*, Hawkshaw might or might not have been interested to learn, had a recurring theme. For *Extérieur* read "posterior". Songs about shit, such as the exuberantly scatological 'La Poupée Qui Fait' (The Doll That Goes To The Toilet), inspired by little Charlotte, only two years old at the time – and farting – his onomatopaeic ode to gas: 'Des Vents Des Pets Des Poums' (Wind, Farts, Booms). Other tracks are about sex and shit – in 'Titicaca', he yearns to drown in an exotic woman's caca and tits. Or sex and farting – the sound effects on the one-night-stand in

'Sensuelle Et Sans Suite' (Sensual And With No Follow-Up). The title track digs deeper still. Yes, he tells a woman, her posterior is beautiful – from the outside. But he has penetrated her, unhappily for him. "Alas, I know everything that's going on inside" – physically *and* mentally "and it's not lovely, it's even quite disgusting/ so don't be surprised if today I tell you to go away."[2]

And yet, among all this toilet activity and talk of strippers and whores and women who are sadly all too human, there are two great romantic classics – 'Je Suis Venu Te Dire Que Je M'En Vais' (I've Come To Tell You I'm Going) and 'Au Mauvais Vent' (In A Bad Wind), inspired by Verlaine's poem (and not, I am assured, a pun).

Some might call it misogynistic. Psychologists – bearing in mind Serge's compulsive tidiness and impeccable bathroom rituals – might diagnose it as anal. But viewed from another angle – as an exploration of what it means to be human, the contrast between man's lofty language and moral consciousness and the base mechanics of this body, and how little, in the end, separates man from beast (an idea which the sleeve design suggests, with its photo of an expressionless Serge surrounded by snapshots of monkeys and apes), it was damn clever. It could also be read as a part-comic, part-serious examination of Serge's own self-disgust. In his interview with Bayon, Serge revealed that he was actually "revolted" by shit. "Every morning when I go to take a shit, it disgusts me. It makes me want to shit!"[3] He said he could not understand how the gods could create beings whose bodies could do such repugnant things, before proclaiming, in almost the very next breath, that "Love is dirty; the dirtier love is, the more beautiful it is. It's an approach," he said, "of the sublime." A complex fellow, Serge. Though he probably would have been just as happy with his description in the newly-attentive rock press: *"l'homme adolescent"*.

Vu De L'Extérieur, wrote *Rock & Folk* magazine in a two-page article on the album, was a "slap on the arse" from a "genius". But the album, needless to say, was not a hit.

* * * * * *

A trawl through the discographies and filmographies for 1974 comes up with a remarkable absence of Serge. No record release of his own, just one new single for Jane ('Bébé Gai' b/w 'Ma Cherie Jane'), and one film, *Les Diablesses* (The Female Devils), in which Jane had a leading role. But he was still what the French call *médiatique*. If you turned on the TV, likely as not you would see him, crumpled, stubbled, waving a smoking Gitane between his yellow fingers and tossing off witticisms on one talk show or variety programme or another – but it was increasingly beginning to look like Jane was turning into the more sought-after celebrity of the two. Their careers seemed to be going off at completely different tangents: as Serge's records gravitated further and further away from the mainstream pop market to become ever more maverick, marginal and dissipated, Jane's films were getting increasingly more family-friendly. Her comedies – in which she'd be typecast as the cute, kooky girl with the funny English accent – were a big hit with children. Film critics started to make jibes about the impossibility of ever being able to see the lovely Jane on screen without having to put up with Serge as well. "I was Monsieur Birkin," he told Verlant. Not easy for a middle-aged man to deal with. Which might have been one explanation for his last album's lyrical misogyny and certainly appeared to have been his motivation for starting work in 1974 on writing a film of his own. While accompanying Jane, as always, to Aix-en-Provence, where she was shooting her latest comedy, *Mustard Goes Up My Nose*, he began plotting his tale of a murderous love triangle between two gay truck drivers and an androgynous young woman. Perhaps for luck, or perhaps for provocation – unless, of course, as he often did, he was just developing an earlier theme – he gave the film the same name as his huge hit record, *Je T'Aime, Moi Non Plus*.

Meanwhile, he was inspired to make a follow-up to *Vu De L'Extérieur*. Heading back to England, still writing words on the Calais-Dover ferry, he greeted Alan Hawkshaw with his latest set of songs. If his record company, or his small, loyal audience, had expected he might have come up with something to remove the taste left by his last album, they were wrong. *Rock Around The Bunker* was a comic, acerbic look at Hitler, the S.S. and the Third Reich, set to cheery '50s American rock 'n' roll.

"A lot of that *Rock Around The Bunker* stuff he did – 'Nazi Rock', 'Zig Zig Avec Toi' – they would be quite basic, and I would have to extend them and routine the album – write down all the parts of at least the outline of the song and get it arranged for musicians to play", said Hawkshaw. "He liked to stick with the same guys, depending on their availability – people like Alan Parker on guitar and Brian Adgers on bass and Dougie Wright on drums. The cream of the musicians really. After one or two run-throughs they'd sound as if they'd been playing together all their lives like an established group; that's how good those guys were."

If once again the lyrics were lost on Hawkshaw, they weren't on the French. The subject of Nazism, particularly when treated with humour, was still a taboo subject in a country uneasy about its war-time past. Hard to imagine another French singer who could have come out with such a provocatively mischievous collection. The lyrics are extraordinary, not just for their subject matter – 'Eva', for instance, where Serge adopts the role of Hitler stuck in a bunker with his lover Eva Braun, driving him insane by singing her favourite song over and over: "*Eva loves 'Smoke Gets In Your Eyes'/ Oh how sometimes I'd love her to go fuck herself with her 'Smoke Gets In Your Eyes'*" – but for their wild punning and rhythmic, alliterated sound. Often he sounds like a one-man percussive jazz band let loose in a Mel Brooks musical. Try reading this fast: "*Otto est une tata teutonne/ Pleine de tics et des totos/ Qui s'autotète les tétés/ En se titillant les tétons/ et sa mitrailleuse fait/ Tatatata tata/ Ratatata*" ('Tata Teutonnne') or "*Y tombe/ Des bombes/ Ça boume/ Surboum/ Sublime/ Des Plombes/ Qu'ça tombe/ Un monde/ Immonde/ S'abîme/ Rock around the bunker*" ('Rock Around The Bunker'). (Trust me, a translation won't help.)

Another song is named after the hated yellow star that he was forced to wear as a boy – but once again it's an exercise in cynical humour, not an outpouring of bitterness and pain. *Rock Around The Bunker* was "clearly an exorcism", he told Verlant.[5] Although, judging by the album sleeve – a sombre self-portrait drawn on a plain, black background – the ghosts of the past were still very much part of him.

And if he chose to make fun of them, it was as good a way as any for self-preservation, and a technique he had perfected through most of his life.

Released in 1975 – a year after the film *Night Porter* and the year before Bowie would declare the Führer to be "one of the first rock stars" – his long-suffering record company had no idea how to market it.

"It was extremely funny," said Jane, "but a great failure. It was too shocking, too ahead." But Serge, undaunted, got straight back to work on another album – this one for Jane. *Lolita Go Home*. Its sleeve shot had been taken from her second nude (apart from high heels and stockings) session for *Lui*, which Serge had photographed for the magazine's Christmas 1974 issue.

"Serge adored pornographic photographs," said Jane, "and he certainly had an eye for what he found attractive or not. And if he thought I was beautiful tied up to a radiator, that was his aesthetic. Because he said what he found really vulgar was when girls looked directly into the camera lens and giggled or were sort of orange-coloured and by swimming pools that were flashy blue. He thought that was not attractive at all and, if he liked pale white people tied up to radiators and looking as if they were victims, well, that was his thing." And if that pale white person was his partner? "He used to laugh and say he had the original. I think he used to like other people to think that you were beautiful in pictures."

* * * * * *

In September 1975, Serge's film *Je T'Aime, Moi Non Plus* was finally ready to roll. He had spent much of the year perfecting it; designing the sets, looking for a place with a sense of isolation and theatricality to shoot what was a highly stylised, mannered, Shakespeare-influenced piece. "It was all absolutely calculated," said Jane. "It was entirely a concept: that aesthetic thing of having that big space with the lorry and the petrol pump and the cafe and dustbins. It was all drawn and painted and then he had it built. None of it was by accident. The dialogue was kept to a minimum, as if it was a song."

Jane took the starring role – against the strongly worded advice of her agent. Although no-one could find fault with Serge's view that she had a more serious side to her acting skills that had been unexploited by the comedy parts that French film-makers offered her, playing the part of Johnny – a girl pretending to be a boy who becomes the love interest of an unsuspecting homosexual trucker, who stirs murderous feelings in his jealous co-driver and lover after sodomising her – might, it was thought, be a little tough for her public to take. Jane shrugged. The film was about "the despair of having to love someone without whom life is unliveable. No-one but Serge could have written this film or treated the theme in this fashion for obvious psychological reasons," she told Verlant. "His sicknesses are infinitely more interesting than other people's health."

The murderous drivers were played by Joey Dallesandro (best-known for his roles in Andy Warhol's underground films) and Hugues Quester. Gérard Depardieu played a tiny role. Serge himself stayed resolutely behind the camera , although wincing with jealousy during some of Johnny-Jane's sex scenes with Dallesandro, just as he had when he had watched her making *La Piscine* with Alain Delon in 1968. This time, though, as its writer and director, he had no-one to blame but himself. For two months, actors, director and crew all lived what Jane described as a happy communal existence in a chateau in the Gard. They would dine together every evening and party every Saturday night. Serge provided the drinks and the music, playing piano and singing while everyone danced.

That *Je T'Aime, Moi Non Plus* was dedicated to the late Boris Vian, the man who had written Serge's first favourable review, turned out to be quite ironic, considering the slamming the film received from most of the critics. The leading newspaper *Le Figaro* dismissed it as "shocking"; others called it *"ordure"*.

"He was horrified when critics said it should be put into a trash can. Others suggested that it should come out in Soho with a lot of vulgar, uninteresting pornographic films," said Jane. "He who was a great connoisseur (of pornography), and who had a collection of black and white ones and went off to see things with Salvador Dali in his hotel when it was very much against the law in those days. The sentiment of the film was Shakespearean for him, and for me too I'm bound to say."

In Britain its only appearance was in a porn cinema in Soho.

"It came out the same year as *Last Tango In Paris*, and I was mortified that the English critics had been so vulgar as to say 'Didn't Mr Gainsbourg know that butter existed?'. Well, if that's all they can remember from a magnificent film like *Last Tango In Paris*, then at least we were in great company."

In France, with a wider release, the film did attract a moderate audience, though it failed to have anything like the success of its eponymous single. "Francois Truffaut and a lot of great, great French names defended it," said Jane. "Truffaut went on live TV saying 'Don't bother going to see my film, see Gainsbourg's. *That* is a work of art', so that helped eliminate all the awful things the other people said about it. But now it's a classic cult film in France and Japan – it's on all year round and it hasn't dated at all, which shows he was avant-garde."

Their daughter Charlotte, incidentally, saw it for the first time a few months before Serge's death. She said she found it "magical".

The soundtrack album, released the following year, included three instrumental versions of 'Je T'Aime, Moi Non Plus', some spaghetti western-esque music with a banjo and the fine 'Ballade De Johnny-Jane'. Jane released the ballad as a single, backed with a song featuring Serge in the role of a heavy-breathing phone pest: 'Raccrochez, C'est Une Horreur' (Hang Up, It's Something Horrible).

BANDE ORIGINALE DU FILM DE **SERGE GAINSBOURG**

je t'aime moi non plus
"ballade de Johnny-Jane"

Musique **SERGE GAINSBOURG**

The aftermath of the film was not entirely beneficial to several of its participants. The cinematographer Willy Kurant couldn't get work for months and ended up going back to the States to work for Roger Corman, while Jane was not offered another film part until *Death On The Nile* in 1978. But Serge, as he usually did, slipped out of the scandal like a man in a rubber suit, and straight into a new line of work: making television commercials. Starting with an ad for laundry detergent.

Chapter 11
UNDERNEATH THE FOAM

A "double agent" is how French newspaper *Libération* once described Serge, and it's an appellation that's hard to argue with. A master of duality, he wrote disposable pop and classic *chansons*, songs about love and songs about shit, quoted trash American TV and movies with the same zeal and acuity as he did Baudelaire, Verlaine and Prévert. So, after writing and directing an anti-commercial underground art film, it only stood to reason that he would make television commercials for prosaic household products.

You can picture the ad-men's thought processes. Here's Serge, one of the best-known faces in France, constantly on TV or in the tabloids looking in need of a grooming or a good scrub-down, a crumpled foil to the beautiful Jane Birkin. Hey, here's an idea: let's get him to advertise laundry detergent, soap and razor blades. You never know, he might even get Jane to appear in the commercials... Which is how Jane found herself following up her appearance as Johnny in *Je T'Aime, Moi Non Plus*, proclaiming to a camera – once again directed by her husband – "Be like me – use Woolite!"

To Serge it must have seemed an exquisite stroke of irony: someone with an immaculate (black) home and painstaking personal hygeine, directing the wife he had only recently photographed naked, to tell the public that what their lives lacked was something that got their clothes clean and soft. And all this set to Gainsbourg music. A wonderful game; positively Dadaist. Certainly Dali-ist. Salvador Dali, after all, had made a far more famous TV ad in France in the '70s, looking totally bonkers and declaring himself "*Mad* for Lanvin Chocolates!" (The painter's addiction to provocation and self-publicity – a requirement, he used to say, of the age he operated in – had led to his dismissal by André Breton, leader of the Surrealist movement, with the anagramised name Avida Dollars.) It was, Serge explained to *Rock* magazine, a perfect exercise in subversion – the advertising world equivalent of *The Great Rock 'N' Roll Swindle*.

"Sylvie Vartan (the popular French singer) does an ad – low on the sound ratings, low on satisfaction ratings, but sales go way up. *I* do one with Jane – it fucks Vartan on sound-ratings, fucks her on satisfaction ratings, but sales collapse ... I vampirise the product by selling Jane instead of the washing powder. My definition of publicity is this: I'm a whore who has an orgasm, and that's why I'm priceless. Because a whore who has an orgasm is extremely rare."[1]

But manufacturers over the years would continue to provide him with more orgasms – among them the makers of Lux soap, Gillette disposable razors, and Bayard suits (which featured Serge in an elegant – if cheap, I'm told – three-piece suit, with the slogan: 'A Bayard suit suits a man, doesn't it, Mr Gainsbourg?'). It made people smile, it put his face on billboards and it helped top up his bank balance, if not quite as significantly as he would boast.

"Contrary to what Serge said, he wasn't very expensive as an ad director," said Gilles Verlant. "He would direct a 'spot' for 100,000 francs (around £10,000) which is not excessive, in these spheres, anyway. Ad-men loved working with him and would have paid more, just to be with the legend."

Although songwriting royalties – not least from 1969's 'Je T'Aime, Moi Non Plus' – made up for the less than stunning sale of his albums, the sliding scale between his income and his outgoings still teetered in the wrong direction. Essentially because, when it came to money, Serge was famously expansive, equally generous to strangers, friends and himself.

"He loved spending money," said Jane. "And he loved spoiling people, because it truly gave him fun. He loved going to nightclubs and taking people off to fancy restaurants and seeing that things were done beautifully for people; getting the best tables and the best rooms in the most luxurious surroundings. He liked to be in beautiful places, so he liked the people he loved to be in beautiful places too. He liked wandering around with an immense amount of cash – it gave him a comfort, I think, because this was the life for the errant Jewish population during the Russian revolution. You tended to have attaché cases full of ready cash.

"Nearly every taxi driver I've met for the past ten years has a sweet anecdote about Serge of some sort. There was one taxi man he saw who was so beautiful but he was missing a tooth. Serge pulled out £300 or something from his attaché case and said, 'Have a false tooth put in – but please, please be very sophisticated and don't make it white like all the really vulgar people who have false teeth that look like false teeth. Get a false tooth that looks like a rotten tooth. Get them to paint it grey with cracks in,' and he drew how the tooth should look so that the rest wouldn't look rotten; the taxi man showed it to me."

Aesthetic concerns also ate into a portion of the proceeds from Woolite. Serge had spotted a sculpture in the window of a contemporary art gallery near his home and it enraptured him. L'Homme A Tête De Chou, it was called – The Man With The Cabbage Head. It was exactly what it said it was: a full-size, seated man with a veg-

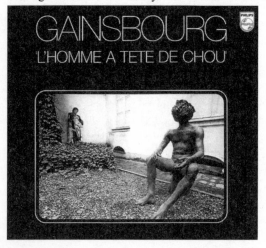

etable where his head ought to have been. Before long it would take up residence at number 5 Rue de Verneuil, set among the surrealist paintings and the English antique furniture, the old masters and the felt monkeys, his collection of CRS riot police medals, and the skeleton in the corner that he bought from the medical shop down the road "and which terrified the children all their life," said Jane, "because they had to run past it to get to the loo."

"The thing totally fascinated him," said Philippe Lerichomme, "and it's where he got the idea for the album." *L'Homme A Tête De Chou* – which borrowed its title from Claude Lalanne's sculpture and pictured it on the front cover – was Serge's second album featuring a complete, linear story, and his first produced by the former engineer Lerichomme.

"He wrote *Cabbage Head* while I was making a very bad film in Milan," said Jane. "I was there for about four weeks, so he took his time on that one. I had made him come under false pretenses. I told him I was in a lovely hotel in the old district of Milan, and he came belting over to find me in a no-man's-land on the outskirts of the city in a ghastly hotel where there were no bathrooms in any bedroom and they were knocking down the buildings next door. He was furious and didn't talk to me for two days. Then he picked a room on the other side of the corridor for himself and while I was off filming all day he sat in there and started writing. There was a fire extinguisher in the corridor. I think that's where he got the idea of killing Marilou and covering her with foam."

Like his 1971 concept album *Histoire De Melody Nelson*, but more musically diverse and with darker, harsher lyrics, *L'Homme A Tête De Chou* is a tale of obsessive love, violent death, sex and self-destruction. In 12 short tracks, a tabloid journalist relates how his life fell apart after the fateful day when he dropped into Mac's Men's Hairdressers for a shave and was "blinded by the beauty and soapy hands" of Marilou, the young black "bitch of a shampoo girl".[2] In a calm monologue murmured over a doomy, almost progressive-metal riff, he tells how he fell hopelessly in love. The lilting Caribbean sway of 'Marilou Reggae' holds out a promise of an unknown world of exotic sexuality. He enjoys some of it to the African beats of 'Transit À Marilou'. But then, in 'Flash Forward', he catches the faithless Marilou having sex with a couple of hippy rock musicians – cue crazed synthesisers, jagged rock guitar and lyrics that choke on a stream of 'ac, ac, ac' rhymes, as if he were slapping her, or slapping himself off. Marilou just mocks him – but he has reached a turning-point. "Insults," he says in the cool, jazzy 'Aéroplanes', "evaporate like a wisp of Gitane smoke."[3] And, taking himself off to a bar, he throws up "my alcohol and my hate"[4] to the African rhythms of 'Premiers Symptomes'. Back at Marilou's room, he spies on her, watching as she knocks back absinthe and masturbates nonchalantly while reading comic-strips. There, to the incongruous accompaniment of a country ballad ('Variations Sur Marilou'), he reveals his decision to murder her. And in the jazzy, percussive 'Meurtre À L'Extincteur' he batters her head in with a fire extinguisher until she slumps underneath the white, sticky foam. The deed done, he serenades her dead body with the lullaby 'Marilou Sous La Neige' (Marilou Under The Snow). Marilou had been condemned to die – like young Melody Nelson before her – on account of her uncontrollable sexuality. But it doesn't end here. Although the journalist – and *Melody Nelson's* Rolls Royce driver – were naturally the victims of corrupting female sensuality, they too must be punished, if only by their own conscience. And so the closing track, 'Lunatic Asylum', finds the journalist in a neuropsychiatric ward. The man has lost his mind. His head, he is convinced, has turned into a cabbage – and the Playboy bunny is devouring it, bit by bit.

And you thought *Tommy* was strange.

Menacing, atmospheric and marvellously mad, part Dostoevesky, part Kafka, part *film noir*, quite surreal and extremely politically incorrect, *Cabbage Head* evinced a heightened sense of morality unexpected in a man whose image had been one of carnal licentiousness. A morality somewhere between the lip-licking prurience of *The News Of The World* and Victorian puritanism. Like *Libération* said, a double agent.

Coming out during the heady days of punk, *L'Homme A Tête De Chou* was greeted by the French rock press as a nihilist masterpiece. Its critical acclaim though, once again, failed to translate into sales, even if it did accord Serge the rare honour of being one of the only old-timers to escape the punk era's cultural Reign Of Terror. He took great delight in finding himself praised in the same publications as youngsters like The Sex Pistols and The Clash.

"Serge liked punk," said Philippe Lerichomme. "He was particularly fond of Sid Vicious. What he most liked about it was its non-conformist element." Not to mention its self-destructive element.

"Serge," said Jane, "kept something that most of us lose, which is being an eternal adolescent. He dared to do things which adults aren't allowed to do and he got away with it. He said, 'The song is a minor art, but I do it for minors'. His great wish always was to be loved by young people."

Nonetheless, after *Cabbage Head* Serge got back to business in 1977 turning out songs for his old clients Françoise Hardy, Zizi Jeanmaire and even Nana Mouskouri. The bespectacled Greek singer had been a young ingenue when Serge last wrote for her, 14 years earlier, but had long since become the kind of straight, old-fashioned singer that young people's parents liked. There was also a spate of movie soundtracks: *Goodbye Emmanuelle* (having turned down a request to score the original soft-porn film, he signed up to do the sequel), *Vous N'Aurez Pas L'Alsace Et Lorraine* (You Will Not Have Alsace And Lorraine), and *Madame Claude*, another quasi-soft porn film about the queen of a celebrated Paris brothel. The *Madame Claude* album featured a song written entirely in English, 'Yesterday, Yes A Day', and the wonderfully-titled 'Ketchup In The Night', 'Fish-Eye Blue', 'Discophotèque' and (a Spanglish pun this time) 'Mi Corasong'.

But then a pathway into the 'youth' market beckoned. Alain Chamfort – the 27-year-old, former '70s teen idol who had since become a kind of tamer, less funky, French Robert Palmer – approached Serge to collaborate with him on his next album. Initially Serge was less than enthusiastic but Jane persuaded him to change his mind. In the end, despite a few hiccups (like persuading Chamfort that singing a song about being sandwiched between two sexy Swedish twins 'Lucette Et Lucie' would not turn off his mainstream audience), *Rock 'N' Rose* turned out quite well. And with 'Baby Lou' (a song later covered by Jane on her album *Baby Alone In Babylone*), he even had a minor hit.

* * * * * *

Not that anyone across the Channel showed the slightest bit of interest. Since 'Je T'Aime, Moi Non Plus' had topped the charts, two other French stars had moved in on the British pop market: Sacha Distel with 'Raindrops Keep Falling On My Head' and Charles Aznavour with 'She'. But Serge, where the British were concerned, had had his moment and done what all one-hit wonders do, disappeared.

"He used to grumble, 'Why aren't there any covers of my songs in England or America?'," said Jane. "But people would say that you can't translate things that have two meanings, if not three; it put them off. Then Serge would say, other people have covers where people just forgot about the lyrics and wrote something completely different, like 'My Way'. But Serge didn't have any covers while he was alive, other than that strange boy who sang in a high voice" – Jimmy Somerville, former lead singer of Bronski Beat, who set his soaring falsetto to 'Comment Te Dire Adieu/It Hurts To Say Goodbye', the song covered by Françoise Hardy.

"Serge was awfully pleased about that. But he was sad because he loved England so much. Every year we would come to England for Christmas, come what may, because he said it was the most exotic country there was, even if it was the closest. He loved everything from the telephone cabins to the taxis and the pubs. He would eat haggis in the kitchen and light it up with whisky. But then he would get a bit melancholic after a week on the King's Road and nobody recognising him, and he needed to get back to Paris to get a shot of being well-known again. Then he would say, 'It's better to be a king in your own country than a second-class citizen in a foreign one'. But he never really got over the bitterness of England."

"He was just too clever," said Marianne Faithfull. "There's a suspicion here of intellectuals. This kind of poet-artist-musician type has never taken on here really. We've got a lot of those people but they've suffered for it, they've had to scale themselves down to the stupidity of the level. There's a really serious intellectual depth to Serge's work that is really beyond English people on the whole, mainly because they can't speak French and can't understand the real genius of the play on words; the double-meanings. The puns are amazing. I don't know anyone in the English-speaking world who has ever achieved that ravishing brilliance in lyrics – not even me!"

Though only separated by a 24-mile stretch of water, the gulf separating U.K. and French popular culture was enormous. The British bands – like their American counterparts – all knew, or at the very least knew of, each other, and knew where each of them fitted into the heirarchy of cool. On the one occasion when Serge met Mick Jagger, for instance, a man described by Marianne Faithfull as one of the few people in the pop world "educated enough to really understand Serge", there wasn't that mutual sizing-up, that flash of inter-celebrity recognition and musicianesque banter. In fact it almost ended ignominiously with Serge getting punched out, until the better-known Jane came to his rescue.

"We were both in a French nightclub when he upset a whole glass of Peppermint Frappé onto Mick Jagger's trousers," said Jane. "Just before Mick punched Serge on the nose I intervened and, thank God, Mick recognised me from the old days in London and a punch-up was narrowly avoided."

A meeting with the composer John Barry – Jane's ex husband – really didn't go much better. "I remember him taking John to a nightclub and asking the disc-jockey to put on one of John's records, saying, 'You must have Goldfinger or something'.

But John didn't want anyone playing his music on a French dance floor and just thought Serge was being an ego freak. They were such different characters. The people in England who really knew Serge were the musicians who played on his albums." Session players. Who, by operating in a place removed from the hierarchy of cool were, just like Serge, outsiders. A fact which may not have been good for his vanity, but it did make for some fascinating records as he moved insouciantly between cocktail-jazz, world music, rock 'n' roll, pomp-rock and electro-pop; lounge, reggae, disco, country and orchestral pop, totally unfettered by rock's unwritten rules about hipness, appropriate behaviour and taste.

Nonetheless, Serge did make another assault on the British charts. In 1978 – the same year, ironically, that disco diva Donna Summer unleashed her 16-minute version of 'Je T'Aime, Moi Non Plus' – he released an English version of his disco song 'Sea, Sex And Sun', about a horny old Frenchman chatting up a teenage girl. The Village People it wasn't, and it failed to make so much as a dent.

Back in France, though, it was a different story. The French version (with the same Anglo title) was a big summer hit – which, thanks to its subsequent appearance on the soundtrack to the successful movie *Les Bronzés* (Suntanned), stuck around well into the autumn. All of which only helped Serge's new youth-press profile. His "honorary adolescent" status was further validated by a visit from the rock power-trio Bijou, a young, somewhat Jam-like band and labelmates at Philips, asking permission to cover 'Les Papillons Noirs' (The Black Butterflies) – the song he had written for Michèle Arnaud back in 1966 – and inviting him to join them in the studio. This time there was no hesitation.

"They were examining the roots of French music," said Bijou's producer, manager and *éminence grise,* Jean-Wiliam Thoury. "And of all the old, established stars he was the nearest they came to rock, in attitude as well as sound. It was a rather obscure song, not one of Serge's best-known songs at the time – the guitarist Vincent Palmer's idea. And they were the first group to ask him to collaborate. He was flattered." Helping them out on the track, Serge found it such an agreeable experience that he wrote a song especially for them, 'Betty Jane Rose'.

"When he worked with them, he left them to their own devices," said Thoury, "acting somewhat like a film director. Since he'd chosen to work with them and liked what they did, he just let them get on with it and arrange it in their own manner, in a rock style. He was very intelligent and wanted people to be able to give their best."

To promote the album that the songs appeared on, *OK Carole*, Philips had organised a showcase in Epernay, in the Champagne region of France, as part of a promotional tour. Serge went along. At the end of the invite-only show, he got up to sing two numbers with them – his first time back on stage since quitting 'Lady In Black' Barbara's tour at the start of 1965. This time, though, his reception was very different. So much so, in fact, that he let the band persuade him to join them on the rest of the short promotional tour.

In the 13 years that separated his performances with Bijou and Barbara, the stage-fright that plagued him had not gone away. "He was very anxious," recalled Thoury. "Very shy. It helped that the first show was in the capital of champagne country!"

A few glasses before grabbing the microphone helped set Serge on his feet. "The dates they did together, around ten in all, gave him the feeling he needed to get back on stage. He made his big comeback straight afterwards," following the release of *Aux Armes Et Caetera*. But that was still another year away; 1978 still held another feather for his cap. *Ex-Fan Des Sixties*, the next album that Serge wrote for Jane, would be her biggest hit so far.

Ex-Fan Des Sixties' underlying theme was departure, loss and being lost. The title track's look back at the '60s was drenched with nostalgia and regret: "Where had those wild years gone?" the song asked, "What had become of its stars?", before reading off a roll-call of dead singers – Brian Jones, Jim Morrison, Eddie Cochran, Buddy Holly, Jimi Hendrix, Otis Redding, Janis Joplin, Marc Bolan and, a last-minute addition to the list thanks to his heart failure in the summer of 1977, Elvis Presley. (Two of those names, incidentally were particularly dear to Serge's heart: "It was my obsession with Eddie Cochran and Buddy Holly that led me into the Anglo trip," he said.[5])

Other songs, though, were closer to home. 'Nicotine' must have been brewing in his head since Jane first slapped him when she caught him smoking after he had had his heart attack; it portrays a woman sitting alone at home, watching the hands turn on the clock, and realising that the man who said he was just popping out to buy cigarettes had gone and left her for good. Closer still were 'Dépressive', in which Jane describes an existence where all of a sudden everything had turned ugly. Or 'Vie, Mort Et Résurrection D'Un Amour Passion' (Life, Death And The Resurrection Of A Passionate Love), where she sings, "We are fucked… And I told you Kill me/ Kill me if you're a man/ But you're just a poor mug/ Because you never could."[6]

Unless it was another game, one more exercise in subversion, on *Ex-Fan Des Sixties*, France's favourite couple, appeared – if you'll forgive the Woolite analogy – to be airing their dirty linen in public. Whether or not things would come out in the wash would remain to be seen.

Chapter 12
FREGGAE

"It wasn't Bob Marley who initiated France in reggae," Serge declared, with some justification. "It was *me.*"

The Seventies were drawing to a close and Serge wanted to end them with a bang. But every time he tried to figure out how, he found himself bashing against the huge monolith that had marked the end of the Sixties for him, 'Je T'Aime, Moi Non Plus'. He had been toying with the idea of a third concept album – this one, said Jane, "about a man having a heart attack in an English taxi and having flashbacks of his past while the taxi meter turned around. And then Philippe Lerichomme, Serge's great artistic director, said 'There are great things going on in Jamaica'. So Serge dropped the concept album and went off to Jamaica and did a reggae album

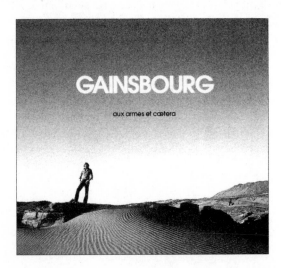

– for the very first time in French!" In doing so, he concluded the decade with the biggest album of his career.

"Reggae had only just started to get going in France when Serge made *Aux Armes Et Caetera* (To Arms! Etc)," said Philippe Lerichomme. "How it came about was I had been asked to go to a club one Sunday night to listen to a punk group, who were due on stage at midnight. So I was in this half-empty club, nothing I heard had interested me, it was midnight and the group didn't come on. The disc-jockey, who was very good, was playing some very hot things in the meantime – punk, and some reggae. And it came to me in a flash. It was two o' clock in the morning, so I waited a few hours and then phoned Serge and said, 'We must go to Jamaica and make a reggae album'. And Serge said 'Good idea!'" He did not need any persuasion.

"He knew all about Rastafarianism," said Marianne Faithfull. "He knew about everything! He was very interested in its spiritual content. I remember having long talks with him about it, as was the way in the '70s. The deepest meaning of Toots & The Maytals!" And he had already made his first tentative steps at playing it on 'Marilou Reggae' on *L'Homme A Tête De Chou*.

So off Lerichomme went to the hippest record shop in Paris, where he bought up its stock of reggae albums, "and I hauled them back – it was vinyl then – and listened to them all, checking out the musicians to see which ones were the best. Then I called Chris Blackwell at Island and said I would like to hire Sly Dunbar, Robbie Shakespeare, Sticky, etc." And so, in September 1978, Serge, Philippe and Jane's father (standing in for his daughter who was busy elsewhere) set off for Kingston, Jamaica to meet drummer Sly and bassist Robbie, percussionist Sticky Thompson and backing singers The I Three, featuring Rita Marley, Bob Marley's wife. *La crème de la crème* of reggae.

A week had been booked at Island's Dynamic Sounds Studio, a place Serge would describe to Jane on his return (with a touch of artistic licence) as the most primitive place imaginable, with chickens clucking about on top of the mixing board.

At the outset it looked like it might turn out to be seven days too long. "It didn't start out too well," said Lerichomme. "When we arrived, the engineer wasn't there and we couldn't really communicate because Jamaicans speak a special kind of English we found difficult to understand. And for a while Robbie didn't know which one of us was the singer and kept talking to me – because Serge was older than me and he was wearing a suit". Naturally they thought the producer was the star. Not that they gave the impression of caring either way.

"It was quite tense, no-one smiling. It was a case of take the money and run. Serge, to try to ease the atmosphere, tried to talk to them and said 'Do you know any French music?' and they started to take the mickey out of us, 'French music? We're Jamaican.' Serge and I looked at each other, crestfallen. This wasn't good. Then Sly said 'We know just one piece of French music, a song called 'Je T'Aime, Moi Non Plus' which has a girl groaning in it.' And Serge said in English '*It's me*'. And that changed the whole mood. We recorded very very fast, and when it was done they didn't want to leave. They hung around the studio to hear the playbacks, smoking their enormous spliffs, saying 'Great! Brilliant!'"

"We got a call from Chris Blackwell that this French guy wants to work with us," recalled drummer Sly Dunbar, "and didn't realise he was the guy who did 'Je T'Aime'. It was very popular in Jamaica. We couldn't believe it. He didn't say why he wanted to do a reggae album. So when we met him here in Kingston we said, 'So, we're going to make it polished?' And he said no, no, no, he wants it raw. It took less than a week to do everything. He just sang and said he wanted us to play reggae, so we just played reggae, and he didn't say anything. He was into the music but he was also having a good time. He was constantly smoking and drinking but he never looked drunk. I didn't see him smoke ganja, it was just his French cigarettes in the blue pack.

"The only time he said anything was when we said we'll overdub some other instruments and he said 'No, no, no, no, no, it's okay, it's what I want – I want it real, raw, no overdubs, just simple'. We couldn't believe it that it was all he wanted, not pretty and polished. But he knew what he wanted once he heard it. He loved everything we did. We laid the tracks and he was singing." Or, as Robbie described it. "It wasn't really singing. He was more like a poet doing French poems on top of popular rhythms at the time."

"He was singing in French," said Sly. "We didn't know what he was singing about but his singing was good and the melodies were great." Perhaps it was for the best that they didn't know. 'Relax Baby Be Cool' – one of the album's perkier tracks, a mix of reggae, '60s R&B and comic-strip *bing boong* noises – is a chat-up routine taking place against a backdrop of hooded Klansmen, morgues, and blood running through the streets. The minimalist lyrics of 'Eau Et Gaz À Tous Les Étages' (Water And Gas On Every Floor) has a man taking his dick out and pissing and farting his way upstairs. The slinky singalong 'Lola Rastaquouère' is an ode to an underage rasta girl whose breasts are "two spheres that threw away two months pay for, just to get to roll my poor joint between them."[1]

Meanwhile, on the mellow opening track 'Javanaise Remake', Serge deconstructs his classic 1963 song, chopping its lyrics into reggae chunks, substituting the recurring phrase "mon amour" with the English "love", and exorcising his much-hated singing on the original with a languid, talk-over that sounds like Leonard Cohen spliffed-out in Quebec. Marilou from *Cabbage Head* is also given another workover in the marvellous 'Marilou Reggae Dub'. (Not just good freggae, good *reggae*.) 'Des Laids De Laids' (Ugly Of Uglies) is a tribute to his beloved Nana, the bulldog for whom he wrote a part in his film *Je T'Aime, Moi Non Plus*, and who had barked her last in the summer of 1978 (and was given full canine military honours, you'll be happy to hear, in a funeral on France's Northern coast). The irony of the dog's cause of death had not been lost on Serge. "It's me who drinks," he mutters melodically, "and she who gets cirrhosis of the liver."[2]

But the song that made Serge notorious, the song which had the album flying out of the shops back home in France, was the second track, 'Aux Armes Et Caetera'. Over a swaying backdrop of laid-back reggae with a patter of percussion and slinky, support vocals from the I Threes, an understated Serge talk-sings the words familiar to every Frenchman: "*Allons enfants de la patrie/ Le jour de gloire est arrivé*". The opening lines of the French national anthem. A master stroke. Hearing a bunch of Jamaicans messing with 'La Marseillaise' was, for the French, The Sex Pistols' 'God Save The Queen' and Jimi Hendrix's 'Star Spangled Banner' rolled into one. And then some.

The lure of doing something provocative with France's revolutionary hymn appeared to have been simmering in Serge's head for some time. Back in 1971, during an interview with *Rock & Folk* magazine to promote *Histoire De Melody Nelson*, when the journalist asked him why he never sang about politics, he replied that politics and hit records don't mix. There had only ever been two big political hits in France, he said: 'L'Internationale' and 'La Marseillaise'. Everyone knew 'La Marseillaise's' orchestration backwards but perhaps, he suggested, they hadn't thought so hard about its sentiment. It was a song to be sung with "a rifle in your hand and ready to take a shot in the gut".[3] The call to arms in the second verse (he'd looked it up in his 12-volume *Grand Larousse*; Serge was an avid reader of dictionaries and encyclopaedias) did not sit well with someone whose family had done their damnedest to avoid gun-toting Frenchmen during the war. However, it did give him a good title for his album.

The outcry over the freggae National Anthem made the scandal caused by 'Je T'Aime, Moi Non Plus' look non-existent. The newspaper *Le Figaro* condemned it as an outrage. An editorial written by Michel Droit (rather apt name, *n'est-ce pas?*) suggested its author would have done more than excommunicate him, he would have removed his French citizenship.

"He called him a 'walking pollution'," said Jane. "He said how someone – and let's not neglect the fact that the name Ginsburg was hardly French – could dare to do the National Anthem with a lot of rastas was poison for him. Serge, I remember was so shocked. He was nearly crying. But then he found it was great fun that he was no longer on the entertainment page, he was on the news page."

That kind of bad press is priceless. Other newspapers in their turn called the record "repugnant". The kids in their turn called it "cool". Released as a single, 'Aux Armes Et Caetera', was on French radio playlists for much of the year. The album was mounting the charts. And Serge, who had been lured back under the spotlights the year before by Bijou, agreed to take the record and its Jamaican musicians (or as many as Robbie could persuade to leave home just before Christmas) out across France on tour.

The tour was a sell-out. It was also plagued by bomb threats from the extreme right. In Strasbourg, an old paratrooper presented the mayor with a petition to ban the show, warning that if it went ahead they would be "obliged to intervene physically and morally with all the strength at our disposal".

"So Serge had a bodyguard with him," said Robbie, "a big guy who weighed about 500 lbs. I remember I didn't sleep for days because whenever I fell asleep someone would call and say 'Monsieur, you have to leave the hotel'. I told him, 'Fuck off, I want to sleep; somebody's playing a joke', until they told me, 'Well Robbie, you're the only one in the hotel, you have to come out'."

"All the Americans (tourists) were furious to find themselves on the lawn at two in the morning with Serge and me in our pyjamas and a whole lot of rastas," said Jane. But Serge declared that the Strasbourg show would go ahead, *with* the National Anthem, despite the noticeable presence in the crowd of a number of none too happy-looking military men. "I hid behind one of the speakers," said Jane, "and I watched as Serge walked on into the middle of the stage. Alone. And in front of all the paratroopers, the ones who had been kicking up all the fuss, he sang the original version of the Marseillaise, white-faced.

"The paratroopers didn't know what to do. They stood up, they sat down, they took their berets off and at the end Serge put two fingers up, like 'fuck you', to cheering. Because he couldn't bear for all the fans to have come and the evening to be fucked up by these extreme right-wingers." And, when Serge closed with the French gesture of contempt – left hand grabs right elbow, and throws right hand over left shoulder, accompanied by disgusted facial gestures and a fart-like expulsion of air – he made sure, he said, "that I had my cuff just low enough to show them my watch." A wildly expensive one, from Cartier; the place where he had bought his platinum Jewish star. What the right-wingers found even more offensive was the news two years later that Serge had purchased the original Rouget De Lisle manuscript of 'La Marseillaise'. "It almost bankrupted me," he told Jean-William Thoury, "but it was a question of honour."

As to why Serge was up on stage on his own, opinions differ. What is certain is that Sly and Robbie left Strasbourg that night to sleep in Brussels. Jane said, "It was because he was such a sweet man, and he said 'Look, these rastas have got enough problems in their own country, I'm not going to have them blown up for me'."

In Robbie's memory it was, "Serge said to me 'I want to play the song' and I said 'Serge, I will play but you have to give us some more dockets, sweeten our pockets', and everybody said 'Yes, we will play if you do that'. But Serge said no. No more money, *he* will go and play, so he went over there by himself and did the National Anthem solo. The next day in the headlines it said 'Sly & Robbie Are Scared Of Paratroopers' but we weren't scared. We are mercenaries!" Serge himself, in an interview with *The Independent*, went along with the newspaper headline theory. The band, he said, had been stoical up until then because they didn't understand the bomb warnings in French, but as soon as the announcement came over the loudspeaker in English, "they all legged it. I don't blame them. They had their kids with them."

By the time they got back to Paris, "Serge," said Jane, "was a hero. Because he had stood up against these racists and right-wingers – he who had never really made a political statement in his life! The only time I think he voted, it was for (conservative) Giscard D'Estaing, because he thought in a naive way that he would not be tempted into taking a bag of gold under the table because he was such a rich man and an aristocrat."

It was an aristocrat, incidentally, who shot the sleeve photo for *Aux Armes Et Caetera*: Lord Snowdon, brother-in-law of H.M. the Queen. Sometimes it's hard to keep up with Serge's contradictions. No matter.

At 51 he was an honorary punk, lauded by youngsters, getting on the covers of magazines *without* Jane (the front of *Hara Kiri* magazine had a staged photo of Serge being bayonneted by French soldiers, with the caption *La Marseillaise Vengée* – the Marseillaise gets its revenge). And, most important of all, he was the proud possessor of his first platinum (eventually to top triple platinum) album.

"He sent us pictures of the platinum discs," said Sly.

"A *picture!*", said Robbie. "We were supposed to get a platinum album. If at that time we had known the business stuff we would have that now. He gave Sly some shoes."

"He bought me four pair of shoes as a gift, two black, two white," said Sly.

"I think I got some too," said Robbie, "but it was a good record. We liked it and Serge treated us nice, you know. He was really, really cool. Every time we were in Paris he would always come and look for us.

"He was a very warm person, very easy-going. The only thing was he smoked so much! He had an attaché case full of cigarettes that I think are called *Goulash*."

(No, *Gitanes!)*

"I said 'Serge, why do you smoke one after the other, not even two seconds pass in between?' And he got vexed with me and told me a cigarette was more than his wife. A wife would get up and leave him and when she left him he would need something to cool down. His cigarette will never leave him."

There was one rather fine track on *Aux Armes Et Caetera* that we failed to mention earlier. The lyrics of 'Vieille Canaille/You Rascal You' (Serge's adaptation of Jacques Hélian's early '50s French translation of the old jazz song) referred to an unnamed man whom he let into his house "with open arms, you old rascal… then I introduced you to my wife, you old rascal… and as soon as I turned my back you left with her."

Like the bookseller in the film *Sex Shop*, Serge's career had taken off at the expense of his marriage. He had wanted to end the Seventies on a high note, and with his freggae album he had done just that. But as the Eighties rolled around Jane was packing her bags.

SERGE GAINSBOURG
CHANSONS ET MUSIQUES DE FILMS

LE PACHA
(Requiem pour un c…)
SEX SHOP
LA HORSE
etc…

Hortensia

Chapter 13
BEHIND THE BLACK DOOR

Let's take a step back for a moment. Life, however inconvenient for biographers, is not a neat pile of discarded pages torn off a calendar marking dates and special events; a steady rise from the depths to a suitably lofty point from which to fall into a heap of discarded bottles and packs of Gitanes. Reality is a far messier business. The route it follows from start to end is more like the one a dog takes walking down a street, sometimes going from one lamppost straight to the next to leave another mark, but more often than not heading back to the first one it pissed on, circling around it, aiming another jet and then flying across the road to spray on a lamppost in a different street. While we've been telling tales of ladies in black, virgin cyclists, Jamaican chickens and paratroopers, real life – something even celebrities suffer from – had been going about its business.

Celebrities are often worse than biographers in their desire to impose order on existence; counting off the days and years by the last headline or magazine cover, airbrushing their history in interviews and press releases, and shining the spotlight on a controlled artificial view of their own reality. This is precisely what Serge wanted to do with his strategically placed lights and opaque window-panes that shut off the world outside.

Serge was particularly fond of control. He needed order, he said, to counterbalance the creative frenzy of words, colours, sounds and images in his head. That was why the interior of his house had to be the undistracting non-colour black, and why no-one was allowed to change the position of the beautiful objects he'd carefully displayed.

"I'm a maniac about it," he said. "I have a horror of coming across a doll or finding a chair moved three centimetres. I know where I have put them. When I come in I can *feel*, right away if I'm at home, or if someone has altered my universe."[1]

That Serge was the one in control of this universe was indisputable; or he certainly could not have felt that it would have been disputed by any of his harem – the tiny Charlotte, the medium Kate, or Jane, who was still a lot younger than Serge and adored him.

"He always used to say 'I want to order everything'," said Jane. "When we went to restaurants, he was the one who decided what to order. I remember one had to dress up like a doll and your hair had to be done just so. He used to sit in places and ask for dresses to be brought to choose which one you would be wearing that night at Maxim's. He said the outside world were our spectators. He wanted to go to restaurants where there were people – not people that he'd know, but like when you make a film and you have the main actors and the paid extras. He used to say, *'C'est pour la figuration'.*" – the walk-on parts in his self-written, self-directed, heightened representation of real life.

"I admit," Serge told *Rock & Folk*, "that there is a certain amount of directing… I don't like an empty nightclub, I need extras."

Why he needed to go to nightclubs in the first place was, he said, because it was "part of the game", a necessity of the business he was in, to put himself on display. "I am neither likeable nor sociable," he said, describing himself as "misanthropic". Fancy nightclubs, as well as having the advantage of better-looking people, were places where he could be "less conspicuous".[2] An understandable sentiment from a misanthrope; but an unusual one from someone who craved celebrity, who would go out and buy the papers and magazines every morning in the hope of finding himself in there, confirmation that he still existed.

During the twelve years that Serge and Jane had lived together, life had always had its own strange kind of normalcy. For a misanthrope, Serge always did a very good job of going out into the streets alone, dropping into bars for a drink or cigarettes, talking to people in the cafes and the shops. Although he was one of the best-known faces in France, he certainly didn't lock himself away like an Elvis. And life for the children, all things considered, was pretty normal too. They got up in the morning, had their breakfast (usually courtesy of one of the revolving door of au pairs, since their parents might still be out enjoying the night before) and went to normal schools, where they were taunted by schoolmates, as kids normally are when they are in the slightest bit different. When Jane appeared naked on the cover of *Lui*, the children told Kate her mother was "a whore"; and later, after Serge scandalously set fire to a banknote on television, Charlotte's classmates burned her homework in retaliation.

On the other hand, "We had lived all those years in a house where we weren't allowed to touch anything. Nothing at all. The children couldn't touch the piano – one of the first things I did when I left was buy a piano and get Charlotte lessons. It *was* like living in a museum. I felt as if I was disturbing the fantastic arrangement of what were mostly presents I'd given him. But once they were there you weren't allowed to move anything. We were allowed to change things in the children's bedroom. The kitchen? Of course not. The bedroom? Of course not. My little room he used to come in and see if it was tidy.

"I remember begging him to buy an apartment on the other side of the road and we could make a bridge or a tunnel or something." But even though it was a good enough system for his beloved Dali and Gala, Serge said no. "He said if I had a room apart it would be the beginning of the end. So I said, for the sake of the children, we should add an extra floor. But all the neighbours kept reminding us that we were 'artists', and that we were in the stables, and not in a house that was considered to be the monument that their apartments were.

"There was no space – but Serge would say 'There are metric cubes of air'. Yes there were. But there were also two children and an au pair girl behind a screen, who was so tall that the children could see her even when she was standing behind the screen, which was unnerving. When Charlotte was too big for her cot, I said to Serge, 'She must have a bed; her feet are poking out of the railings', and he said, 'Put socks on her'. In the end I got a double bunk-bed that was made of mahogany, so I thought that would go with the taste of the house."

Au pair girls – usually English – came and went with alarming rapidity. Serge's rather old-fashioned 'no boyfriends' rule didn't help. Not that they would have much opportunity to do anything, having to share their bedroom with two children. And they had to be inordinately tidy. When they used the bathroom, "they had to take away all their soap and flannel and things when they'd had a bath because it would ruin the beauty of the bathroom and hurt the eye."

All that she craved was "a certain form of liberty". After a long pause, Jane added, "When people die, it makes them sort of above everything, because you can only remember the good things, not the tiresome or irritating or the very, very bossy things – when you used to start a story and he used to whistle, as if to say 'Pipe down!'. I didn't really think I'd got much of a character next to him. But he was never knowingly cruel or violent. He was the most generous man I've ever known. Sometimes when he had been drinking he would say things that were clever and hurt people, then he would call them up and tell them he was sorry – and he *was* sorry. But then he couldn't resist saying it again a second time when he was a bit pissed. But afterwards, like a child, he thought he could be forgiven easily. He used to do wonderful things to be forgiven – fill a room full of flowers, get musicians to come to the room. So how could you not forgive him? And so it went on.

"Yes of course he drank too much. If you ask anybody who drinks a great deal, they are usually people who are extremely interesting to know and very shy, very *pudique* (an untranslatable word people often used when describing Serge, its meaning resting somewhere between reserved, discreet, shy and chaste). It puts the barriers down; he would dare to hold somebody's hand, kiss them, say something imprudent that otherwise he was too timid to do. I've seen it on other people who did not necessarily have Serge's genius, but people who were very intelligent, great writers, and you think, why do they get plastered like that? Because it's not really what they do to themselves, it's what it does to the other person.

"Serge told everybody I'd left because he was so drunk and difficult – which he was. Toward the end, I used to rush off to hotels with the children in the middle of the night because he sort of – he didn't know what he was doing. But dramatically we were very well-matched. When I got into a rage when he was writing a song for another girl – I was the one who was jealous – and I kicked in a present I'd given him, he kept it and told everyone with relish, 'Janette did that because she was so jealous' – but in fact he never went off with anybody else. He was an absolute darling."

On what was probably the most spectacularly dramatic occasion, after an argument in a nightclub, Jane threw herself in the River Seine. "He had turned my basket upside-down at Chez Castel, the nightclub, which meant that all my tampons and everything fell out. And he had made a slur over my past life with John Barry in front of everybody. I was humiliated. And he wasn't loved at that time – he wasn't the saint that he is now for people. He was someone who anybody in the room thought was very lucky to be with a very pretty and very young girl like me – and the posh group that were by the bar couldn't wait to see me getting my revenge.

"So a few days later when we were back at Castel, and we stayed up in the bar, there was a group of people and they were having a bit of a giggle about Serge. I don't know what about. And there was a custard tart on the table. I don't know why, but irresistibly my hand was drawn towards this custard pie, egged on by these stupid, giggling people. I was fairly drunk myself . And in a second I'd thrown it at Serge's face. Whereupon he stood up – he didn't do the ridiculous Laurel and Hardy gesture of flicking it off – he went straight towards the front door, tart falling off of his face bit by bit as he walked, totally dignified, all the way back to the Rue de Verneuil. And I was running after him, thinking, what can I *do* to say sorry to have humiliated him in the most unforgivable way in front of these silly, nightclubby people. And even in my quite drunken state I thought, I know what I can do: I can throw myself into the Seine.

"So I ran past him," (making sure he had seen where she was going, because she couldn't swim) "and I flung myself into the Seine. It was very cold, I was out of my depth and there was a terrible current. Whereupon the firemen came out to fetch me. Serge, very kindly, waded in too. My top, a rather pretty St Laurent I remember, had retracted somewhat because these garments were not made for being in water – it said dry cleaning only and I saw that that was perfectly true. And of course Serge forgave me."

In the end it was, ironically, the banality of their celebrity existence that made Jane decide to leave.

"The monotony of coming back at exactly the same time as the dustmen, having finished a decaf and a croissant first thing in the morning in Pigalle, and the children waking up just as you roll in. After years and years and years you can't resist pushing them a bit at the front door because they're so drunk they can't get their key in the lock. I tapped him on the back of the head and he fell and cut his eyebrow on the door moulding. The next morning he saw the black eye and asked me what had happened – he couldn't remember anything. I told him he had fallen over and he said, 'That's strange, drunks don't usually hurt themselves when they fall,' and I thought, 'Right, unless some evil person gives you a shove.' You get fed up… He was always so clever about tiny things and yet he didn't see the enormous thing coming." That she would actually leave.

When Jane told Serge she was depressed, he could not understand it. *He* wasn't depressed; his career was going better than ever. "He said '*Why* are you depressed? You have everything, you have money, you have the children, you have this house, you have *me*'."

His reaction to Jane's misery didn't help; he turned it into a song – 'Dépressive'. And he got her to sing it on her 1978 album *Ex-Fan Des Sixties*.

"It wasn't a very good song," said Jane, "because it didn't feel like me. He didn't understand that the outside me didn't correspond with the inside at all. Then someone came along who understood how unhappy I was." Jacques Doillon, an acclaimed young film director whom Jane first met in the summer of 1979 after Anne-Marie Berri, the wife of director-producer Claude Berri, had suggested that the two work together. They did the following year, in Doillon's fine film *La Fille Prodigue* (The Prodigal Daughter). First Jane fell in love with his films; then she fell in love with Doillon. He was already in love with her.

In 1980, Jane moved out of the black museum and into a hotel with the film-maker. "But I was ready to go – I think it didn't really matter who came by at that moment. I suppose it was my age or something. I was 34, 35, and I had only ever known two men, John Barry and Serge, and he was 20 years older and had known me since I was 19 or 20, practically a child. You're always expected to be the same and all of a sudden you weren't. I thought, 'Nobody's ever going to understand me. I don't want to be a doll anymore'."

Serge's reaction to her departure was perfectly Sergesque. He wrote a song about the man who had taken her away from him, 'Vieille Canaille/You Rascal You'. And he showed up at the hotel with a gift for Jane, a silver Porsche convertible – his way of apologising, perhaps, for not having been able to understand. And he took the blame for everything – telling everyone that it had been his shortcomings that had driven her away.

"He told everyone that I'd left because he was so impossible, because he drank so much, because he bashed me up – that's the sort of mythology he put about. Perhaps it was easier to take it that way. And he then based all the rest on the mythology of a sort of eternal love that he would have for you, and he had me moulded in bronze in his sitting room."

One afternoon Serge took Jane off to a sculptor's studio. She was led to a glass booth, like the one where she had sung 'Je T'Aime, Moi Non Plus', and the assistant poured in the material to make the mould.

"I remember very well being stuck in that telephone booth with two little heels that I was supposed to stand on as they shot in a lot of jelly stuff to model my body exactly. They were going to send up compressed air from the heels which was going to liberate the body from it, but I'd slipped off the heels – because the weight of jelly was so violent – which meant that I was stuck in a whole lot of jelly and when they sent the air through it just made a lot of rude noises. Whereupon some inspired person said, 'Let's do her head', and I said, 'Under no circumstances. You can make the head up later'. Once they'd pulled me out, I was covered everywhere with what looked like love-bites, because the jelly had stuck. And then they filled the mould up with a sort of plastic; I'd been weighed before so it filled it exactly.

"It's still there, at Serge's house. He took the head off – it was a very silly head they made later, so he was quite right to do so – and then he cut the arms and legs off because they didn't look particularly attractive. Then Serge rang me up after I was living in the Rue de la Tour and said, 'You've got blisters – or your statue has. It's like Dorian Gray! I'm going to file it down and have it dipped into bronze'. And so he did."

When Jane walked out, Serge called after her, "Jacques will make you into a nobody!" But Serge made her into a flawless, nude, unchangeable work of art, something that time or circumstances could never corrupt. With her legs cut off, the Jane de Milo would have no way of running; without a head, his Perfect Jane could never conceive of such an idea.

In an interview he gave *Rock & Folk* back in the mid 1970s, Serge had said: "If Jane leaves me, it wouldn't hold together any more. I am a very cold being, very suppressed, and suppressed passions, when they explode, are the most terrible."

Initially, Kate had told Jane she wanted to stay with Papa; she didn't think he could look after himself, and she was probably right. After Jane left, said Philippe

L'enfant

Self portrait

La Revolte Des Esclaves

Serge at work.

J.L. Rancurel / O. Medias

Chez Serge

With B.B. on the Bardot Show

Alain Nogues / Sygma

Serge and Jane

The Masterpiece

Photo by Giancarlo Botti, Camera Press

Serge and Jane demonstrate La Décadanse

Photo by Philip Lerichomme, reproduced with his kind permission

Serge as crooner

Serge and Jane en famille

Call to Armes *in Kingston, Jamaica*

At the birth of Freggae

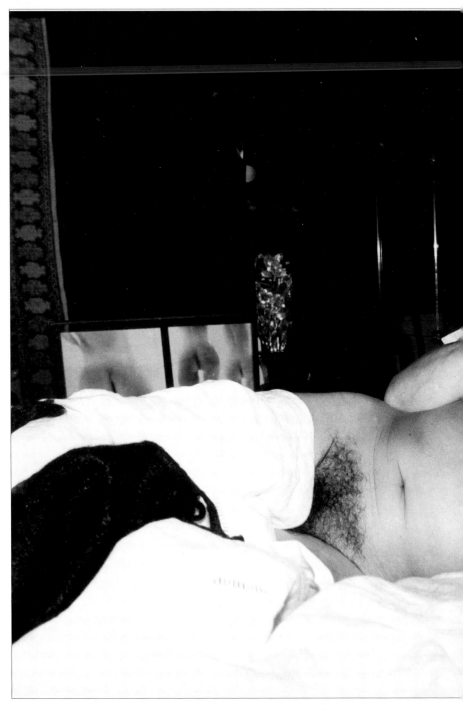

Au naturel

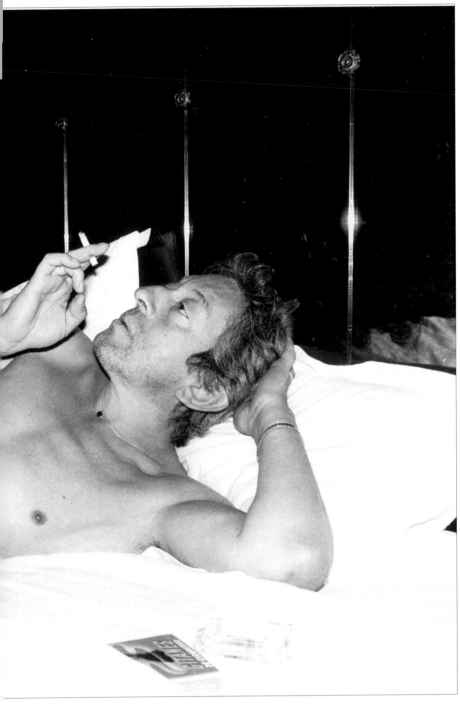

Photo by Patrick Duval, reproduced with his kind permssion.

With Catherine Deneuve on the set of Je Vous Aime

Serge and Bambou

Serge and Charlotte

With lolycéenne Vanessa Paradis

Geral / O Medias

Lerichomme, "he changed a lot. Of course he did." A long pause. "They both made a choice: she decided to leave, but he decided to stay alone as well. He liked that too, to be alone. He had a sad side to him. And to have been abandoned like that – it was somehow heroic for him, to be brave in the face of solitude. I think there was something of that to it – something poetic, something very Slavic, tragic, but a heroic sort of tragedy.

"He once said something that explained everything. If you take a camera and aim it at the sky and the weather's great, the sky is blue, everything's wonderful and sunny, you look at the photo and there's nothing there, it's just blank. But on a stormy day when there's lots of clouds, you take a photo then and you'll have something. And for him it was like that. The fact that Jane left and he missed her gave him the storms and the clouds that allowed him to create something wonderful."

It also allowed him to create something rather less wonderful: his dissipated, alcoholic alter ego *Gainsbarre*.

Chapter 14
THE ART OF FARTING

Jane had gone, Serge was shattered, yet at the same time his star had never shone so brightly. To his record company's astonishment – and to his own enormous satisfaction – the odd cult artist that they had pretty much left to his own devices since they had no idea how to market him, was suddenly outselling his unquashable label-mate Johnny Hallyday. The success, and subsequent scandal, of Serge's 1979 album *Aux Armes Et Caetera* had a knock-on effect on the back catalogue. First to be re-examined and elevated to gold album status were his two concept album masterpieces *Histoire De Melody Nelson* and *L'Homme À Tête De Chou*. A live album – *Au Théatre Le Palace* (At The Palace Theatre) – recorded with his "rastas" in Paris and released in 1980, ensured that the media attention continued. A good time, all in all, to publish his first – and only – novella: a quasi-autobiography set to, as he put it, "a soundtrack of farts".

Evguénie Sokolov is an erudite, tragi-comic tale of how a young man transcends suffering – in this case violent intestinal gas – by harnessing it to art and becoming in the process a huge success. Being Serge, it operates on a number of levels: an exposure of the often vile depths from which exquisite art can be created, an examination of the duality of the human condition (à la *Vu De L'Extérieur*), and an astute comment on fame and how successful artists are adulated for producing, quite literally sometimes, shit.

That last thought had become a popular subject with Serge in press interviews. "Records, TV, newspapers, having an impact on millions of kids, it's hallucinatory," he told one journalist. "A painting by Raphael will never sell as many tickets as Michael Jackson – *never*. Hallucinatory – a minor art screwing a major art up the arse."[1]

The way his producer Philippe Lerichomme saw it, Serge didn't really believe that what he was doing was 'minor': "It was just a game; when he died on 2nd March and we were going to leave on the 20th March for New Orleans, it wasn't in order to paint pictures." Perhaps not, but there was still something about Serge of the painter *manqué*, the would-be great artist who found himself feted for the lesser – and as he saw it less artistically significant – skill of writing pop songs.

Which is not an uncommon stance. Over the years, this writer has interviewed a number of successful, sometimes brilliant, rockstars who have expressed similar discontentment, and have tried their hand at writing novels, making films, taking photos or painting pictures, usually with unfortunate results. Being natural songwriters, they belittle what comes to them so easily on the presumption that something that takes such little effort can't be valid art. Although Serge had always made it patently clear that for him the frontiers between audio and visual, music, film and writing, simply did not exist, it was only his music that was lauded. It was a situation that the publication of *Evguénie Sokolov*, sadly, was not about to alter.

The story opens in a hospital where the narrator, lying in a shit-stained bed surrounded by buzzing flies, looks back over his life and the part played in it by the particularly odiferous and incessant wind he had been stricken with since birth. As a young schoolboy, by dint of an innocent face and a carefully placed, muting finger, he had avoided too many repercussions. But as he grew up, life as a farter had become increasingly more complex. It was not helped by his burgeoning sexuality. At the art school he attended, inflamed by the sight of nude models in the life-drawing class, he was obliged to visit a prostitute for oral relief, then farted at the poor girl as he climaxed. He was called up for military service, where the officers took his flatulence as insubordination and packed him off to military camp; but the rank and file admired his farting skills and he became so popular in the army he was almost sad to return to civilian life,

Back home he tried to distance himself from the vile-smelling gas by getting a bulldog to blame it on. And he continued painting pictures, if none too successfully. He'd had to take a job as a comic-strip artist to make money, an illustrated story about a superhero propelled through the air by his own farts. Then one day, when his body was shaken by a particularly powerful emission, he looked at the canvas and saw that the electrical tremors it had sent down his arm to his paintbrush had produced something magnificent. Just as the surrealists had devised the technique of 'automatic writing', Sokolov had invented automatic painting. Constructing a device that controlled the timbre and intensity of the fart, he set about producing a series of what he termed 'gasograms', which sold for fortunes and made him a star.

With his new-found wealth he bought a Bentley, hired a black valet, wore the best English jackets and American jeans. When, one terrible day, his farts stopped coming, he read up furiously on all matters intestinal and added so much fibre to his diet that he had to wear a protective mask just to be around himself. Even if fame and art were suffocating him, he needed them both to live.

The critics adored him; "They talked of hyperabstraction, formal mysticism, mathematical certitude, philosophical tension... and certain others mystification, bluff and crap. Three-quarters of my works were sold in two weeks, most of them to Americans, Germans and Japanese." Women loved him too. He became promiscuous to avoid becoming so close to a woman that she would discover his secret. This only earned him a reputation as a great seducer (though he knew himself to be a misogynist; had been since he first set eyes on the nude art-school models with their varicoloured pubic hair and, on one memorably repugnant occasion, a protruding tampon string). The first time he ever felt love was for an underage deaf-mute girl with an underdeveloped sense of smell. In his dreams he fantasised about recording his farts and turning them into a full symphony.

But eventually his intestinal problems led to hospitalisation: two rectal operations and an attempted suicide (by attaching a rubber hose to his gas mask and the other end up his behind). The third operation killed him. At his funeral two days later, the lid blew off his coffin when a passer-by lit up a cigar, igniting the gas that still orbited his body. "Sokolov had just passed his last anal sigh, his final, poisonous, posthumous flatulence to the memory of man." (My translation; I have since discovered the existence of a 1998 English-language version by John and Doreen Weightman, which boasts an afterword by Russell Mael of Sparks).

Anyone with an *I-Spy Book Of Gainsbourg* would have spotted any number of autobiographical moments. Serge himself referred to it in an interview with an art magazine as "an autobiography with distortions – horrific distortions which recall the manner of Francis Bacon".[2] His book – like his house, for that matter – was a fusion of Serge, Dali and Huysmans. The formal, straight-faced writing of *Evguénie Sokolov* aped the style of the *fin de siècle* Decadent. And since Dali's autobiography was appended with a novella-length essay titled 'The Art Of Farting', one can't help but suspect an homage or (like the pocketing of those pictures on his visit to Dali's apartment with Elisabeth) a shameless, if artistically motivated, theft.

Serge and Dali had always had a good deal in common. Dali, like Serge, had become a connoisseur of Paris's brothels on one of his first visits to the city. They shared an interest in scatology (something Dali referred to as "a terrorising element"), with Serge's song about shit-encrusted underwear echoing Dali's early painting of the figure similarly clad. Both Serge and Dali had a fascination with America, Hitler, films, fame, provocation and porn. (From time to time, Dali would organise an illegal Super 8 porn-film screening at the Meurice Hotel. Serge would go along – with Jane once; she didn't like it enough to go back a second time; and even Serge admitted to watching with one hand over his eyes.) Book critics, however, failed to pick up on any such artistic or literary references. When *Evguénie Sokolov* was reviewed at all, it was generally along the lines of Annette Colin-Simard's critique: "It is Gainsbourg's first novel and, let's hope, the last one he will write. The grossness of its subject is beyond the imagination. As for talent, absolutely none."[3]

But extracting art from farting (which, after all, had something of a noble tradition in France, perhaps best known through the famed music-hall flatulent Pétomane who could fart a good half-dozen notes of the 'Marseillaise') remained a firm interest. The 1980 album that Serge wrote for Françoise Hardy's husband Jacques Dutronc, *Guerre Et Pets* – a pun on the similarly pronounced Tolstoy novel *Guerre Et Paix*, *War And Peace* – translates as 'War And Farts'.

Songwriting commissions had come pouring in, in the wake of the success of *Aux Armes Et Caetera*. With Jane gone, Serge had no excuse not to write them. For some time, *chez Serge*, it was like post-Eurovision all over again. When Claude Berri, his old friend and neighbour, started work on his new film *Je Vous Aime* (I Love You) starring Catherine Deneuve, he called Serge to do the music. This included a Deneuve-Gainsbourg duet, released as a single, 'Dieu Fumeur De Havanes' (God The Havana-Cigar Smoker). In it Serge tells his *chérie*, See, God smokes all night, just like me; to which she replies, "You're only a Gitanes smoker" but "you are my master, after God."

Serge and Deneuve had actually become good friends – though no thanks to Serge, who turned up on the set blind-drunk and tried, unsuccessfully, to pick her up.

The actress was astute enough to see that he was suffering – to such an extent that she called up Jane to try to talk her into going back to him. Jane, who could never refuse Serge, went back to the Rue de Verneuil to attempt a reconciliation; in a fit of pride, Serge sent her away. But he credited Deneuve for being the reason he did not kill himself after Jane's devastating departure – a sentiment which Jane corroborated, praising her fellow actress for the way that she would regularly drop in at Serge's house to make sure that he was eating, sleeping and "not walking too close to windows." Jane too joined the regular care patrol, coming by with casseroles of his favourite home-cooked food.

British men might be forgiven a deep sigh of envy at witnessing how even badly behaved old Frenchmen could find themselves the object of such attentions from beautiful women. Even Serge's second ex-wife Béatrice – the mother of his children Natacha and Paul – had made moves to get them back together. Serge declared roundly that he had abandoned the monogamy of his Jane years for polygamy. But the spring of 1981 found him at the start of another new relationship. Caroline Von Paulus, aka Bambou, was 21-years old, a model, and – if that was not attractive enough – also a big Gainsbourg fan; one of the fans who could often be spotted outside his house at 5 Rue de Verneuil. As the newspapers ran pictures of Jane Birkin and her young partner Doillon, along with rave reviews of *La Fille Prodigue*, their film together, which was finally released, Serge was photographed close-dancing in a Paris nightclub with his new, even younger lover, Bambou.

* * * * * *

With the summer came thoughts of making another album. Another reggae album, Serge decided, with Sly Dunbar and Robbie Shakespeare. And so in September 1981, Serge and Philippe Lerichomme packed and got on a plane – this time to Compass Point Studio in the Bahamas. The far more upmarket location marked Sly & Robbie's upturn in fortunes in the short period of time since they'd worked with Serge in Kingston, Jamaica on *Aux Armes Etcaetera*. The pair were now highly in demand as producers.

"I didn't want to do a second reggae record," said Serge's producer. "I tried to always make sure that he was *en avance* – ahead – never behind or following. But Serge wanted to do it, as of course was his right." Lerichomme, though, was right to feel uneasy. The second experience was very different – and altogether less agreeable – than the first.

"They had become stars. They'd done an album with Joe Cocker, I think, and perhaps Dylan already, and Robbie – who before couldn't talk to us in English – was walking around reading *Billboard* and *Cashbox* like a businessman. That was the difference, a really a big difference in character."

In Serge's character too. By this time he was drinking very heavily – in the studio as well as after hours. As for their take on it, Robbie Shakespeare could only offer, "It felt a little bit different from the first – it's kind of hard to explain." While Sly Dunbar claimed to have remembered nothing about it at all.

"But they played very well," said Lerichomme, "and it's a good album," though not a jot on its predecessor *Aux Armes Et Caetera*.

Nothing, of course, could top the shock value to the French of the reggae 'Marseillaise', but on *Mauvaises Nouvelles Des Etoiles* (Bad News From The Stars) Serge did his best, with songs name-checking God, rastas, Jews, joints, sperm, poppers and his daughter's soiled underwear. In 'Juif Et Dieu' he claims God as a fellow Jew, 'Evguénie Sokolov' is a truncated attempt at the fart symphony that his novella's narrator dreamed of writing (fart noises set to a reggae beat), 'Mickey Maousse' turns the innocent Disney critter into a paean to his cock and sperm. And 'Ecce Homo' introduces for the first time the character 'Gainsbarre', the cool, bestubbled smoker that you might run into in *des nightclubs et des bars*.

"When I left," said Jane, "he started calling himself Gainsbarre – a made-up name, which could mean a complete nihilist. Gainsbarre used to laugh about Gainsbourg and mock Ginsburg, but they were always there inside him, like a Russian doll. I know that I was in love with Gainsbourg; I don't know about Gainsbarre. I never really understood. I remember when I saw him at the Palace where he sang with his rasta band – which was the first time he had sung in public in years and a comeback at quite an advanced age – I went to see him afterwards and, I don't know, perhaps I was a tiny bit reticent over something and he said something curt like, 'Well the *crowd* thought it was okay'. And I remember thinking, 'Yes, that's how it is now, he's become *un homme public*. So you lose Lucien Ginsburg and you lose that old Serge a little bit."

Serge himself had a wonderful phrase ready for when anyone asked him about the Gainsbourg/Gainsbarre duality, something along the lines of fellow-drinker Tom Waits' line about preferring "a bottle in front of me to a frontal lobotomy" but with a few added layers: *"Gainsbourg se barre, Gainsbarre se bourre"*. (For the non French-speakers, 'bourre' is pronounced like the 'bourg' bit of Gainsbourg. 'Se barre' means to cross yourself, shut yourself out or disappear, and 'se bourre' means to get shit-faced drunk, something usually achieved in *un bar*).

Gainsbarre was Gainsbourg's badly behaved alter ego, the *Docteur Jekyll* to his *Monsieur Hyde*. He was the battered, booze-soaked body-double he could send out to do his interviews and TV appearances. A good game and a good means of self-protection; a buffer between Serge and the real world and a way of stopping people (especially journalists) from getting too close. But the line separating Gainsbourg and Gainsbarre would become increasingly blurred. The Doors' keyboardist Ray Mazarek used to talk in a similar manner about singer Jim Morrison's alter ego 'Jimbo', the dissolute genie that lived in the bottle and that used to come out when the game got too much for the sensitive artistic genius Jim. Jim was the best person you could ever want to meet, he said; Jimbo could be amusing but was more often an offensive drunk. And there were times when Serge seemed to have become more addicted than was healthy to his dissolute twin. He certainly seemed to have a far closer relationship with him than he had with his real twin, Liliane. Perhaps he was making up for lost time.

As Philippe Lerichomme no doubt predicted they would, when Serge insisted on a second reggae album, some of the reviews of *Mauvaises Nouvelles Des Étoiles* (named after the Paul Klee painting that hung in Serge's house) accused him of having run out of ideas; hell, he'd even got Lord Snowdon back to shoot the cover. But Serge simply shrugged and said, "Brassens scratched away at his guitar all his life; surely I can do a second reggae album."[4]

And it has to be admitted that in 1981 Serge left his mark on a good deal of music that had nothing to do with reggae. There was another collaborative album, this time in Los Angeles, with Alain Chamfort, *Amour, Année Zéro* (Love, Year Zero) which produced three singles: 'Baby Boum', 'Chasseur D'Ivoire' (Ivory Hunter) and 'Bambou' (in honour of his new girlfriend, who flew to keep him company, since even the sun and blue sky failed to lift his mood). Another collaboration that year was with Alain Bashung – one of France's more interesting rock stars of the period and improving with the years. The pair shut themselves away, drunk, in a room and somehow kept on working, emerging with *Play Blessures* (Play Wounds), a very good album and rightly critically acclaimed.

He also made an album with Catherine Deneuve, *Souviens-Toi De M'Oublier* (Remember To Forget Me), which had some fine songs – including the revisited 'Ces Petits Riens' and 'Overseas Telegram', the jazzy Franglais 'What Tu Dis Qu'est-ce Que Tu Say' and 'Dépression Au-Dessus Du Jardin' (Depression Beneath The Garden), a song he once named as one of his favourites. But the album – unlike the film on which they had met – was not a success, which upset Deneuve far less than it did Serge.

One of his most unusual projects that year – resulting in a soundtrack single – was a cinema short, *Le Physique Et Le Figuré* (The Physical And The Figurative, with a few other meanings besides). In his first brush with the French beauty business since the attempt by a cosmetics company to launch the Baby Pop line named after his France Gall hit, Serge accepted a commission from The Organisation Of French Beauty Products to make a five-minute film for screening before the main movie in cinemas. It showed a model in a bathroom, brushing her hair and applying unguents. Really it was little more than a glorified arty commercial – one of several commercials he had signed up to do. By now his range of products had expanded; there were TV ads for Maggi soup and Gini lemonade. Just one item related to cleanliness – Brandt dishwashers. His ad for it – a mini *Gainsbourg Percussions* featuring Serge in a kitchen snapping his fingers, shaking packets of rice, hitting bottles and making a jazzy, percussive symphony of sound – won him a *Lion D'Argent* at Cannes for best commercial.

Another gong to add to the growing pile. But nothing could have topped the ceremony that had taken place earlier in 1981 at the Musée Grévin, Paris's ornate waxwork museum. Postcards issued to mark the occasion show a beaming Serge watching as his Madame Tussauds' style model was unveiled. Dressed in his trademark pin-striped jacket, jeans and soft white shoes; a Gitane in his hand, his face sweaty and pale, his wax twin stands by a fake EXIT door, looking oddly uncomfortable, as if he would like to run out of it. If you should go to look for him, he's downstairs, somewhat hidden in a corner, the last figure you pass before the you collide with the camera-wielding crowd snapping the spotlit splendour of the dummy Michael Jackson – upstaged by the man whom Raphael would never outsell.

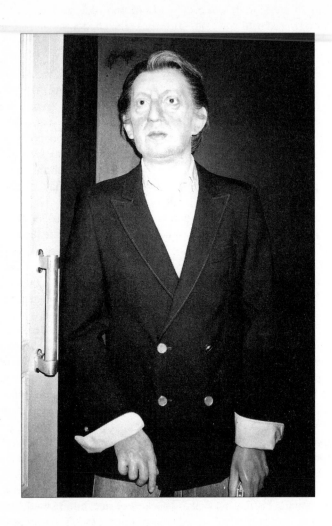

Chapter 15
STARS AND STRIPES

As Bambou's position in Serge's life became increasingly more established, he immortalised her in a book of nude photographs. *Bambou Et Les Poupées* – those dolls again – was a study of beauty, prostitution and forbidden eroticism as told through Serge's pictures and accompanying text. He was very pleased with the result; he told people it inspired him to go back to painting and writing and that he would turn Jane's old room in the house on Rue de Verneuil into a workroom. Since the day she walked out, he had kept her room exactly as it was: "No-one could touch anything I had left there," said Jane. "Hairpins, my stockings, dresses, underclothes, the Birkin shampoo from Germany which was pretty revolting but he thought it was funny, all my bits and pieces and toys from when I was small."

What Bambou made of her partner's shrine to his former love is anyone's guess. But it was evident that his interest in Jane hadn't waned, whether it was professional, personal or part of "the mythology" Jane said he had invented "of a sort of eternal love". In 1983 he wrote his first album for Jane since *Ex-Fan Des Sixties* five years earlier: *Baby Alone In Babylone*.

Jane: "After an initial, well, horrible time for him, I still used to go off and see him in the Rue de Verneuil. I couldn't resist. I used to bring him lunch. One day, when I'd brought him an enormous casserole of Lancashire hotpot, I said, 'Do you notice anything about me?' and he said 'No, did you cut your hair? Is it because you're wearing a dress?' and I said 'No, please look carefully. I'm having a baby, Serge'. And his response was: 'I forbid you to see my mother'. I would always go and see his mother, whom I adored, every Sunday, but he was furious and wanted to do something which would hurt me. To ban me from seeing his mother is rather a sweet reproach, when you think about it. It could have been infinitely worse."

When she gave birth to her daughter Lou, Serge was the first person she called from the hospital. "I said, 'It's a little girl,' and he said 'Thank God for that, because I can't see myself being a godfather to a little boy'. And packets and packets of bonnets and Russian fur booties arrived at the American hospital."

He would later tell Lou to call him *Papa deux*: – dad number two. "I realised that in an incredible way that he was managing to make the separation work – something as extraordinary as making a marriage work.

"After the intense pain of the first year, he came along while I was making a film in Marrakesh and I gave a party for Serge and Lou, who was a year old. That was all a bit peculiar, because Jacques was there... Serge took the royal suite at the end of the corridor which was for the King of Morocco, and from time to time, as I was filming in the same hotel, he would send glasses of champagne along and write on the little mat underneath, 'C'est pour les vitamines,' just in case I was lacking vitamins. And then he would lure the crew and people from the film to come along to the royal suite and listen to my record to hear what they thought. He was more than gentlemanly about everything. It was the same when I'd left him and he wanted me to be in the best hotel. I said, 'You can't pay for the hotel that I've left you to go into,' and he said 'I refuse for you to be in this third-class hotel' – where I'd shacked up with the children – and made me go to the Hilton. So it was a very curious affair."

In a reprise of the opening paragraph, one also has to wonder what Jane's new partner Jacques Doillon made of all this. Though the news that he reversed his car over Jane's famous basket – the one whose public emptying by Serge made her throw herself in the Seine – might give some indication.

Serge had decided to make *Baby Alone In Babylone* at the exact same time he undertook writing an album for Isabelle Adjani. "His only naughtiness," said Jane, "was he let Adjani come in first to the Rue de Verneuil to choose, so when I came in he used to play them and I would say, 'That's pretty, Serge', and he said *'Ah c'est pour Adjani'*..."

"Did he do it so the two would fight over him? Good question," said Philippe Lerichomme. "I think it was mostly an accident of planning, but I think too that he would have found that very stimulating. It was quite exciting for him to see two magnificent women interpreting his songs at the same time." Fortunately, their tastes were so different, said Jane, that unseemly squabbles were avoided.

"He'd done all the orchestrations in England before I got into the studio to meet Serge and Philippe. It was the first time that I hadn't gone to London with him, which was sad. And the first song he played was 'Con C'Est Con Ces Conséquences' (Stupid Consequences), which was just one of the saddest things to sing."

Although the music had been written and recorded earlier, the lyrics, as was usually the case, had been last-minute additions, done with his back against the wall.

"Apart from *L'Homme À Tête De Chou*, which he worked out in advance, all the others I know of were written at the last moment," said Lerichomme. "He always started out with the title – he'd see something around him that would appeal to him, something on a sign or a poster or a word or two here and there. I used to invent fake deadlines for him, because it made me sick to see him so worn out, especially with his health problems. But Serge could only work like that. "If Jane was booked to sing at two o'clock, he would come in at one o'clock with the thing he'd written in the night, and we'd get it in shape, put everything in the right order, make any edits."

The health problems he mentioned had stemmed from a recent trip to Africa, where Serge had been directing his second film, *Equateur*. Making the suspense story based on a Georges Simenon novel had not been an easy or a pleasant experience. His initial choice to play the starring role, Patrick Dewaere, had killed himself a few days after Serge approached him, added to which funds had dried up and Serge, like several of the participants, had caught a tropical bug. But, back to the studio. "Serge would lie down on the sofa while Philippe wrote it out in capital letters and I wrote it down in phonetical writing to understand what he had written," said Jane. "Every night he worked all night with black coffee and Gitanes cigarettes and would come in like a ghost the next day and say, 'Here's three'. One time he came into the studio and slammed two songs on the table that he had written in the night – two absolute, perfect beauties, 'Les Dessous Chics' (Chic Lingerie) and

'Fuir Le Bonheur De Peur Qu'il Ne Se Sauve' (Run Away From Happiness For Fear It Will Run Off). When I realised the meaning and what he was saying in songs like 'Fuir Le Bonheur', I was crying on my side of the glass and he was crying on his side of the glass, while Philippe Lerichomme was writing down which were the best takes. Serge was pleased with anything. He'd say, *'Non, mais c'est bien, il y a de l'émotion, je m'en fou'* (it's fine, there's emotion, I don't care) and Phillipe would say, 'No, I want her to sing *juste*, or she'll be cross with herself if she doesn't pronounce it properly because the lyrics are so exquisite.'

"I realised that he was in fact asking me to sing words about his pain and the separation – that I was singing his wounded side, his feminine side, the B-side of Gainsbarre. I actually asked him whether it was all right to say that and he said, 'Yes', he thought that was right, and that it was unusually bright of me!"

Apart from their soul-baring aspect, the lyrics also displayed Serge's trademark in-built rhythm and plays-on-words. 'Haine Pour Aime', for example, sounds like 'N for M' while meaning 'hate for love', while the syllables of 'Con C'Est Con Ces Conséquences' (pronounced con-say-con-say-con-say-cons) sawed like a sad old violin.

Baby Alone In Babylone went gold, as did Isabelle Adjani's eponymous debut (which featured one of Serge's most painful puns, 'Beau Oui Comme Bowie'. But Jane's also took first prize from *L'Academie Charles Cros* – the same prestigious award which Serge had received for *Du Chant À La Une!* 25 years earlier, and which he accepted, on Jane's behalf with tears in his eyes as she went off to shoot another film.

✳ ✳ ✳ ✳ ✳ ✳

Jane may have been taking care of Gainsbarre's B-side, but the A-side was still very much at large. In March 1984 it was responsible for one of the biggest scandals of Serge's career. When it came to TV shows, Gainbourg increasingly 'barred' himself, handing the reins to his debauched twin; the results would be either hilariously funny, wickedly witty, provocative, pertinent or alcoholically pathetic, depending on the occasion and one's viewpoint. Most of the time, when he stepped over the limit, people just shrugged and said it was Serge being Serge. But it was a different matter when, railing against "the whore called socialism" on prime-time TV, he set fire to a 500 franc (£50) bank note, blowing out the flames when only a quarter of the note remained – the amount he had left, he said, after paying his tax.

No big deal, you might think, even if note-burning is illegal in France, but it caused the kind of telly-smashing outrage that greeted the Pistols' TV appearance with Bill Grundy. It wasn't just the patriots who were upset, the ones who had objected before to the reggae 'Marseillaise', but normal, working-class French people with no money to burn. Serge was unapologetic. He had no regrets, he told journalists, he loved scandals, they kept his life interesting. Privately though, the vehemence of the reaction rattled him, according to Jane. "Serge paid his taxes; he didn't have a company in Switzerland. He used to go off to the tax man himself, on foot, at the end of the Rue de L'Université and fill out a cheque and, towards the end of his life, when he didn't see very well, he made Fulbert fill it out for him, and he said he made Fulbert cry because he couldn't bear that Serge paid so much tax." Fulbert was the new valet Serge took on following the passing of Mamadou.

Under the circumstances, it was probably with some relief that Serge agreed to Philippe Lerichomme's suggestion to go off to America to make his next album. "Serge had only ever gone to England to work," said the producer. "He adored recording in England; the sound was different and the culture among the musicians wasn't the same as it was in France. I think that that's changed now – in France today there are some great musicians among the young generation – but back then, the English musicians with whom he worked, although they were the same age as him, had cut their teeth on rock music, whereas in France they'd cut their teeth on the accordion. So working in England was very, very important to what he did, but although he had been to the States several times to do other things, he had never recorded an album there for himself."

Lerichomme had been listening to a record an associate had sent him – *Trash It Up* by Southside Johnny & The Asbury Jukes, the band championed by Bruce Springsteen. It was co-produced, Lerichomme noted, by Nile Rodgers of Chic fame and Asbury Juke guitarist Billy Rush. Having tried, unsuccessfully, to recruit the busy Rodgers, he turned to Billy Rush, who had even less knowledge of French pop music than Sly & Robbie, claiming an ignorance even of 'Je T'Aime, Moi Non Plus'. But after some initial awkwardness, their first endeavours at Rush's home studio – a converted garage in New Jersey – went well. Serge and his producer played him some tapes of the songs' basic tunes and Rush went right to work.

"We didn't speak," he told Verlant. "I sensed he was unsure and measuring me up... I chose a rhythm, stuck on a bass, threw in some keyboards and guitars." Serge took the tape back to his hotel and returned the next day and said "Great, let's keep going." Rush was given the job of choosing the musicians – including Peter Gabriel's synthesiser player Larry Fast, plus Stan Harrison and Steve and George Simms from David Bowie's band. Despite their long experience in the business, they were nevertheless dumbfounded at how much Serge drank during the recording ses-

sions in New York's Power Station studios. "Enough," Rush said, "to knock out a horse. I had to move my family out and turn my house into a giant bar. He'd make incredibly strong piña coladas. And did he smoke! If I get lung cancer it's his fault."

Love On The Beat's English title came with the added delight for Francophones of 'beat' being a homonym for 'bite', French for penis. The song titles were all-English too, even if the hard-edged lyrics were not. "New York music is very hard, so I have to align myself", explained

Serge. "The kids aren't afraid of words any more, nor of ideas. Through intellectual necessity, I have to go along." One of the themes of the album was homosexuality – 'Kiss Me Hardy', for example, which namechecks the painter Francis Bacon, and takes Admiral Nelson's dying words and turns them into a love song to his faithful assistant – which was underlined by Serge's decision to appear on the sleeve made up as a woman (and since, aesthetic as ever, he wanted to be a beautiful woman, he claimed to have stopped drinking for a fortnight to try to lose the bags under his eyes).

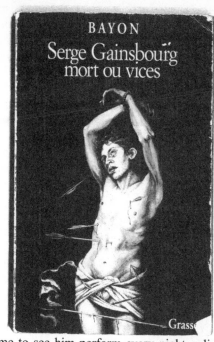

He had spoken, in his interview with Bayon in *Mort Ou Vices*, of how older men had fancied him as a child, and claimed that most beautiful declaration of love he had ever received had been from a good-looking young man who came to see him perform every night, religiously, when he was still a nightclub pianist. An attempt at a sexual relationship, with Serge on the receiving end, had ended in *abjection totale*; that he had never managed to play the "chick", he said, was one of the greatest regrets of his life.

But by far the most controversial aspect of the album was his duet with his 13-year-old daughter Charlotte. The love song, based around a Chopin Étude and fleshed out with throbbing bass and funky beat, had the title 'Lemon Incest'. Sensing another *cause celèbre*, and the possibility of another *Aux Armes Etcaetera*-type success, Serge's record label launched the electro-funk album in 1984 with a huge media blitz. 'Lemon Incest' – released as a single the following year – went to number one, while its video, featuring Serge and Charlotte side by side on a circular bed, hit another ten on the scandalometer.

"How could people have imagined that he would have been a father that could have abused his children in any way!" protested the girl's mother. "Charlotte, whom he loved so, he who always found it so difficult to actually say that he loved someone. It was a love song to Charlotte, to show her off, and to have play on words like lemon zest and put it to classical music, was something Serge couldn't resist. Of course he knew he was being provocative, but he was horrified that people would actually think –." Jane, clearly horrified herself, was for a moment lost for words.

"He was the most unlikely person to touch anyone. He was easily shockable. You couldn't get anyone that was more *pudique* – it makes me mad that I can't translate that word, you will have to put it in French. The children never, ever saw him naked in his life. *No-one* ever saw him naked. I never saw him naked. Bambou didn't. He always covered himself with the dressing-gown that he'd brought off the film

Romance Of A Horse Thief. He was the most modest of men."

As Serge told Bayon, he didn't even like to see his penis in the mirror and would always hide it with his hand. When he was in hospital and the nurses came to clean him, he would cover his genitals with a towel. "I am extremely *pudique*," he said, "I always have been."[1]

As for incest, "I am a man subject to vertigo and I think that incest is – vertigo," he said. "I imagine that it could be superb, but at the same an atrocity."[2] As he pointed out, the key words in the song were "The love that we will never make together".[3] As for paedophilia in general, he couldn't understand the attraction, he said; little girls smell of piss on one side and shit on the other. He was certainly in love with Charlotte, just as Jane had been in love with her father and, as was normally the case in father-daughter relationships, Charlotte was in love with him too. But to degrade it with the sex act, he said, would be "an abomination". As for Charlotte herself, she recalled the experience as "completely innocent and easy," and had no memory at all of "any of the scandals that it caused".

One more scandal before we leave 1984 (one, it must be said, that did not upset the French anywhere near as much as the note-burning incident, though it did tweak the attention of tabloid newspapers in the U.S. and U.K.): the infamous Whitney Houston incident.

It was one of those live variety shows with which French TV is still infected, of a type that make the Parkinson programme look like the very apex of the avant-garde. The line-up that night was a prestigious one: Serge, Eddy Mitchell (the chunky, post-menopausal, but still gainfully-employed French rock 'n' roller) and Whitney. The diva, following the fluff format of these shows, sang her song then sat down next to Serge, beatifically smiling, ready to indulge in the standard chat that was part oleaginous flattery, part new-product plug. Whitney spoke in English, the other guests in French, while the beaming host Michel Drucker lobbed translations back and forth like a manic tennis pro. Serge, looking like something poured out of Tom Waits' whisky bottle and bristling at Drucker's deliberate bland mistranslations of his various mutterings, suddenly interjected, in plain English, "I said I want to fuck her."

"WHAT DID HE SAY?" screamed Whitney. The pale-faced presenter tried to smooth things over, offering more fake translations in English, assuring La Whitney that what Serge had really said was he found her "great" and "very pretty". To clear up the confusion, Serge repeated his statement in French: *"J'ai dit que j'ai envie de la baiser."*

Drucker, a strained rictus stretched across his face, suggested that his mother might want to switch channels. Since it was live TV and the damage had already been done, and there were still ten minutes left to fill with a Gainsbourg-Mitchell duet, Serge survived the evening without being thrown off the show.[4]

"I saw it live!," said Nicolas Godin of Air, a youngster when it was broadcast. "I was watching it with all my family at my godfather's house and all of a sudden he said that he wanted to fuck Whitney Houston! It was amazing – very shocking and very funny." And a lot of people agreed with him. Serge had got away with saying something that no doubt a lot of people thought but would never have dared to put into words – his reputation not only intact but enhanced.

The following year Serge was back on TV, atoning for the earlier scandal of the note-burning, handing the presenter a cheque for 100,000 francs (£10,000) made out to the charity Médecins Sans Frontières. It was an expensive retribution for the destruction of 500 francs, but that was not the reason why Serge looked so sober. He *was* sober. Just a short time before, his mother had died. She was 90 years old, but the shock still knocked Serge sideways, to the degree that for a while he put the bottle aside. But his period of abstinence clearly seemed to be over when he appeared at the Casino De Paris that autumn, stumbling down a flight of steps before standing in front of the microphone to a standing ovation from the crowd.

When Serge decided he was going to tour with the *Love On The Beat* album, he asked Billy Rush to once again put together a band. They were somewhat surprised to find themselves travelling in France in a style they were unaccustomed to in America. Serge, who brought with him as many of the comforts of home as he could fit in the removal van that tagged along behind them, took the musicians to fancy restaurants and bought them gifts. "He treated them like kings," said Jane. "He was sincerely appreciative of their talents. And, though he loved his English musicians, he felt more familiar with the Americans because he felt less intimidated talking to them; he didn't feel like he was not speaking correctly. Serge was a proud man and he was always afraid to be less brilliant in English than he was in French."

The show at the Casino De Paris resulted in the live album released the following year. But the tour also came with another bonus. Serge, Billy Rush recalled, was delighted to find himself mobbed by young girl fans. "Look," he would point out to the musician, "they're fainting over me."

Jane: "It was the most important thing to Serge that teenagers loved him – and that only really happened after I left. He would ring me up and say, 'Did you see me on the television last night?' And when I would tick him off and say it was rather rude, he would say 'I don't care what you think, the young ones thought it was great'. I used to be so conventional. I'd say, 'Serge, that is a horrible, horrible jacket' – he'd had one made out of snakeskin – and he said, 'I don't care what you think, the kids love it.' Good old Serge, he was right."

Chapter 16
SUCK BABY SUCK

In January 1986, at the age of 57, Serge became a father again. Photographs show his crumpled face, smudged with stubble, smiling proudly down at the tiny baby in Bambou's lap and offering him his first Gitane. Spurred by tradition, one imagines, rather than some 'Boy Named Sue'-esque effort to toughen him up, Serge named his second son and fourth child Lucien and nicknamed him, naturally, Lulu. He marked the occasion by writing a song for the new baby and handing it to its mother to sing; which is how Bambou found herself in a glass booth in a recording studio making her first single, 'Lulu'.

For Lulu's half-sister Charlotte, meanwhile, Serge wrote a film. The plot of *Charlotte Forever* revolved around an adolescent girl whose mother is killed in a car crash (a sports convertible not entirely dissimilar from the one Serge bought Jane after she left him) and who now lives alone with her father Stan, an alcoholic and suicidal screenwriter whose career, life and liver are all on the skids; his one success in life has been his daughter. Stan throws up, pisses blood and then crawls into bed to sleep next to the girl – there's a sexual tension, but it's unconsummated. Charlotte had the role of the daughter, while Serge played her father. Although still barely 15 years old, Charlotte, quite the pro, had already been making her name as an actress, but Serge's film was hard-going. She was too young to appreciate her father's sophisticated aesthetic and, with matters further complicated by the blurring of real life and make-believe and her own *pudique* nature, she was reduced to tears when Serge undressed her in the film. Her memory this time was that it "was not very comfortable. Because it was a bit too close".

But "I think Serge was more frightened of Charlotte than the other way round", said Jane. "I had no qualms whatsoever about *Charlotte Forever*, in fact I rather pushed Charlotte into doing it. I knew that Serge, when he loved somebody, wanted to make a record about them, write a film for them, put them in the spotlight and make them look beautiful. And, just as for me there was no question of Jacques (Doillon) saying no when Serge said he wanted to use him in a film, even though Jacques said, 'But I'm a bad actor and I don't want to do it' – thank goodness, that film didn't come about! – there was no question for me of Charlotte saying no to *Charlotte Forever*, even if it meant her losing her first trimester at school. It was only when Catherine Deneuve said, 'Why is she crying?' and I said, 'because Serge is going to do a film in September and she wants to go on doing her school classes' and Catherine said, 'So she should', and I said to Catherine, 'We can't do it to Serge', and she said 'But we can't do it to Charlotte!' that I went back home and phoned Serge and repeated what she'd said. And Serge said, 'Oh, I hadn't thought of that', and he fixed for it all to be done a month earlier. Catherine of course had been right. She'd put up resistance in a motherly way and I'd put up none, because I somehow thought only of him."

When the reviews appeared, several of them labelling the film "distasteful", "unhealthy" and "sick", Serge was the one who was in tears, Jane said. This time even some of his supporters seemed to feel he might have broken one taboo too far.

To compensate, he wrote his daughter a touching album with the same name. The title track and 'Plus Doux Avec Moi' (Gentler With Me) are affecting father-daughter duets, while in 'Pour Ce Que Tu N'Étais Pas' (For What You Were Not) Charlotte sings, "I took you for what you weren't and left you for what you are"[1] – a variation on the theme of Serge's oft-repeated quote about taking women for what they're not and leaving them for what they are. In the Anglo-French hybrid 'Oh Daddy Oh' she has him pinned down as a guy who "fucks too much, smokes too much, drinks too much" and who takes himself for "Huysmans, Hoffman, Rimbaud and Edgar Allen Poe".[2]

"Charlotte seemed perfectly comfortable in the studio," said the album's engineer Dominique Blanc-Francard. "As did he. When Serge was singing alone and it was just him, Philippe Lerichomme and me, he always seemed a bit lost – he didn't like to hear himself sing alone in the cabin with his headphones – and he was much harder to please. But when he was with Charlotte or the other singers he wrote for – Birkin, Adjani – he would be in there directing, making sure that everything went well. On his own he struck me as much more timid but when he worked with these women he was much more strong and forceful; there was a kind of seduction going on."

That year a two-decade-old seduction was resurrected, in the form of the Gainsbourg-Bardot version of 'Je T'Aime, Moi Non Plus'. B.B. – who had hung up her head-phones some years before after recording around 70 songs – finally gave the go-ahead for its release to raise money for Greenpeace and her animal shelter. Also in the shops was a compilation album of Serge's songs sung by Jane Birkin. If Bambou – who had waited three years before getting to record a Serge song, far longer than his ear-lier female associates, singers or oth-erwise – felt she was in second or third place, publicly she just said "I love him, therefore I forgive every-thing". Quiet and dignified, in spite of the image 'Bambou Et Les Poupées' might have given, she was uncomfortable with the tabloid attention that Serge so loved. "With

VERSION ORIGINELLE

JE T'AIME MOI NON PLUS
BARDOT · GAINSBOURG

45T N° 884 840-7 – 45 T GÉANT N° 884 840-1
ENREGISTREMENTS ORIGINAUX

Jane," she told Verlant, "they made the ideal media couple – much less so with me. It's not the same, I'm not a public person. Without him I don't exist – and I'm well aware of that."[3] Releasing a single had evidently been Serge's idea, not hers.

Serge's own 1986 releases included a soundtrack album from *Tenue De Soirée* (Evening Dress) – Bertrand Blier's somewhat 'Je T'Aime, Moi Non Plus'-themed film in which Gerard Depardieu's character fucks a man (Michel Blanc) dressed as a woman – a riot of alliteration with its titles 'Travelling', 'Traviolta One', 'Traviolta Two', 'Traviolta Three', 'Travaux', 'Travelure', 'Entrave', 'Travers', 'Travelo', 'Traverse', 'Travelinge', 'Traveste', 'Trave' and 'Traveling', all based around the prefix *trave*, meaning transvestite. There was also the *Live* album from the previous year's Casino De Paris show with his American band, and a single 'My Lady Héroïne' (My Lady Heroin). The words of the song – which had first appeared back in 1977 – about the beautiful 'lady' from the Far East who had come to lead him to paradise, took on a new significance bearing in mind that it hadn't been that long since Lulu's half-Asian mother had quit shooting up. Perhaps Serge had revisited it as some sort of badge of merit for Bambou.

He was to receive another of those himself that year when he was presented with the prestigious Croix D'Officier de L'Ordre Des Arts et Des Lettres medal by the French Minister of Culture, Jack Lang. It was Gainsbourg, not Gainsbarre, who turned up to accept it; these days his alter ego couldn't be trusted. He had shown a particularly unattractive side on a TV programme where his fellow guest was Catherine Ringer, the singer with the fine French art-rock group Les Rita Mitsouko. Many years earlier, when Ringer wasn't making enough money from music to support her drug habit, she had acted in some porn movies under a pseudonym. Serge wouldn't let the matter drop; he turned on the singer – as it happens, a long-time Gainsbourg fan – and called her "disgusting" and "a whore". A bit rum from someone who claimed to have enjoyed enthusiastic and ongoing relations with prostitutes since adolescence, and who had not only scored music for soft-porn films but sat in the audience at several more distinctly hard-core ones. Ringer handled it calmly and articulately, while Serge, looking utterly dissipated, could barely sit upright and slurred his words. What appeared to be on display here was either unfortunate over-acting on Gainsbarre's part or a neon display of self-disgust by Gainsbourg. Afterwards, brazening it out, he said he behaved "according to my moods – because I am impulsive. Not aggressive".[4] But there was beginning to be a look of corruption about him. Like a negative image of *Dorian Gray*, as his work stayed fresh and invigorated, his appearance became more worn and debauched.

His next project was another new album for Jane: 1987's *Lost Song*. "I remember I had come back from Japan," said Jane, "and I said to Serge, 'I don't know where I am in life. They ask me, do you feel more French than English – always the same old questions – and I don't know. It's like I'm not 20 any more but I'm not yet 40 – I'm just somewhere in the middle'. Serge said, 'I don't want to talk about age, ever', and I said, 'Well, I don't know if I'll be left'. And he said, 'We will never mention that you would ever be left; there'll be no question of another man or another girl, ever. You are ageless. But I suppose what you really want is a lost song'. And I asked him to write a song about my friend Ava, who had died a few years before, and he came up with the breathtaking 'L'Amour De Moi' (The Love Of Mine) which was an old French song from Elizabethan times which he changed."

Jane was to make her solo singing debut onstage that March. In spite of nerves, she had been keen to do it, in response to the bad press Serge had received from the film with Charlotte. "There was a journalist who had written that Serge was a finished man; I wanted to get up there with his songs and say, is *this* a finished man? And to stay stoically faithful to Serge the way he always stayed stoically faithful to me." The show was a triumph, and captured in a live album *Au Bataclan*.

✳ ✳ ✳ ✳ ✳ ✳

Another event that same month was decidedly more unsettling. Charlotte was the victim of a bungled kidnap attempt. And a very singular one at that: on her way home from school she was grabbed by a three-man aristocratic gang led by a 24-year-old French prince named Edouard Faussigny-Lucinge. It ended with a shoot-out in the Latin Quarter. The would-be kidnappers later claimed to have been inspired by watching Serge set fire to the bank-note on television, figuring if he had money to burn, he would happily hand over the French equivalent of half a million pounds for his daughter's safe return. According to "friends" quoted in *The Express*, Serge collapsed under the strain.

But his work-load had not eased up. In August 1987 Serge flew back to New York to make another album with Billy Rush and the *Love On The Beat* musicians. *You're Under Arrest* – a rap album this time – borrowed its title, accidentally or otherwise, from Miles Davis. The arrest-sheet under the police mug-shot on the cover included *"détournement des mineurs"* – corrupting the young. In 'Suck Baby Suck', Chuck Berry, Bob Dylan and Bill Haley CDs and Tex Avery cartoons are judged equally effective blow job soundtracks. 'Five Easy Pisseuses' (a "pisseuse" being a weak-bladdered female) managed to encompass a Jack Nicholson film, golden showers, Serge's sizeable erection and an Anglo-French pun all in one song. Several numbers also featured the appearance of yet another of the young female characters that populate his albums – this one a black Lolita named Samantha. It was while scouring the Bronx looking for Samantha in the title track that Serge was hauled over by the cops.

"You're under arrest" rap the backing singers, "Cause you're the best". The song also namechecked – in a torturous pun on the Bronx – Bronski Beat, the group whose frontman Jimmy Somerville had brought joy to a 60-year-old French rockstar's heart by covering 'Comment Te Dire Adieu/It Hurts To Say Goodbye' and taking it into the U.K. charts. (The impossibly high-voiced singer had discovered the song on the Françoise Hardy record that his French boyfriend had given him as a gift.)

Coming across the epic anti-drug song 'Aux Enfants De La Chance' among all this filth and fun might have raised a few eyebrows, particularly bearing in mind Gainsbarre's increasingly evident alcoholism and his addiction to Gitanes. Significant, perhaps, that weeks after the album's November 1988 release, Serge and Bambou were plastered over the papers under the headline: 'Gainsbourg-Bambou: Drogue!' (Drugs) after Bambou was intercepted by police leaving a dealer's house.

You're Under Arrest's song-titles and tough, edgy lyrics were written variously in

French, English and Franglais. "You must not forget that French is a guttural lan-guage." (Not something that the *Académie Française* or A-level teachers would have been pleased to hear.) "Then, I love that," said Serge, "I've become pretty strong in English since touring with my Yanks."[5]

Rush and the band had been flown over in March 1988 for a second tour, which would take in three nights in Paris, where Serge was a star. The American noticed how much Serge seemed to have aged in the few years since they'd seen each other. He looked tired and worn down, said Rush, and if he was continuing to work, it was only because taking a break would have somehow been even worse.

The video shot during Serge's seven-night stand at the Zénith in Paris in March 1988 (recently remixed and upgraded by Lerichomme and Blanc-Francard to DVD) shows a puffy-faced man with stubbled double chin, rheumy eyes and a waxy com-plexion, and that kind of sweat that seems to come from the eyes that only very sick people or serious addicts get. But however bad he looked, hunched over the micro-phone like the victim of repetitive shrug injury, he still looked in control, his spoken vocals contrasting perfectly with the precision of the backing singers as he prome-naded through his back catalogue.

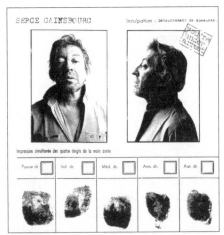

But in interviews at the time, he did sound depressed. "I had everything and I no longer have anything," he said to Verlant. "The idea of happiness is a stranger to me. I cannot conceive of it, therefore I don't look for it."[6]

A journalist from *Rock* magazine was told, "To be honest, I am not at my high-est point. I feel perishable and I want nothing of me to remain when I die."[7] He even sounded negative about the one thing he seemed to have always striven for – eternal fame. Although it was probably the "eternal" bit that dismayed him. For someone who didn't believe in death, as Jane put it, or at least didn't believe it would ever happen to him, he seemed very much aware that time was running out. "I don't want to go down in posterity. What has posterity ever done for me? I fuck posterity." All his career had been, he said, was "a search for the truth via an injection of perver-sity", before rallying enough energy to declare, as if chiselling out his own epitaph, "I have remained intact. INTACT. That is my strength."[8]

Intact, but with a lot of hairline fractures. The cumulative effect of the alcohol had brought on D.T.s, nightmares, even a coma. In December 1988, British writer and rock journalist Nick Kent found himself sitting next to Serge in the ski resort of Val d'Isères. It was one of those annual French music industry get-togethers, and Serge, Kent and the filmmaker Julien Temple were part of a panel judging the current crop of rock-related films, among them the John Lennon documentary *Imagine*, Prince's *Sign 'O' The Times* and The Pet Shop Boys' *It Couldn't Happen Here*.

"He looked like he wasn't taking care of himself. His eyes had that bloodshot, unfocused look of someone who was not so slowly poisoning himself with alcohol. One of the other people on the panel was staying in the room next door to Gainsbourg's suite, and he told me that every night he was awakened by Gainsbourg in the next room screaming – *screaming* – 'I'm going blind!' He was in a terrible state. I'd been clean for about eight months when I saw Serge Gainsbourg", said Kent, a former heroin addict, "and it reminded me of all the reasons I gave up substance abuse. Most of the time he was either hungover or on another drunk, so it was very hard to have a conversation with him, though he didn't really want to talk to anyone English anyway. I got the feeling that his grip of the language wasn't as strong as he wanted and that he preferred to be around French people who just kissed his arse all the time and thought he was great.

"In my opinion, he was being corrupted by the alcohol and also by his genuine iconic status. And he loved being an icon, he lapped it up. He understood how to stay on top and stay well loved. He knew how to deal with the media, the right people in the media to talk to, and he knew how to appeal to the French people's sense of the artist as this kind of beautiful loser. He had all the classic symptoms: the *joli-laid* figure who was very earthy on one level and a romantic poet on the other, and he was drinking himself to death. There was a tradition to this; it was something that the French related to very intensely. British people, I think, reach a point with drunks where after a certain level, when they're just not functioning and become sad old drunks – Shane MacGowan or George Best for example – we just don't tolerate it. Whereas Gainsbourg went way beyond that. I think that's what helped kill him."

Serge, incidentally, was very taken with the Prince film but finally gave his vote to *Imagine*. "He loved it. Here was an icon watching another icon and he was in tears, just incredibly moved by the whole thing." As for the Pet Shop Boys' opus, "he fell asleep".

Chapter 17
REQUIEM FOR A TWISTER

In 1989, Philips Records launched their monumental nine-CD, 207-track, Serge box-set *De Gainsbourg À Gainsbarre* with a poster campaign proclaiming: "Gainsbourg is not waiting until he's dead to be immortal".[1] Rather unfortunate when an ambulance was screaming past the men with the paste pots and brushes, taking Serge to hospital after another heart attack.

That year he would be in and out of the American Hospital five times. The first time, in January, the doctors warned him that if he didn't stop drinking he would be blind in six months and dead in twelve. "My back's against the wall, but I don't give a fuck," Serge shrugged.[2]

It takes a toughness as well as a weakness to drink the amount that he did and, if alcohol didn't agree with him, he seemed more than happy to continue the debate. There were some powerful reasons for doing so. There was his image to consider, for one thing. As Serge told a British journalist who made one of the rare pilgrimages to Paris for an interview, "What is rock 'n' roll all about, if not sex and drinking?" And what is a rock 'n' roll poet if not – as Verlaine once described Baudelaire – "a modern man with senses sharpened and quivering, his painfully sensitive awareness, his brain soaked in tobacco, his blood burning with alcohol"?

On a more personal level, it was also his mask and crutch. Said Dominique Blanc-Francard, "I think it was a way of hiding his shyness, and a bit of despair as well in a world in which he did not feel completely fulfilled in the role that he had. He was a poet, but they wanted him to play this image. What he told me once was, 'People expect me to be like this – badly shaved, a bit dirty and shocking', and whenever there were journalists in the recording studio he was impeccable at playing this role. I remember him being offered a TV thing once and he said 'It's not worth going because it isn't live. If I make some filthy remark, they'll take it out'. But in the end it was his choice; he was the one who decided to be like that."

"He was very much in control of his image," Charlotte confirmed, if not quite so much so with the drinking. "For a child the alcohol and what it did to him wasn't very pleasant." "And he said he couldn't stop completely," said Blanc-Francard, because all his life he'd drunk and smoked regularly to get into the rhythm of writing, so if he deprived himself of the lot, it just wouldn't happen."

A British star – or certainly an American one – told that his lifestyle would kill him, would have checked into rehab, gone to the gym and appeared on TV shows as a spokesman for clean living. When friends suggested detox, Serge countered that he sang and wrote better when his voice and brain were ruined. Instead he made an album for his young partner Bambou, another one with the even younger Vanessa Paradis, and went on TV shows flopped over the arm of a sofa, blue smoke spilling from his slack Gallic mouth, carrying on in his role as *raconteur-provocateur*, albeit an increasingly incoherent one. A fatalist more than a nihilist, a man who knew that "death is *always* present, if one isn't a fool",[3] but who was equally convinced that somehow it would not happen to him.

"I don't think he tried to do himself in wilfully," said Jane. "He used to very dramatically say to me that he'd got a gun and he'd taken the bullets out so that he would resist the temptation of blowing his head off. But Jacques (Doillon) said a rather odd thing: *'C'est un suicidaire optimiste'* – he's an optimistic suicide – and I think he was right. He always thought he would get a second chance."

In April Serge was back in hospital, this time for an operation. Two-thirds of his liver were cut out; newspapers prepared their obituaries. But to everyone's surprise – perhaps even his – he made a remarkable recovery and on his release went straight onto a TV show to turn the op into another Gainsbourg anecdote. He was in sparkling form. He was even resourceful enough to give a plug to his new live album, relating how, when he came to from the anaesthetic, he thought he was onstage at the Zénith and was asking the nurses what had happened to his band. He dismissed the reports that, like his dear departed bulldog Nana, he'd had cirrhosis of the liver or cancer, and offered to beat up anyone who said otherwise. It was all the result of a bug he'd picked up filming *Equateur* in Africa, he said. But if he appeared to be in denial, at least he seemed to be taking the doctors' instructions seriously. Instead of going home to the Rue de Verneuil, he took a suite at the Hotel Raphael, where he issued the staff with strict instructions not to serve him alcohol. And where he also got straight back to work.

He was working on lyrics for the new album by Vanessa Paradis. The young blonde pop singer who looked like Tweety Pie if Tweety Pie were a sex doll, and who was just 14 when she broke into the U.K. pop charts in 1988 with 'Joe Le Taxi', had laid claim in a radio interview to being a Gainsbourg fan since infancy, while Serge, in a separate radio interview, had declared that she was one of the few contemporary *'lolycéennes'* (Serge's nifty French compound of schoolgirl and Lolita) that he would like to write for.

They finally met face-to-face on one of those dreadful TV variety shows, where thirty children dressed up as Serge, right down to the fake Gitanes, sang to him as if paying posthumous tribute to a corpse they'd propped up on the chair, "Nous sommes venus te dire que nous t'aimons" – we've come to say we love you – a play on words on his classic 'Je Suis Venu Te Dire Que Je Me'en Vais' (I've Come To Say I'm Leaving).

Serge and the *lolycéenne*'s collaboration, when it eventually came about, was a nightmare. Vanessa, who had always worked with the same composer and lyricist, was left with a pile of wordless melodies after her lyricist's wife suddenly died.

"It was very difficult for Serge," recalled his friend François Ravard, "because he hadn't written the music, and his lyrics didn't fit the metre," and – something else he wasn't used to – four of his texts were rejected; even though he had sweated blood over them, determined, however tired and weak he was, to prove that his work was still of the highest quality. Working with her on *Variations Sur Le Même T'Aime*, he told people, had been what had driven him back to drink. "That's why he called her *L'Enfer* (hell)," said Ravard, "instead of *Paradis* (paradise)."

Lyrically, the Paradis cuts showed a different mood to the those on Bambou's debut album, released the previous year. An Anglo-French mix of somewhat geographically muddled references to his partner's ethnic background – from Sony Walkman to sake, Chinese crackers to King Kong and Serge's Far Eastern take on 'Cry Me A River', 'J'ai Pleuré Le Yang-Tsé' (I've Cried The Yang-tse) – it casts Bambou as variously an Asian hooker ('Hey Mister Zippo'; 'How Much For Your Love Baby') and a 'China Doll'. By all accounts, Bambou was as enthusiastic about making this album as she had been about recording her debut single two years earlier. She knew that she wasn't a singer – as judging by its sales, did the French public. Admittedly it didn't help that its release coincided with the massacre in Tiananmen Square.

***** *****

In the Hotel Raphael, sitting in the bar, a glass of water and a Gitane to hand, Serge was also writing a film: *Stan The Flasher*. The plot, as he pitched it to its producer Ravard, was a sexually deviant and blackly humorous, Shakespearean study of the blurred line between innocence and experience in adolescent girls and the profundity and strangeness of love. Stan, an English teacher, is besotted with one of his pupils. Since life at home isn't good – he suspects his wife is having an affair and anyway he can't get it up for her – he fixates on the young Natacha and plots to follow her home from school where, at the perfect moment, he will open his raincoat and flash. Adding to the layers, the English teacher is named after the father in *Charlotte Forever*, and the pupil after Serge's (by this time 25-year-old) daughter by his second wife Béatrice.

"As usual," said Ravard, "like a lot of his songs, it was a metaphor – taking this character Stan as a metaphor for trouble in life and unfulfilled desire. There were a lot of recurrent themes with *Charlotte Forever*, as there were in all of Serge's work. There was always a bit of Oscar Wilde and Daniel Defoe – there are excerpts from Defoe in *Stan The Flasher* and in *Charlotte Forever*" – plus quotes from

Shakespeare and from Serge's own songs.

"He was very disappointed in the reaction to *Charlotte Forever* – I think a bit bitter that even though he was such an institution in France and a legend in the music business, the film world didn't recognise him as one of them – so he really wanted to make a new movie."

Ravard – a friend and drinking partner of Serge's since 1979 – had made the jump himself from music to film; the manager of the hugely sucessful French rock band

Telephone (and the current manager of Marianne Faithfull) he had set up his own production company and offered to raise the cash.

"He wrote the script in a couple of weeks. At first he just had the story. I had to send him my secretary – he only liked to work with people he knew – and she had to go to his place three times a week, because he was a maniac about having the script typed a certain way and on his own typewriter. It was a thin script, but he was very proud of it. He wrote the role of Stan with just one person in mind to play it: Claude Berri. It was quite a trick to get him."

For one thing, Berri no longer acted; the last time he had set foot in front of a camera was in 1983's *L'Homme Blessé* (The Wounded Man). Since they had worked together in *Sex Shop* and *Je Vous Aime*, Serge's neighbour had gone on to become one of France's leading directors (with international hits like *Jean De Florette* and *Manon Des Sources*) and was a big-shot movie producer for whom the words "low" and "budget" were only the dimmest of memories.

"But Serge really wanted Claude Berri; he thought that Berri had this kind of face of a flasher," Ravard laughed. "For him nobody else could play Stan. And, it's hard to say now, but probably somewhere inside him he had the feeling it was going to be his last movie, and my job was to make the movie happen. It was a really difficult thing to convince Claude to do it. At the time he was producing *L'Ours* (The Bear) by Jean-Jacques Annaud, with a maybe $100-million budget. But we went over to his house with the script and Serge's box set, which he signed to Claude, and finally he said 'Yes, okay, I'll do it'. After that I kept on calling him – or one of his many secretaries, as he was always busy, impossible to get hold of on the phone – and it went on like that until the first day of shooting. And Claude didn't show up.

"We were all ready on the set and there's a phone call from Claude Berri's assistant saying, Mr Berri is in Milan or somewhere, and he couldn't come. So we did something else, but Serge was upset of course. Then the second day he showed up. He came straight to me, grabbed my arm and said 'I need to speak to you', threw me into a dressing room and said 'I came to tell you I won't do the movie. I can't. I'm too busy. And I've read the script. Serge should do it, it's for him, it's about him, and no-one will be better.'

"So I went to Serge and whispered in his ear, 'Claude doesn't want to do the movie'. And when Claude arrived and said the same thing to Serge, Serge fainted! He clutched his chest going, 'Oooh, my heart, my heart!' – giving me a big wink – and Claude said 'What's happening?' 'Oooh, I've just come out of the hospital, I've written the thing for you, you said yes, don't do this to me!' So Claude said, 'All right, all right! I'm here, I'm going to do it for one day, and if the dailies are good we'll go on, but you'll see I'm right and the dailies won't be good and you should do it'. So we did the first day – which was a nightmare, because Claude kept on telling Serge where to put the camera, like he was directing, so it was a big fight".

But Berri liked it enough to stick around for the rest of the shoot, after which it all went well. So well that when it came to the point where Stan was to flash at his young prey, while Serge was debating what reaction he might get if he suggested to Berri that he might consider showing his naked penis, Berri was already voluntarily removing his underpants.

Ravard, meanwhile, heaved a sigh of relief that everything had worked out in the end. "It had been a very difficult film to finance, because film business people didn't like him intruding into their territory and Serge was seen as a complete misfit." But Serge's fourth and last film brought some of his most favourable reviews, washing out some of the bitter aftertaste left by the reaction to *Charlotte Forever*. There was talk of making a fifth film with Ravard, a new take on Defoe's *Robinson Crusoe*, where Friday – an old black man playing a banjo – actually teaches Crusoe (a part planned for Christopher *Greystokes* Lambert, dressed like Rambo) about manners, sophistication and culture. The only reason it didn't happen, said Ravard, is because a year after *Stan The Flasher* Serge died.

"We had a fantastic time when the film was shown in a festival in Canada and we went there to present it, just him and me – when he was with a bit of an entourage, like a lot of artists he felt he had to put on a performance, but when it was just two or three people he was just the best company, one of the kindest and funniest guys. He had the kind of ironic and cynical humour that comes from someone who faces reality and who knows that this world is a terrible place, but instead of committing suicide decided to live and really enjoy every second of his life."

✳ ✳ ✳ ✳ ✳

But, all things considered, there was not an awful lot of joy to be found in Serge's final months. On the surface he was still the *bon viveur* – drinking again, joking that his box set was a "sarcophagus" and that his entry in the encylopaedia *Larousse* would be perfect if it weren't for the hyphen and gap that followed his date of birth. But when the spotlight was turned off, he was a lonely alcoholic on the wrong side of 60. When he wanted someone to drink with in the early hours of the morning, he would drop by his local police station.

"Even your closest friends don't want to get phone calls every night at three or four in the morning," said Jane. "So they put on their answering machines. And you find yourself slowly isolated from the other world, and the only people that you can go and see at four in the morning are policemen who've got nothing else to do and are delighted to hear all the latest Belgian jokes, have someone take them Krug champagne and have a good laugh. He used to use the police van like a taxi. He liked to have the little light on the top. He would ring them up and say, 'Take me over to Jane's house' and tell them that they had to taste my home cooking, and he would turn up with two unknown policemen for dinner at 11pm and crash around in our house where I had kept a room for him, just as he had kept my room, even though I had Jacques and he had Bambou and Lulu."

His relationship with the police, particularly for such an anti-authority figure, was remarkable. Dominique Blanc-Fancard recalled an incident during the vocal recordings in Paris for *You're Under Arrest*, where Serge, bored during the mixing, popped out for a drink "and came back to the studio with two cops – hats in hand, very shy – and said, 'I'm bringing them down to hear my new record. Come on, sit over there and listen'. When he saw the cops loved it, he looked at one of them and, with his face on the verge of tears like a little kid, went, 'Oh what a great badge that is. I wish

I had one like that'. And the cop was all upset: 'We can't give you one, they'd give us hell when we get back to the station'. And Serge said 'But can't you say you lost it?' By the time they got out of there, the cops had given him their badges, holsters, the lot!"

Like Elvis, Serge appeared to have a thing about uniforms, guns and authority figures. Unlike Elvis, and despite his firm anti-drug stance, as displayed in "Aux Enfants De La Chance", he wasn't volunteering to be a good patriot and secretly help them fight crime.

The cops loved Serge. But then everyone did. When he walked down the street – as he still did, leaning on his cane now, peering carefully at the pavement through his half-blind eyes – young people, old people, everyone would stop him, not for an autograph but to say hello, as if they knew him, and to ask him how he was. Another of his in-built dichotomies: so loved, but so alone.

He hated being on his own, but at the same time living with anyone was near impossible. Bambou and Lulu had been installed in an apartment some way off in the 13th arondissement – what Serge referred to as his "country house" – on the pretext that he hated to be disturbed when he worked. They were regular visitors – as of course, were Jane, Charlotte and Kate – but the only constant in his life was his gay valet Fulbert, whose job description had expanded to take in housekeeper, secretary, confidant and personal assistant. When journalists came to the house – as they still did (however private and reclusive Serge would become, he was still highly media-conscious right to the end) Fulbert would let them in. He would also let in the occasional devotee hanging outside the Rue de Verneuil when Serge was lonely and in the mood to talk, and he would turn off the doorbell, unplug the phone and shut out the world when Serge wanted to work. He looked after the regular sacks of fan-mail and begging letters, dug out the bills and made sure they got paid, and kept the house exactly the way Serge wanted it, the food placed in the refrigerator aesthetically – Serge had a special one made with a transparent door and it had to be kept just so – and all the furniture and *objets d'art* kept immaculately dusted and never, ever moved from their original place. A tidy house to help ease the torment of an increasingly disordered mind.

"He couldn't stop at a *petit verre* – a glass or two. He had to finish the bottle. Then another bottle. And as he didn't used to eat at midday, if you have a Pernod as your breakfast then you're usually pretty well slaughtered by tea time. When he turned up at my house," said Jane, "I used to try to push food down him. I remember once I'd made some dish with lentils, and I remember watching him stick his fork in, but by the time it got to his mouth he was so plastered that there was not one lentil left on the fork. And then he would wander around with a silver teaspoon, make himself sick in the loo and then come back and have some more like a Greek emperor. Somehow I think he thought it sort of washed it all out and he could start again. The 'optimistic suicide'. He always thought he could have another go."

Somehow, through all this mess, he continued to work. There was a third stab at the Eurovision Song Contest – 'White And Black Blues', sung by Joelle Ursull – which made a respectable second place, despite its extremely weak lyrics. He had been approched by director Bertrand Blier about doing the music for Charlotte's new film *Merci La Vie* (Thank You Life), and there was talk of a collaboration being set up with Dylan – Bob's music, Serge's words. Serge was reportedly mad for the idea, and producer Phil Ramone had volunteered to act as a go-between. It was just a case of co-ordinating timetables. He also made a TV appearance, playing piano to accompany Jane, who was promoting the new album Serge had written for her that year, *Amours Des Feintes*. Serge also took the opportunity of debuting a new song titled 'Un Homme Dans L'Ombre' (A Man In The Shadows) – written about his modest and low-key producer Philippe Lerichomme, who was hiding in the wings. Hard not to see it as a parting gift.

"No-one, not even his record company, knows to what exent Philippe was not only of major importance but kept Serge alive, out of pure morale," said Jane. "He gave him projects, found him covers of magazines, because Serge needed to be on covers, he needed to feel that he *existed*. Philippe had an extraordinary way of knowing how to balance things – that if Serge was on flash and extremely chic TV programmes at midnight, he also had to be there for the rest of the population of France because he was *populaire*. He would guide him. In the commercial breaks he would come dashing down to remind Serge of something they'd discussed earlier and, when people tried to ban him so they could catch Serge on the hop, he didn't give a damn. He understood if Serge needed a glass of something and not two glasses. And the time Serge went on television and couldn't even sing the song – which was 'Vieille Canaille', 'you pinched my wife, you dirty devil', the song that was written so pointedly to Jacques – Philippe watched it, appalled, from his house. It had been the one time he couldn't go. And Serge rang up Philippe – as he often did if he'd done something naughty, and said 'I wasn't very good on the television last night, was I? But if you had been there it wouldn't have happened' – like a little child."

* * * * * *

Serge's last album for Jane had gestated earlier that year in his room at the American Hospital, which had started to become a home from home. *Amours Des Feintes* has two meanings – love of pretending and love of the dead – and when Jane went to visit him, she wasn't sure which one it was.

"It's strange; I didn't realise he was dying. I went to see him and he drew my picture on the album cover. He asked me to get him some paper of the exact right size and because he couldn't see very well, I had to come terribly close. The first one he did I said 'That looks exactly like Bambou!' He said, 'Oh, does it?' and started again. I pulled my hair back and he did my face and I said, 'One of my eyes has a tiny pupil; you've given me an evil eye.' Then he did a third one and that wasn't so good, so he went back to the second one, then *paff!*, the pen broke, ink spattered onto the paper, and it was marvellous. Serge thought so too because he wrote 'Gainsbourg' on it rather big."

Perhaps if she had been more aware quite how seriously ill he was, Jane might not have told him off when he gave her the song 'Love Fifteen'. "I didn't want to sing something I thought was just being clever with words. I said, 'Serge, I want to sing sad songs, songs that make my heart bleed,' and he said, 'If you just have sad things, people will get bored. In life, things go up and down. You need something a bit pushy to put the really sad things *en valeur*. It's like a line drawing, you need fine lines and thick lines'."

She had also initially been reluctant to do 'Un Amour Peut En Cacher Un Autre' (One Love Can Hide Another) which she found difficult to sing. "It's what the signs on French railways always say: 'Watch out, one train can hide another one.' He always twisted the language. In one of his most interesting interviews he said, 'There's everything to be discovered. There's a new way of French-speaking.' Serge has made up more French words in his lyrics than Shakespeare made up in English."

Jane had been in England, starring in a play, when she was summoned back to Paris in November to make the album. "I grumbled to Philippe, 'Why do I have to do this record so fast? Why can't he wait until Christmas when I get off the play and can do it? Perhaps Philippe realised there was something terribly wrong with Serge, but he said 'Serge wants to do it now.' People used to say to me, 'But couldn't you see how ill Serge was? But no, because I used to see him nearly every day. In the end we became like an old married couple, sitting around and gossiping; he always used to know all the wicked, scandalous things that were going around and I used to absorb them with relish. Yes, the last month he'd slept at my house and when he woke up in the morning he'd fallen against the lamp and burnt himself, and then I saw how terribly thin he was because he didn't have a shirt on. When I said, 'Oh my God, Serge, you're so thin!' he said, *'Non, Janette, je suis svelte'*. Was he aware that things were very very wrong? I don't know – some days yes, I should think, other days no."

Serge was sufficiently aware to figure out that there was probably only one way of stopping his conjoined twin Gainsbarre from killing him. As the autumn of 1990 turned to winter, Serge decided to leave Paris for a country retreat – Vézelay, population 400, in Burgundy.

He had tried this before in August, telling Fulbert he was going there to write a book. He had been pondering two titles since the early '80s, or so he told interviewers: *Le Journal Fictif,* (Fictional Diary) and *Les Techniques De L'Amour*. He must have felt it had done him some good, for despite the far less clement weather, he instructed his valet to reserve the same room in the same small hotel, and once again customised it with photographs, ornaments, a couple of old masters and his childhood teddy-bear brought from home. There, once again, he took daily walks by the river. Even when there was snow on the ground, he would stroll about in his thin white dancers' shoes and his glasses – he could barely see – leaning on a cane.

"He had rung me up to say, 'They're going to cut my legs off'," said Jane. "I thought he was just being dramatic, but they *were* – because if you smoke far too much you get artereosclerosis in your legs."

Taking comfort in simplicity and ritual, he fell into the routine of eating twice a day at the same table in the hotel restaurant, his back to the room, looking out at the garden. At night he would either watch TV or write in his room or, if he was feeling sociable, sit at the piano in the lounge and ask anyone if they minded if he played; even at that point he wanted an audience. At weekends, Bambou and Lulu, Kate or

Charlotte would come by to visit. When he returned to Paris at the beginning of 1991, he continued the simple life. No more nightclubs, just strolls along the Rue de Verneuil and quiet nights at home in front of the television.

"Every night," said Jane, "I would go off and do my play. I used to ring him up in the Rue de Verneuil on my car telephone, because I knew he never used to move, just as I used to ring up my father, because he never used to move either. I used to ask him what he was doing and he'd say, 'Fulbert bought me some frozen cod so I'm going to put it on a little bed of spinach with a dribble of olive oil and then I'm going to watch an old Western that's on at 8.30. What are you going to do?' And I said, 'I'm in this play, of course' and he said, 'But you were there last night! Watch it or it will be like *The Mousetrap*.' It's strange, now I'm on my own, these last few years, I found myself the other night going to the fridge, picking out a little thing of frozen cod, putting it on a bed of spinach with a dribble of olive oil and watching *Night Of The Hunter*, one of Serge's favourite films, with Robert Mitchum, and I thought, how funny; I used to think how sad and tragic to be eating a piece of frozen cod on spinach and watching the television..."

Serge told her that the surgeons had decided to operate on him, but that it wasn't due to happen for a few more months, giving him time to go to New Orleans to make his next album. His producer's idea, but one he seconded wholeheartedly.

"We were due to leave on 20th March," said Lerichomme. "We had the musicians ready, everyone," – The Neville Brothers and Louisiana session stalwarts Tony Hall, Willy Green and Brian Stoltz. "I think it would have been an excellent record – a blues album, not pure blues, but quite pure all the same." Serge, as always, was waiting until the very last minute to write it. Philippe, meanwhile, was working with Blanc-Francard on a remix of Serge's 1968 song 'Requiem Pour Un Con' (Requiem For An Idiot); another device, Jane believed, of keeping Serge's pecker up.

"We started doing it in December 1990 – Serge didn't know anything about it, we only let him listen to it when we'd finished it in February. We had some difficulties with the owner of the tape because it was originally written for a film, *Le Pacha*," said Lerichomme. "He found it fantastic. We were working on the sleeve and everything when he left to go away with Charlotte." His daughter had persuaded him to get away from the cold, wet European winter and go on holiday with her to the Antilles. "It was the last thing I talked about with Serge; I had been to hear it played in a club, to see what it sounded like, and the young guy at the club put it on and said it was fantastic; it would go down great in the clubs. I told Serge that on the Friday night. And the next day he was dead. And the record – incredibly – came out on the Monday. A lot of people found it shocking that there should be a record out two days after his death called 'Requiem Pour Un Con'."

Ten years earlier, Serge had done a "posthumous" interview for *Libération* with Bayon. The newspaper had challenged him to prepare the edition that would appear after his death. He described being inside his dog Nana's stomach, looking out at the afterworld through her butthole. He had just fucked one young woman and there were another five on call. He had died, he said, on a cold night in 1990. He was one year off the mark. On Friday 1st March he had been out celebrating Bambou's birthday. He went back home alone. When Bambou couldn't reach him on the telephone later, she went over to the Rue de Verneuil. He didn't answer the door. She couldn't let herself in because she didn't have a key; Serge wouldn't give her one. A neighbour summoned the fire-brigade. The *pompiers* broke in through the first-storey shutters and found him laid out on his bed, hands curled into child-like fists, dead. For someone so accustomed to spotlight and to scandal, it was a remarkably prosaic, almost *pudique*, death. No under-age sleeping partner, no drunken vomit, no smoking mattress from a carelessly discarded Gitane, just a cardiac arrest in his sleep, one month short of his 63rd birthday. In death, as in life, Serge Gainsbourg refused to conform or to be so easily summed up.

Jane: "I got the first flight back to Paris from London. I had been looking after my father. It must have been eight in the morning; France hadn't realised he was dead yet. I could see on people's faces that life was going on as usual so I thought perhaps it wasn't even true, perhaps it was a nightmare. But I saw Philippe Lerichomme waiting for me and he said 'I'm afraid it is true'. So I went back to the Rue de Vernueil where I found Kate, Charlotte and Bambou and we stayed there for about three days until they took Serge away. And going into the bathroom and seeing all these things that he loved so much, which were so artistically put so that they could never be moved, and they never would, because he was next door, dead. Four days later I went back to my house with everybody and the telephone rang to say that my father was dead too. The two pillars, the people who had loved you, quite blindly, in spite of anything you had done, had collapsed in one week.

"Serge wrote a record for me which said, 'one thing among other things that you don't know is that you've had the very best of me'. I remember thinking: it's true. We were like two old ladies sitting on a bench, nattering about who's left who and who did what to whom, and my little old lady had gone, and that was that."

L'EVENEMENT

VIOQUE, PORTIER AU ROX-Y HOTEL, SI JE DEBLOQUE »

Gainsbourg raconte sa mort

En novembre 1981, cet éternel provocateur avait accepté ce pari extrême : préparer carrément l'édition du journal de sa mort. A l'époque, le créateur de « Requiem pour un con » publiait « Mauvaises nouvelles des étoiles », nous l'interviewions dans son appartement noir sur sa disparition. Un testament.

« a sent le sapin », répétait-il toujours. Pour dire que l'échéance, éthylo-Seitama-nie aidant, approchait. Sinon depuis toujours, depuis une éternité (dix ans), Gains-bourg ne nous intéressait plus, qu'ainsi. Mort à crédit. Son trépas dans sa dernière vie. Entre deux alertes (1973, 1989), nous lui avions du coup demandé froidement, en prévision de cette mort annoncée, le plus cyniquement possible, à ce Diogène du rock français qui ne jurait que par son chien, crevé du cirrhose, de mettre en scène son propre décès. Littéralement. De l'anticiper, le plus précisément possible, de le peindre, de le rapporter. Le principe, morbide certes, était le suivant : Serge Gainsbourg est mort, nous communiquons avec son ectoplasme, il nous raconte de l'au-delà comment, pourquoi et quand il est mort. En exclusivité.

Des *Mémoires d'outre-tombe* qui choqueront peut-être, émouvront à coup sûr, et qui, coûte que coûte, avec certaines provocs plus ou moins attendues, facilités d'ailleurs typiques, prennent çà et là un tout pour le moins troublant, voire étonnant. Quand l'intéressé, trans pour rire en 81, annonçait catégoriquement, entre deux « 102 » (deux « Pastis 51 » en un), qu'il frôlerait la mort en 1989... Ou quand le même, dans cette véritable communication avec l'au-delà, flottant déjà « dans l'éther sans oiseau », se rappellera au futur antérieur qu'il mourrait « juste après la Troisième Guerre mondiale »... On peut le dire.

SERGE GAINSBOURG. — Bon, je suis mort. Je fais un bilan...

LIBÉRATION. — C'est déjà une appréciation.

S.G. — Un mort avec la parole, il fait le bilan... De toute façon, je suis à côté de mon chien puisque je l'ai perdu, je l'ai donc retrouvé. Il est mort d'une cirrhose...

LIBÉRATION. — Peut-être était-ce par osmose ?

S.G. — Ouais, oui, c'est vrai. *(Sur la bande on entend le pétillement du champagne rosé que Gainsbourg se sert généreusement.)*

LIBÉRATION. — Quand est-ce que ça s'est passé ?

S.G. — Il n'y a pas longtemps. C'est le cœur qui a lâché. Non, c'était plutôt une overdose de plomb (rire).

LIBÉRATION. — Un « Sid Vicious » (1) de plomb...

S.G. — Ouais, c'était un allumé...

LIBÉRATION. — On est en quelle année ?

S.G. — On est en... quatre-vingt... dix.

LIBÉRATION. — Comment ça s'est passé ?

S.G. — Ça s'est passé en octobre. Un jour froid. Une nuit froide. La nuit c'est mieux, hein ? Canicou.

LIBÉRATION. — Comme Nerval...

Tu étais en train de faire quoi ?
S.G. — Draguer.

LIBÉRATION. — Draguer ?
S.G. — Je ne me souviens plus très bien — c'était assez foudroyant — si c'était un coup au cœur ou une over-dose de plomb. Flash. Et puis j'étais exceptionnellement faible.

LIBÉRATION. — Ça s'arrange, depuis que tu es mort ?
S.G. — Ce qui ne s'arrange pas, c'est que je vois en dessous. C'est le merdier.

LIBÉRATION. — Ça ne sert à rien, alors ?
S.G. — Ben... Ha oui, la cécité ? Pour être heureux ? Heureux... C'est pas un but, le bonheur... Moi je trouve ça absurde, l'idée d'un nirvana.

LIBÉRATION. — On est peut-être délivré. On n'a plus à se...
S.G. — ... A se branler ? Si. Ça dépend. S'il n'y a pas de gonzesses, on continue à se branler. Non, non, y'a plus rien. La queue qui part en couille.

LIBÉRATION. — Tu peux décrire l'endroit où tu te trouves ?
S.G. — Je suis à l'intérieur de mon chien. Il y a des gaz. Des gaz inflammables. Alors, j'allume une allumette...

LIBÉRATION. — Tu ne risques plus rien ?
S.G. — Justement : c'est pour voir les boyaux de mon chien. Je suis content parce que je l'aime beaucoup. Comme lui, de mon vivant, il était dans ma tête, j'ai décidé d'aller dans son ventre.

LIBÉRATION. — Ce ventre, c'est un ventre de remplacement du ventre de ta mère, non ?
S.G. — Exact.

LIBÉRATION. — Donc, ta mère était un chien ?
S.G. — Non, absolument pas ! Ma mère est vivante. Et je tiens à ce qu'elle le reste. (2)

LIBÉRATION. — Oui, mais on parle au passé.
S.G. — Ouais, on parle au passé et elle est toujours vivante. *(Malaise très net.)*

LIBÉRATION. — Comment réagit-elle à ta mort ?
S.G. — Je ne sais pas. Je ne voudrais pas lui faire de la peine... Bon enfin, passons. *(Silence. Tension grandissante. L'entretien semble capoter et Gainsbourg se ferme...)*

LIBÉRATION. — ... Bon, bon. Donc, tu n'étais pas seul au moment où ça s'est produit...
S.G. — Non, puisque j'étais avec une gonzesse.

LIBÉRATION. — Ce qui ne veut pas dire que tu n'étais pas seul... Quel âge ? 12 ans ?
S.G. — *(Rire).* Non. En 89, elle avait... trente ans de moins que moi... Ça lui fait 26 ans.

LIBÉRATION. — Rousse ? Blonde ? Brune ?
S.G. — Eurasienne.

LIBÉRATION. — Est-ce que tu étais ivre au moment où ça s'est produit ?
S.G. — Non, mais mon verre s'est brisé avant moi.

LIBÉRATION. — C'est le dernier bruit que tu as entendu ?
S.G. — Non ; j'ai entendu un coup de pétard.

LIBÉRATION. — Un verre en cristal ou bien en Sécurit de cantine ?
S.G. — Je ne bois pas dans du Sécurit. Je préfère le danger.

LIBÉRATION. — Est-ce que tu aurais aimé que ça se passe autrement ?
S.G. — Oh... Le coup de la pipe qui tue. C'est un supplice chinois qu'on trouve dans *le Jardin des supplices*, d'Octave Mirbeau, qui consiste à faire sept pipes. A la septième, on crache son sang. C'était acceptable, comme mort.

LIBÉRATION. — Ça n'aurait pas pu être un accident ? C'est une overdose de plomb...

LIBÉRATION. — C'est le « cynisme » absolu... Tu restes tout le temps dans ton chien, ou tu peux sortir ?
S.G. — Je jette un œil par le trou... L'œil était dans l'anus et regardait Caïn.

LIBÉRATION. — Comment t'es-tu retrouvé là ?
S.G. — Par une force de volonté fulgurante.

LIBÉRATION. — Et c'est quoi, ce ventre ?
S.G. — Des tripes. C'est un trip.

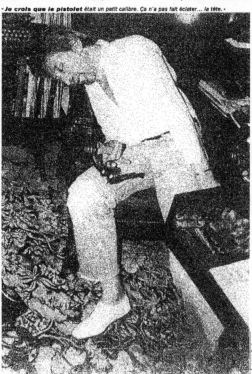

« Je crois que le pistolet était un petit calibre. Ça n'a pas fait éclater... la tête. »

GAZETTE

OBITUARIES

Serge Gainsbourg

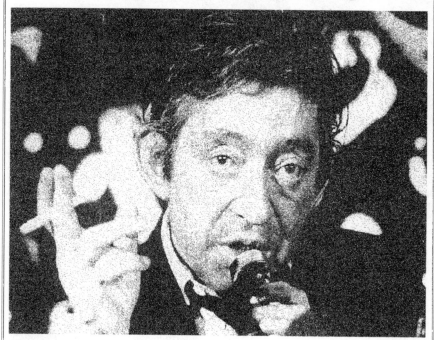

THE DEATH of Serge Gainsbourg, just before midnight on Saturday, at the age of 62, leaves France without one of its best-loved artistic figures.

Outside his house in the Latin Quarter, police held back weeping crowds that gathered yesterday, but allowed through Jane Birkin, mother of Gainsbourg's daughter Charlotte, and Catherine Deneuve, who had come to pay their respects to the sordid Svengali of French pop.

Brigitte Bardot, who has not made a public statement in two decades about her charity work with animals, said she was not surprised to hear of his death, given the way he lived, and Jack Lang, the Minister of Culture, said the nation was deeply grieved by the news. Virtually half of this morning's issue of *Libération* has been given over to a memorial to Gainsbourg.

Bardot was one of the Lollycennes — a contraction of lollipop and *lycéenne* — who recorded under the tutelage of Gainsbourg, a list that began with France Gall's "*Les sucettes*" and ended recently with an album for Vanessa Paradis. When Bardot refused to record a Gainsbourg song called "*Je t'aime (moi non plus)*" — because she thought the lyrics too bold — he enlisted Jane Birkin, the British actress he had met on the set of the film, and earned world-wide notoriety in 1967 with an opus of strings, signs and sexual innuendo.

He had already been awarded the respect of peers like Boris Vian for songs such as "*La javanaise*" and "*Le poinçonneur de Lilas*" — wry, bittersweet little pieces in the French *chansonnier* tradition that marked his début in 1963. The *enfant terrible* of French pop in the Sixties, Gainsbourg and his friend the singer Jacques Dutronc used to compete in nightclubs to see who could take home the ugliest girl.

He wrote, produced and directed promo films for a series of pop hits for Brigitte Bardot including the celebrated "Harley Davison", stretching out into quasi-symphonic albums with Jane Birkin. *The Story of Melodie Nelson* from 1970 was an extended ode to his fantasy nymphette, the *gamine* figure who recurs, played by Birkin; Isabelle Adjani and Catherine Deneuve, throughout his *oeuvre*. Gainsbourg's girls perfected a breathy whisper on discs as the old dog growled his desires — and perhaps those of a whole generation of Frenchmen too. His most *risqué* offering on these lines was "Lemon Incest", in which the object of Serge's lust was none other than his teenage daughter Charlotte.

Born in Paris of Russian *émigré* parents, Lucien Ginsburg wanted to be a painter. He went to the Ecole de Beaux Arts, becoming an art teacher. "Song-writing is a minor art," he often grumbled. "None of it is worth a line of Picabia." Taught to play piano by his father, he nonetheless found he excelled at this art, and signed his songs "Serge".

He created his own musical form out of his lack of a singing voice and his personal obsessions, a kind of ongoing autobiographical erotic novella. His albums sold by the millions in France and his career as a *provocateur* found him much in demand for television appearances, where he was guaranteed to double ratings. The public appetite for his drunken scandal-mongering didn't seem to trouble him. He burned a 500-franc note on one show rather than give it to the taxman and made obscene overtures to a shocked and uncomprehending Whitney Houston.

A Dionysian figure for the French, Gainsbourg represented their libido at play and so was tolerated in a way that he would not have been elsewhere. For many in France, his calm demise at the end of a long career of public outrage and equally public self-abuse was the vindication of a debauched life, wreathed in cigarette smoke and reeking of alcohol.

He showed no remorse at his excesses, though he did give up drinking towards the end, after a serious operation.

"Ugliness is superior to beauty," he once said, apropos of himself, "because it lasts longer." The French are going to miss him.

Paul Rambali

M

aigré un tirage
exceptionnel,
« Libération » n'a pu
répondre hier à la
demande de tous ses
lecteurs. Des
contraintes techniques
nous ont empêchés
de procéder dans la
journée à un nouveau
tirage. Nous
republions donc les
pages consacrées à la
mort de Serge
Gainsbourg.
Il avait, en 1981,
imaginé sa mort.
Dans l'interview qu'il
avait alors accordée à
« Libération », il disait :
« C'était très beau. Ça
se passait à la fin de
la Troisième Guerre
mondiale... On est
en... quatre-vingt...
dix... Une nuit froide.
La nuit c'est mieux,
hein ? »
Il est mort dans la
nuit, le samedi
2 mars, dans son
appartement, rue de
Verneuil. Il avait
62 ans. Peintre
insatisfait, il devient
pianiste de bar. Puis
compose et écrit ses
premières chansons :
« Le Poinçonneur des
Lilas », « la Javanaise »,
« Poupée de cire,
Poupée de son »... En
1968, il rencontre
Jane Birkin. C'est « Je
t'aime moi non plus »,
le scandale, le
triomphe. Suivent
« Melody Nelson »,
« Initials B.B. », « Rock
Around The Bunker »,
« la Marseillaise
reggae », « Marilou »
« You're under Arrest »
et, ultime succès.
« Tandem », chanté par
Vanessa Paradis.
Parallèlement, il
circule des deux côtés
de la caméra,
acteur dans vingt-deux
films et réalisateur de
quatre (« Je t'aime
moi non plus »,
« Équateur », « Charlotte
for Ever »,
« Stan The Flasher »).

**GAINSBOURG
POST MORTEM**

L I B E R A T I O N .

SERGE GAINSBOURG
TIMES - 4. III. 91

Serge Gainsbourg, French pop singer and composer, was found dead in his Paris apartment on March 2 aged 62. He was born on April 2, 1928.

SERGE Gainsbourg is likely to be remembered less for his contribution to French pop music than for the degenerate image he cultivated. As a singer he started out in the mainstream of French popular music as it was in the Sixties and thereafter adapted skilfully to changes in public taste to retain for himself a following among successive generations of pop fans. None of this would have brought him much standing in the international — that is to say largely English-speaking — pop world, without the series of shocking gestures which accompanied the output of songs.

These were presented as the natural fall-out from a dissolute and riotous life but were carefully calculated. Thus the 1969 song "Je t'aime, moi non plus" which made him notorious in Britain through its being ostensibly a recording of an erotic encounter between Gainsbourg and his companion of that time, the British actress Jane Birkin, was, of course, a studio construction with both being passionate on *their* own in separate booths. But it worked on the fevered imagination of Sixties Britain, the fact that one of the participants was a British girl doubtless adding to its titillating effect on the Anglo-Saxon mentality. Thereafter an attack on the song by the Vatican newspaper, *Osservatore Romano*, and a ban on the song in Italy only doubly ensured its runaway success in the charts of many countries.

Serge Gainsbourg was born Lucien Ginsburg, the son of a Russian émigré nightclub pianist, Joseph Ginsburg. He was educated at Paris's Lycée Condorcet, from which he was thrown out for indiscipline, and at the École nationale supérieure des beaux arts. He started his working life as a pianist and guitarist at the Paris cabaret Milord l'Arsouille in the 1950s. He also began composing and won the grand prix de Académie Charles-Cros for his first album, *Du Chant à la Ine* in 1959. Besides his more singe writing he also created songs for vocalists such as Jetula Clark and Juliette Greco.

In 1960 he began a film career with a part in *Voulez-vous danser avec moi?* and thereafter appeared in a number of features with such characteristic titles as *Erotissimo* (1969) and *Cannabis* (1970). He also composed the scores for a number of films, notably *les Loups dans la bergerie, l'Eau à bouche* and *le Jardiner d'Argenteuil.*

He met Jane Birkin on the set of the film *Slogan* (1968) which was being directed by Pierre Grimblat. Their relationship lasted 12 years and produced a daughter, Charlotte, who is herself a cinema actress.

Gainsbourg also had a career as an actor and presenter on television where he seldom failed to come up

with behaviour calculated to scandalise audiences. On one occasion he was criticised for burning a 500-franc note on a live show. On another — this time the popular family music programme *Champs Elysées* — he made earthily explicit suggestions to the singer Whitney Houston to the predictable outrage of 17 million viewers, his employers at Channel 2 and Miss Houston herself. But such affronts were a carefully calculated part of his broadcasting persona, as was a reggae version of the French national anthem the Marseillaise, which brought threats of violence from right wing groups in France.

Gainsbourg's health suffered badly from his excessive drinking and smoking and he suffered a succession of heart attacks as well as having to have two thirds of his liver removed in 1989.

In recent years he had lived with Caroline von Paulus (better known as the model Bambou), by whom he had a son. A marriage earlier in his life to Françoise Pancrazzi was dissolved.

Chapter 18
AFTERLIFE

Go past the tombs of Baudelaire and De Beauvoir and the stone double-bed where Charles Pigeon, inventor of the unexplodable gas lamp, perpetually prepares to mount his sleeping wife; head for the roundabout where the avenues Principale and Transversale cross, and you'll come to a plain, flat concrete slab, hidden, like an existentialist *Crackerjack* episode, beneath a mound of metro tickets, cabbages, fluffy toys, a glass, a Pastis bottle, and cigarettes. On Thursday 7th March, Serge's body was brought to Montparnasse cemetery and buried alongside his parents Joseph and Olia, mere feet away from Sartre and Serge's beloved Huysmans.

Paparazzi, a couple disguised as undertakers for a closer look, snapped a procession of French popstars and public figures. Jane and Bambou of course, were among them, and Charlotte and Kate, Isabelle Adjani, Françoise Hardy, Johnny Hallyday and Catherine Deneuve, who read the words to 'Fuir Le Bonheur De Peur Qu'il Ne Se Sauve' over his grave as an oration.

"When police threw open the gates to the public," read the Reuters report, "ageing hippies, shaven-headed young trendies and tearful teenage girls clutching single red roses" crushed their way through. There were two wreaths sent by his local police station. The tube tickets were in homage to Serge's classic song 'Le Poinçonneur Des Lilas', the vegetable offerings a tribute to 'L'Homme À Tête De Chou'.

The announcement of Serge's death in the early hours of Sunday morning brought Paris to a standstill. Police blocked off the streets around the Rue de

Verneuil as thousands flocked, just as John Lennon's fans had gathered at the Dakota building.

"The whole place was in tears," recalled Bob Stanley of St. Etienne, who was visiting Paris at the time. "Nothing on TV but Gainsbourg all day long. It was like a head of state had died." The radio was one continuous rotation of Serge songs, broken only by yet another eulogy.

President Mitterrand pronounced, "I learn with sadness of the death of Serge Gainsbourg. Through his love of language and his musical genius, he has raised the song to the level of art which will pay witness to the sensibility of a generation."[1] Jack Lang – the minister who had given Serge his medal – called him "one of the greats of French poetry and music", speaking of his "sensuality" and "Rimbaudian sense of liberty".[2] A touch less grandly, Jacques Chirac, Mayor of Paris, revealed that his favourite song was 'Harley Davidson' – "imprinted in my heart, because it was sung by Bardot, whom I liked very much." (He also confessed to being rather fond of the album Serge did with Vanessa Paradis, assessing that no further explanation was necessary.)

Bardot's own eulogy to her former lover spoke of "a very, very vulnerable being, full of shyness and humour, perpetually questioning himself about everything he did. He wasn't at all sure of himself and when one sees the marvels he could write and the beauty of his music – whether interpreted by him or us – one cannot understand this lack of self-confidence. He is a man who lived in an extraordinary manner. His death touches us enormously because we have lost someone irreplaceable."[3]

This side of the Channel, although it would be wrong to say that his death went entirely unnoticed, it was greeted with somewhere between blithe indifference, a warm flush of memory of making out to 'Je T'Aime, Moi Non Plus', and an excuse to dust off the old innuendoes about randy old Frenchmen and young girls.

Reported *The Times*: "Serge Gainsbourg is likely to be remembered less for his contribution to French pop music than for the degenerate image he cultivated." Wrote *The Independent*: "The enfant terrible of French pop in the 60s, Gainsbourg and his friend, the singer Jacques Dutronc, used to compete in nightclubs to see who could take home the ugliest girl... 'The Story Of Melodie Nelson' (sic) was an extended ode to his fantasy nymphette, the gamine figure who recurs, played by Birkin, Isabelle Adjani and Catherine Deneuve, throughout his oeuvre. Gainsbourg's girls perfected a breathy whisper on discs as the old dog growled his desire... The French are going to miss him." That much at least was right.

But it failed to acknowledge the overseas cult of Serge that has been steadily swelling this side of the Channel, as well as further afield in the U.S., Australia and Japan. Unusually, the U.K. Gainsbourg cult following appeared to be a grass-roots rather than a media-generated one, and divided into three main, occasionally overlapping, sects: the dance crowd attracted to the Easy Listening kitsch element; musicians (mostly young and indie) fascinated by his intricate arrangements and wild eclecticism; and would-be popstars, drawn to his impossibly cool style. Jarvis Cocker of Pulp might have modelled himself on Serge; Brett Anderson of Suede duetted with Jane Birkin on a benefit album. The Serge Effect permeated Britpop and beyond – through Divine Comedy, Bloody Valentine, Black Grape, St Etienne,

Luna (who covered 'Bonnie & Clyde' with Laetitita Sadler of Stereolab), The Bollock Brothers (Johnny Rotten's brother's band, who covered 'Harley David Son Of A Bitch'), The High Llamas (who have been waving the banner since their first album), Momus (who dedicated 1991's *Hippopotamomus* album to Gainsbourg) and Baby Birkin (who formed after the frontwoman saw Jane Birkin in concert singing Gainsbourg songs, and whose repertoire is largely based on his back catalogue). The most recent Serge-related U.K. hit has been David Holmes's album *Let's Get Killed*, featuring samples from *Histoire De Melody Nelson*.

David Holmes: "I was knocked out by everything about the album; I'd never heard anything like it in my life. It was just one of those records that you wanted everyone to hear after you'd heard it. But there was so much other stuff Serge did; one brilliant thing about him is that he did everything – funk tracks, soundtracks, psychedelic, jazz, dub, kitsch 60s pop and luscious strings. He was totally ahead of his time. And he was always seen with the most beautiful women. The one thing that Serge's music doesn't lack is sex appeal. If you find a good woman and you have dinner, and you put a bit of Serge on, you're laughing."

Nick Currie/Momus: "I think Gainsbourg above all is someone who intrigues other artists. People who work hands-on with music every day really appreciate the genius of his arrangements, the beautiful coloration that sometimes sounds like Satie, other times like some generic English 1960s rock band. Gainsbourg had a sensuality, an intimacy and an arty perversion which was equally informed by surrealist painting as mainstream pornography. Sometimes his sexual jokes and obsessions could seem perverse and masturbatory, but then you look at his life and saw that he hung out with the most beautiful women in the world so you thought, if this is masturbation give me more of it! And then there were these incredible feats of wordplay. That French model is appealing to a whole generation of new-wave musicians. It's also very inspiring for musicians over 30 to realise they can still be cutting-edge and influential and sexually attractive in their old age!"

Sean O'Hagan, High Llamas: "Don't you find it really annoying when some twatty little Sunday journalist goes on about how 'the French, of course, are no good at pop'? Gainsbourg had literally three or four decades of working within the mainstream with big record companies, but working outside the mainstream with the subject matters he employed. He had a wonderfully nasty view of the world linked with a fantastic harmonic grip on 20th century music and in this country he is massively overlooked. I always picture this guy in a studio with a 50-piece orchestra, everyone on double time at one o'clock in the morning, and you can't see the brass section through the smoke because Serge is at the piano, smoking himself to death."

Bob Stanley, St. Etienne: "Linguistic isolation and the national trait for battening down the hatches and getting on with, well, being French resulted in a quite unique and wonderful take on 1960s pop... Gainsbourg incorporates everything I love about pop music into what he does, and at the same time doesn't sound like anybody else at all. What is really amazing about him is he obviously got into writing pop songs as a sideline which he found quite comical – something he could do at the drop of a hat, like writing a Eurovision winner – and as soon as he realised that he started becoming much darker and writing incredibly cynical lyrics and getting these

poppets to sing them. But while that was happening, at the same time he was becoming quite smitten with the music, so by the time it got to *Melody Nelson* he had this unique style which is very dark, very intense and humorous, but also sounds like someone who loves what he's doing."

In Australia, Mick Harvey of Nick Cave's Bad Seeds tried to do something about the linguistic isolation factor by translating Serge's song into English and gathering them on two tribute albums, *Intoxicated Man* (1995) and, two years later, *Pink Elephants*.

Mick Harvey: "I think his greatest strength lies in his lyrics, and that obviously is immediately confounded by the language barriers. That those same language barriers don't seem to dog Bob Dylan or Leonard Cohen, whose music is also strongly lyrically-based, is probably down to the predominance of English as a world language or American music as a force, but Serge really suffered from that. But what gets lost in translation is just his character and the way he was such a personality and cultural figure in France, which doesn't quite translate into other cultures. He's a great songwriter, someone I've gotten a lot of entertainment from, who has something very special to offer which has gone pretty much unnoticed outside of France."

"Like all the great songwriters," said Françoise Hardy, "Serge was equally as strong on lyrics as on melodies. To appreciate him fully, one must be able to understand his lyrics, his plays on words. If Serge is more well-known today in your country, it's because he was an innovator, ahead of his time, and also because the music scene these days is increasingly more internationalised."

In the U.S., Serge's devotees include the seminal post-punk, hardcore art-rock band Sonic Youth. They in turn introduced the equally influential Beck to Gainsbourg's music while they were touring the U.S. together. Beck recently duetted in Paris with Jane Birkin on 'L'Anamour'.

Beck: "Every night for two weeks we'd sit on the bus watching all his videos. I took to Serge immediately, because I grew up with Françoise Hardy records and being taken to Truffaut and Godard films, and I already liked that whole era of French pop culture. In America he's been trendy for the last few years, but people only grab onto the playboy image, the international stud. But I responded to the

other thing that was going on: the humour and the perversity and the poetry and the attitude. I think on my last album I went a bit for that sense of humour, attitude and sexuality and toying with perversity. Finding beauty in the bottom of a garbage can, making something sublime out of something mundane is what I think everybody strives for, and Gainsbourg was able to do that."

New York girl group Luscious Jackson covered '69 Année Érotique' on *Ain't Nothin' But A She Thang*. Art-Americana band The Walkabouts recorded an English version of 'Bonnie & Clyde' on *Trail Of Stars*, rewritten by former Dream Syndicate frontman and solo artist Steve Wynn, who had sung it on his own album *Dazzling Display*.

Steve Wynn: "In 1991 I was on a French promotional tour; my publicist spoke very little English and I spoke almost no French. One day she played a compilation of Gainsbourg's biggest hits on the car stereo and I was very intrigued. I knew 'Je T'Aime, Moi Non Plus' from the novelty-status limited radio play in the U.S. when I was growing up, but I was unfamiliar with the rest. Despite having no idea what he was singing about, I was immediately hooked by the sound of his voice; the exotic and alternately dark or playful arrangements and the obvious. 'Look,' she said, pointing to a large billboard by the side of the highway, 'there's a picture of Gainsbourg.' He was hawking one product or another. When our day of promotion was done and we went to a local bar to relax – obviously a trendy gathering point; the patrons, mostly in their late teens or early twenties were decked out in various outrageous, envelope-pushing attire – at one point the music stopped and the DJ made an announcement. All talking ceased; there was a pretty intense reaction, some people actually crying. I asked my host what he had said. 'Gainsbourg has just died'. I took this weird string of events as a sign that I had to seek out more of the man's music and I was especially taken by 'Bonnie & Clyde'. I found out later that Gainsbourg had, in fact, taken the lyrics from the poem written by Bonnie Parker for the newspapers during their crime spree – so the lyrics had been translated and amended from English to French and back to English!"

John Zorn, the American underground jazz saxophonist, released a compilation album to Gainsbourg, the second in his series of 'Great Jewish Music'; (the first was Burt Bacharach). Alternative artists who paid homage to Serge included Fred Frith ('The Ballad Of Melody Nelson'), Faith No More frontman Mike Patton ('Ford Mustang'), Blonde Redhead ('Slogan'), Shelly Hirsch ('Comic Strip'), Medeski, Martin and Wood ('Intoxicated Man'); Zorn himself tackled 'Contact', while Cibo Matto, with the help of Sean Lennon, took on the mighty 'Je T'Aime, Moi Non Plus'.

John Zorn: "Serge Gainsbourg is one of the world's great eccentrics."

In Japan, the Gainsbourg cult has thrown up a number of art-rock acts with well-defined Serge influences, among them Pizzicato Five and Kazuko Hohki. In France, of course, his influence is everywhere – three to be getting on with are MC Solaar (the rapper sampled 'Bonnie & Clyde' on 'Nouveau Western'), Mirwais (the godfather of French Nu-Disco sampled 'Cargo Culte'); and Air, whose whole oeuvre shows the impact of Serge. To mark the tenth anniversary of his death, Serge's French record label released a tribute album, *I Love Serge*, featuring remixes of his songs by leading electronic artists, including The Orb ('Requiem Pour Un Con'), Stratus ('L'Hotel Particulier'), Herbert ('Bonnie & Clyde') and Howie B ('Ballade De Melody Nelson').

Nicolas Godin/Air: "In England everyone's a popstar, in France we don't give a shit, France is not a country of rockstars, and me I prefer to be a composer. Everyone loves Serge. He's like the grandaddy, always doing something crazy, funny and provocative. He's a part of our culture so it was just natural that when I learned to play the piano, I learned his songs. It's unconscious."

MC Solaar: "I first discovered Serge when I was 12 or 13, during his reggae period, and what struck me straight away about him were his words. Later I could see the way he chose them, how he'd put them in the right place, never gratuitously, always with a concern for the sense of rhythm. There are a lot of stylistic touchpoints between Gainsbourg and rap – his song 'Brigade Des Stups' for example, where he plays around with the terms 'spliff', 'chnouf', 'cops', 'scoop'. Pure rap! And his way of referring to his origins – 'Nazi Rock' for example is the same as the black rapper talking about slavery."

Beck: "His influence is all over the place. Because Serge was all over the place – so renegade that you can be influenced by him stylistically, but really I think it's more about the disregard and abandon behind what he was doing. It's really about *him*. I remember growing up with it being a given that there was no good music from France. Maybe my generation just got tired of the canon of what's acceptable music and decided to go and search elsewhere; maybe we're more curious. I do get frustrated that for the next generation up from me, what's considered tasteful is only Dylan, Neil and Bruce and maybe Patti Smith and Joni Mitchell, who are amazing, but there's many other artists as well. Serge is definitely up there with all those artists. I hear a bit of Leonard Cohen and Dylan in there, even a little Frank Sinatra, but it's almost impossible to compare him with anyone."

The British rock writers who have been coming out of the woodwork lately to sing his praises have offered everything from a hybrid of "Charles Bukowski and Barry White, Jim Morrison and Leonard Cohen, Scott Walker and Chet Baker" (*The Guardian*) and "somewhere between Cliff Richard and Malcolm McLaren" (*Q*) . As widely recognisable in France as Elvis Presley (except an Elvis who wrote his own songs), as musically changeable as Bowie (though his appearance, from *Melody Nelson* on, never changed), as provocative as Johnny Rotten (but the cops loved Serge, and his provocation lasted so much longer), and as musically literate as Burt Bacharach (but with songs about cabbage heads and turds). You see the difficulties. Over to the experts.

Dominique Blanc-Francard: "He's so many things, a bit of a mutant, someone who keeps changing forms – jazz, pop, rock, sometimes all three and more of his own invention. I think he was the first man in France who did a real 'swing' with French lyrics – he had a technique of cutting the words in the middle and replacing them with a rhythm and accent that was very English but with a meaning that was completely French. For him the sound of words were as important as the sense, and that was completely new in France."

Françoise Hardy: "Serge Gainsbourg's inspiration has been so rich that it cuts the

grass from underneath the feet of all the songwriters who have followed on from him. It is impossible to undo his influence; he found everything before everyone else."

Philippe Lerichomme: "He was unique."

Jane: "Damn, he wrote some beautiful songs!"

✳✳ ✳✳✳✳

And so we find ourselves back where we started, on the Rue de Verneuil. Charlotte, who bought out her siblings' share of the house, has applied to the Minister of Culture to turn Serge's "museum of my memories" into a real museum, honouring his life, his work, and all the strange and wonderful furnishings and ornaments that are still feather-dusted and kept immaculate by Fulbert's friend, after Serge's valet passed away. The Ministry said no. The tiny house could not meet bureaucratic requirements of fire exits, wheelchair access and toilets. Family debates came up with the idea of scooping the house out with a giant crane and depositing it on the outskirts of Paris, "where they would cherish it", said Jane, "because the 7th arondissement doesn't deserve Serge. Even when we used to live there, they kept on reminding us that we were in what was used to be the stables, so would we mind keeping that in mind. They keep writing foul letters to Charlotte saying that the graffiti on the wall brings down the tone of the neighbourhood." An architect they consulted – who had designed the Cartier Centre – proposed putting the whole place under a glass dome. "A wonderful idea, but I know in advance that the neighbours would just love to have a dome on the top of Serge's house and people lining up outside the door!"

So the latest plan is to make it a Virtual Museum. Put its tiny black rooms onto the Web so that fans can wander about at will, open the drawers, rattle the skeleton hanging by the door, and see Jane's room, which is still exactly the way it was when she left it 18 years ago, "even the half-tubes of toothpaste and hairpins have been preserved. It's like the Sleeping Beauty."

Barring any unforseen problems, fans can drop by and visit Serge through cyberspace some time in 2001. Meanwhile, ten years after his death, fans still drop by in person to leave messages on the wall outside and, in some strange way, to keep him company.

I last paid a visit to Gainsbourg's grave on a crisp Autumn day in 2000, while writing this book. The Montparnasse Cemetery Fulberts, tiptoeing around quietly with their buckets and rubber gloves, had not yet come to tidy it, and, cul-de-saced between three imposing black marble slabs belonging to the families Simon, Grinberg and Lamouroux, it looked rather rakish, as if caught in the middle of a birthday party. There was a red rose, a stuffed donkey, a plant leaning from its pot at a drunken angle, scores of metro tickets and a business card from a beauty salon in Limoges (where the Ginsburg family had fled in the war), all held down with tiny stones. Propped at the back was a message board on which someone had scribbled a shopping list: tea-bags, butter; no cabbage though. There was a glass with a few drops of cloudy liquid in the bottom that looked like someone had just emptied it. And, next to it, a newly opened pack of Gitanes.

APPENDICES
Source notes

Chapter One

1 "Ma mère m'adore. Voilà. Elle est idolâtre de moi" – *Actuel*

2 "Je me dis, 'Il doit se passer quelque chose, avec une fille; je ne sais pas ce qu'est'" – Bayon, *Mort Ou Vices*

3 "Pour moi c'est indélébile. C'est comme un taureau qu'on a marqué au fer rouge. Un petit garcon qui portait l'étoile." – *Actuel*

4 "Toi, tu n'as pas le droit d'etre dans l'orchestre parque que tu est Juif. Casse-toi. Ils voulaient lui piquer sa place."

5 "Je n'arrive pas à oublier que j'aurais dû crèver en 41, 42, 43, 44." – Verlant, *Gainsbourg*

Chapter Two

1 Bayon, *Mort Ou Vices*

2 Bayon

3 "J'ai vraiment le regret de ne pas avoir vécu cette époque." – *20 Ans*

4 "C'est un univers de mecs. On se pétait la guelle, on grattait la guitare, on chantait des conneries et on allait aux putes" interview with Jean-William Thoury.

5 "Je suis entré dans l'armée française sans jamais avoir touchée une goutte d'alcool, j'en suis sorti treize mois plus tard, alcoolique." – *20 Ans*

6 "Pianiste de bar, c'est la meilleure école." – Gilles Verlant, *Gainsbourg*

7 "Je voulais avoir du génie et je n'avais que du talent." – *Rock & Folk*

8 "Je ne me sentais pas bien dans mon nom." – *20 Ans*

9 "une des dernières qui avait conservé l'esprit rive gauche." – *20 Ans*

10 "Je me suis rendu compte avec Vian que la chanson n'etait peut-être pas un mode d'expression mineur, que mon potential agressif pouvait exploser à travers la chanson." – *20 Ans*

Chapter Three

1 "Une vraie guele d'assassin" – *Libération*.

2 "C'était atroce. La souffrance! Peut-être, de là, vient ma misogynie... Une salope, quoi." – Bayon, *Mort Ou Vices*

3 "Serge Gainsbourg est un pianiste de 25 ans qui est devenu compositeur de chansons, parolier et chanteur. Il chante l'alcool, les filles, l'adultère, les voitures qui vont vite, la pauvreté, les métiers tristes. Ses chansons, inspirées par l'expérience d'une jeunesse que la vie n'a pas favorisée, ont un accent de mélancolie, d'amertume, surtout la dureté d'un constat. Elles se chantent sur une musique un peu avare où, selon la mode de notre temps, le souci du rhythme efface la mélodie. Je souhaite à Gainsbourg que la chance lui sourie surtout qu'il le mérite, et qu'elle mette dans ses chansons quelques taches de soleil." – Liner-notes

4 "Bordel, vous êtes des cons si vous n'achetez pas le disque de Gainsbourg." – *Le Canard Enchaîné*

5 "Il me dit, en ouvrant un livre de Cole Porter, 'Vous avez la même prosodie, la même technique du rejet et de l'allitération'." – Gilles Verlant, *Gainsbourg*

6 "blême physique et voix blanche" – *Libération*

7 "Mes musiques sont judéo-russes. C'est toujours quelque chose de triste." – Gilles Verlant, *Gainsbourg*

8 "J'aurais aimé avoir les racines. Il faut des racines pour etre un homme. Je suis un déraciné" – *Actuel*

9 "C'est un garcon qui ne ressemble à personne – et qui fait des chansons comme personne. Il

est grand, tres frêle, timide d'aspect, de voix – vous parle si bas que vous l'entendez à peine… Mais il fait des chansons qui vous arrivent dans le coeur et l'estomac comme des coups de poing. Il y exprime tout, rien ne l'arrête, ni la pudeur inutile, ni la peur de choquer… Il n'imite personne, ne cherche jamais a faire joli ou gentil, aimable ou commercial. Avec lui, rien de banal, de convenu, L'idée est toujours étonnante et le mot celui qu'on n'attendait pas.".… "rien d'un chanteur, mais qui dit ses chansons mieux que personne. Il nous apporte quelque chose de nouveau, de bizarre, de tourmenté, de profond, d'ultra-moderne… On l'adore ou on le déteste, mais même alors on doit reconnaître, Serge Gainsbourg est quelqu'un!" – *La Semaine Radiophonique*

Chapter 4

1 "On n'a pas su m'employer comme acteur. On m'a attribuait tous les rôles de méchant à cause de ma sale gueule" – *Actuel*

Chapter 5

1 "J'étais très pudique et je l'ai chantée avec une innocence dont je me vante. J'ai été peinée par la suite d'entendre qu'il retournait la situation à son avantage, en se moquant" – Gilles Verlant, *Gainsbourg*

2 "C'est la chanson la plus osée du siècle." – *Rock & Folk*

3 "C'est France Gall qui m'a sauvé la vie, car j'étais vraiment en perdition … avec tous ces jeunes… Moi, je ne regrette pas cette partie de ma vie. Du coup j'existe toujours" – Verlant, *Gainsbourg*

4 "Je suis incapable de médiocrité. Je suis capable de faire de nombreuses farces commes 'Les Sucettes'. Mais écrire des choses médiocres, même pour beaucoup d'argent, je ne pourrais pas." – *Rock & Folk*

5 "de prendre les gens à la mode, de travailler pour eux et de m'en sortir habilement sans me compromettre vraiment. Cela m'a ouvert le marché du disque et cela m'a permis de sortir ensuite tout ce qui me plait" – *Rock & Folk*

Chapter 6

1 "Il y a une trilogie dans ma vie. Un triangle, dirons-nous, équilatéral, qui est: la fumée –

enfin, les Gitanes – l'éthylisme, et la fille. Je n'ai pas dit isocèle, j'ai dit équilatéral. Mais tout ça avec un background de mec initié à la beauté, à la peinture" – Bayon, *Mort Ou Vices*

2 "C'est un cocktail de nonchalance gestuelle et évidemment d'aura de célébrité… Et puis le sense du mouvement dans l'espace, cette espèce de – je dirais – une classe." – Bayon

3 "Les titres de Brigitte et moi sont autant de chansons d'amour. Amour combat, amour passion, amour physique, amour fiction. Amorales ou immorales, peu importe, elles sont toutes d'une absolue sincérité." – liner notes *Bonnie And Clyde*

4 "J'en ai connue beaucoup à l'horizontale mais je ne peux pas dire qui." – *20 Ans*

Chapter 7
No source notes

Chapter 8

1 "Picasso est espagnol; moi aussi. Picasso est un génie, moi aussi. Picasso est communiste, moi non plus."

2 "Moi? Jamais. Je le sens mais je ne sais pas le dire. Mais j'aime bien l'entendre." – Bayon, *Mort Ou Vices*

3 "Brigitte et moi, c'était trop… chaud; et Jane et moi, hyper-technique. Eh bien, c'est comme la baise: quand on baise à chaud, on baise mal, et quand on baise technique, on baise mieux… (Avec Bardot) c'était une espèce de copulation effroyable et je crois que c'était *too much*." – Bayon, *Mort Ou Vices*

4 "Je connais certaines personnes proches de la princesse Margaret qui pensent qu'il s'agit de sodomie. Ils en sont très heureux. C'est peut-être pour ca que j'ai été numéro 1 en Angleterre." – *Rock & Folk*

5 "une chanson anti-baise … une musique presque liturgique … Quant à prendre mon pied, je me suis refusé, parque que j'aurais pu en faire un 30cm" – *Rock & Folk*

6 "Je n'ai pas honte de montrer ma femme nue" – *France-Dimanche*

7 "mon petit androgyne…ils vont t'aimer, eux non plus… Tu vas leur ruiner la santé." – *Lui*

8 "Ces vieilles Rolls sont ce qu'il ya de plus eshétique dans le domaine de l'automobile." *Rock & Folk*

9 "Avoir des millions d'auditeurs est assez impressionant... j'ai du fric; passons aux choses sérieuses" – *Rock & Folk*

Chapter 9

1 "Et c'est leur couleur naturelle" – lyrics 'Melody'

2 "N'ayant plus rien à perdre ni Dieu en qui croire" – lyrics 'Cargo Culte'

3 "J'ai une fixation sur Marilyn, sur sa beauté. Mais parce qu'elle est morte" – *Actuel*

4 "Comme toutes es histoires d'amour, finit mal" – *Rock & Folk*

5 "Melody, c'est Jane. Sans Jane, il n'y aurait pas de disque" – *Rock & Folk*

6 "J'ai aimé Lolita. J'avais même demandé à Nabokov si je pouvais mettre ces poêmes en musique. Il a refusé parce qu'à cette époque on était en train de tourner un film d'après son livre..." – *Rock & Folk*

7 "pour moi ce n'est pas une couleur, c'est une valeur, un 'no man's land'" – to journalist Eric Vincent

8 "les champions de l'anti-conformism" – *Paris Match*

9 "Je lis: 'Salut pauvre conne/ Adieu c'est fini'" – lyrics 'La Baigneuse De Brighton'.

Chapter 10

1 "Regarde cette cigarette. Bien sûr ça me ronge les poumons. Qu'est-ce qui peut me donner un climax physiologique pareil qui se renouvelle toutes les cinq seconds, toutes les cinq minutes? Il y a le gestuel, le briquet qui claque. Il y a le plaisir du goudron et de la nicotine qui me rongent. Et ce sont des plaisirs violents et des drogues mineures... Comment arrêter une drogue mineure qui est une plaisir?" – *Actuel*

2 "Tu es belle vue de l'extérieur/ Hélas je connais tout ce qui se passe à l'intérieur/ C'est pas beau même assez dégôutant/ Alors ne t'étonne pas si aujourd'hui je te dis va-t'en" – lyrics, 'Vu De L'Extérieur'

3 "Ça me revulse, chaque matin quand je vais chier. Ça me fait chier... L'amour est dirty. Plus l'amour est dirty, plus l'amour est beau... C'est an approche du sublime." – Bayon, *Mort Ou Vices*

4 "Eva aime 'Smoke Gets In Your Eyes'/ Ah comme parfois j'aimerais qu'elle aille/ Se fair foutre avec 'Smoke Gets In Your Eyes'" – lyrics, 'Eva'

5 "Pour moi cet album était évidemment un exorcisme" – Gilles Verlant, *Gainsbourg*

6 Gilles Verlant, *Gainsbourg*

Chapter 11

1 "Sylvie Vartan tourne un spot: indice d'écoute moyen, indice de satisfaction moyen et indice de vente incroyablement élevée. Moi j'en tourne un avec Jane: l'indice d'écoute baise Vartan, indice de satisfaction baise Vartan, mais l'indice de vente s'effondre. Un plan d'escroc – j'ai vampirisé le produit en vendant Jane au lieu de vendre la lessive... De tout façon, en pub ma définition c'est ça: je suis une pute qui prend son pied. C'est pour ca que je suis hors de prix: une pute qui prend son pied, c'est hyper rare." – *Rock*

2 "Chez Max coiffeur pour hommes/ ... Je tombe sur cette chienne/ Shampooineuse/ Qui aussitôt m'aveugle par sa beauté paienne/ Et ses mains savonneuses" – lyrics, 'Chez Max Coiffeur Pour Hommes'

3 "Qu'importe, injures un jour se dissiperont comme volute Gitane" – lyrics, 'Aéroplanes'

4 "Je m'allais enfermer dans les water-closets/ Où là je vomissais mon alcool et ma haine" – lyrics, 'Premiers Symptomes'

5 "Cest ma fixation sur Cochran et Buddy Holly qui m'a émmené dans le trip anglais." – *Actuel*

6 "Nous nous sommes foutus/ ... Et je disais tue-moi/ Tue-moi si tu es un homme/ Tu n'es qu'une pauvre pomme/ Car tu n'as jamais pu" – lyrics 'Vie, Mort Et Résurrection D'Un Amour Passion'

Chapter 12

1 "deux sphères entres lequels j'abandonnais de mois de salaire pour y rouler mon pauvre joint" – lyrics 'Lola Rastaquouère'

2 "C'est moi qui bois/Est c'est lui qui est morte d'un cirrhose'" – lyrics 'Des Laids De Laids'

3 "fusil à la main et prêt a prendre une giclée dans les tripes." – *Rock & Folk*

4 "Je t'ai reçu à bras ouverts/ Vieille Cainaille/ … Puis j't'ai présenté ma femme/ Vieille Cainaille/… Puis t'es parti avec elle…" – lyrics, 'Vieille Cainaille'

Chapter 13

1 "Moi, je suis maniaque. J'ai horreur de retrouver une poupée ou une chaise deplacée de trois centimètres. Je sais où je les ai placées. Quand je rentre, je sens tout de suite si je suis chez moi ou on a modifié mon univers." – interview with Eric Vincent

2 "J'admets qu'il y ait une certaine mise en scène, des figurants don mon film. Je n'aime pas une boîte vide, j'ai besoin de figuration… je passe plus inaperçu … Je suis ni aimable, ni sociable, je reste toujours aussi misanthrope." *Rock & Folk*

3 "Si Jane me quitte, ça ne collera plus. Je suis un être très froid, tres contenu, et les passions contenues, lorsqu'elles éclatent, sont les plus terribles." – *Rock & Folk*

Chapter 14

1 "Les disques, la télé, les journaux, un impact sur des millions de gamins, c'est hallucinant. … Jamais une toile de Raphael ne fera autant d'entrées que Michael Jackson, jamais, jamais. Hallucinant, un art mineur qui encule un art majeur." – *Actuel*

2 "Une autobiographie… avec distorsions, distorsions atroces qui peuvent rappeler la manière de Francis Bacon." – *Art Press*

3 "C'est le premier roman et ésperons-le, le dernier qu' écrira Serge Gainsbourg. Le sujet est d'une grossièreté qui dépasse l'imagination. Quant au talent, il est parfaitement nul." – review, Annette Colin-Simard

4 "Brassens a bien gratté de sa guitare toute sa vie, je peux quand même me faire un deuxième album de reggae!" – France Inter radio interview, reported in Verlant's *Gainsbourg*

Chapter 15

1 "Je suis extrêmement pudique. Je l'ai toujours été." – Bayon, *Mort Ou Vices*

2 "Je suis un mec sujet au vertige et je pense que l'incest c'est… vertigo… J'imagine que ça pourrait etre superbe, mais ça peut aussi etre une atrocité." – Bayon

3 "L'amour que nous n'f'rons jamais ensemble" – lyrics, 'Lemon Incest'

4 An audio excerpt from the show can be accessed on the website www.prioryv.demon.co.uk/media6.trm

Chapter 16

1 "J't'ai pris pour ce que tu n'étais pas/ T'ai laissé pour ce que tu es" – lyrics, 'Pour Ce Que Tu N'Étais Pas'

2 "Tu baises tu fumes tu bois trop… Tu te prends pour Allan Poe/ Huysmans Hoffmann et Rimbaud' – lyrics, 'Oh Daddy Oh'

3 "Je l'aime donc je lui pardonne tout… Avec Jane il formait le couple médiatique idéal, beaucoup moins avec moi, ce n'est pas pareil, je ne suis pas quelqu'un de public, sans lui je n'existe pas et j'en suis quand même conscience" – Verlant, *Gainsbourg*

4 "Selon mes humeurs parce que je suis impulsif – pas agressif" – Verlant, *Gainsbourg*

5 "Il ne faut pas oublier que le français est une langue gutturale. Et puis j'aime ça. Je suis devenu assez fort en anglais, surtout depuis que j'ai tourné avec mes ricains" – to Jean-William Thoury

6 "J'ai tout eu, je n'ai plus rien. L'idée du bonheur m'est étrangère. Je ne le conçois pas donc je ne le cherche pas." – Verlant, *Gainsbourg*

7 "Il faut être honnête, je ne suis pas à la hauteur. je me sens périssable et je veux qu'il ne reste rien de moi quand je crèverai." – *Rock*

8 "Je ne veux pas passer à la postérité. Qu'est-ce que la postérité a fait pour moi. Je fucke la postérité" …"une recherche de la vérité par injection de perversité"…"je suis resté intact. INTACT. Voilà ma force" – Verlant, *Gainsbourg*

Chapter 17

1 "Gainsbourg n'attend pas d'etre mort pour etre immortel" – Philips slogan for *De Gainsbourg À Gainsbarre*

2 "Si je bois, dans six mois je suis aveugle et dans un an je suis plus là. Alors je suis dos au mur, mais je m'en fous" – *Rock & Folk*

3 "La mort est *toujours* présent, si on n'est past con." – *Libération*

Chapter 18

1 "Serge Gainsbourg avait élevé la chanson au rang d'un art qui témoignera de la sensibilité de toute une génération". – Mitterand.

2 "Il incarnait avec sensualité l'idéal Rimbaldien de la liberté libre." – Lang

3 "C'était un être très vulnerable, plein de timidité, plein d'humour et se posant perpétuellment des questions sur tout ce qu'il faisait. Il n' était pas sûr de lui du tout, et quand on voit les merveilles qu'il a pu écrire, la beauté des musiques qu'il a interepretées ou nous a fait interpréter, on ne comprend pas ce manque de confiance en lui. C'était un homme qui a vécu d'une façon extraordinaire, qui a eu une vie merveilleuse. Sa mort nous touche énormément parce qu'on perd quelqu'un d'irremplaçable." – Bardot

Further Reading

For those who read French, there are shelves full of books on Gainsbourg. Besides the invaluable and much-cited *Gainsbourg* by Gilles Verlant and *Mort Ou Vices* by Bayon, you might also like to check out: *Gainsbourg – Voyeur De Première* by Frank Maubert (about Serge and art), *Au Pays Des Malices* (a selection of Serge's) writings and aphorisms (Le Temps Singulier, 1980), *Gainsbourg Ou La Provocation Permanente* by Yves Saalgues, and a paperback containing all of Serge's lyrics, *Dernières Nouvelles Des Etoiles*. For those who don't read French, there is but one other book that I know of, in English, *Serge Gainsbourg: View From The Exterior* by Alan Clayson (Sanctuary). There is also a English language fanzine called *The Serge Gainsbourg Gazette*, available from 60's Scene, 1 Wellington Avenue, St Ives, Cambridgeshire PE27 3UT.

Selected Discography

This stands as a selective introduction to Gainsbourg's major albums.
A more complete discography follows afterwards. All inclusions are by
Serge Gainsbourg unless alternatively stated.

1958 DU CHANT A LA UNE! (10" LP, Philips)
*Le Poinçonneur Des Lilas/ La Recette De L'Amour
Fou/ Douze Belles Dans La Peau/ Ce Mortel Ennui/
Ronsard 58/ La Femme Des Uns Sous Le Corps Des
Autres/ L'Alcool/ Du Jazz Dans Le Ravin/ Le
Charleston Des Iménageurs De Piano*

1959 **NO. 2** (LP, 10" Philips)
*Le Claqueur De Doigts/ La Nuit D'Octobre/ Adieu,
Creature!/ L'Anthracite/ Mambo Miam Miam/
Indifférente/ Jeunes Femmes Et Vieux Messieurs/
L'Amour A La Papa*

1959 **Juliette Gréco**
**JULIETTE GRECO CHANTE SERGE
GAINSBOURG** (EP, Philips)
*Il Etait Une Oie/ Les Amours Perdues/ L'Amour A
Papa/ La Jambe De Bois 'Friedland'*

1961 L'ETONNANT SERGE GAINSBOURG
(10" LP, Philips)
*La Chanson De Prévert/ En Relisant Ta Lettre/ Le
Rock De Nerval/ Les Oubliettes/ Chanson De
Maglia/ Viva Villa/ Les Amours Perdues/ Les
Femmes, C'est Du Chinois/ Personne/ Le Sonnet
D'Arvers*

1962 **NO. 4** (10" LP, Philips)
*Les Goémons/ Black Trombone/ Baudelaire/
Intoxicated Man/ Quand Tu T'y Mets/ Les
Cigarillos/ Requiem Pour Un Twisteur/ Ce Grand
Méchant Vous*

1963 **VILAINE FILLE, MAUVAIS GARÇON**
(EP, Philips)
*Vilaine Fille, Mauvais Garon/ L'Appareil A Sous/ La
Javanaise/ Un Violon Un Jambon*

1963 **Brigitte Bardot**
L'Appareil A Sous (Single, Philips)

1964 **GAINSBOURG CONFIDENTIEL**
(LP, 12" Philips)
*Chez Les Y-y/ Sait-On Jamais Où Va Une Femme
Quand Elle Vous Quitte/ Le Talkie-Walkie/ La Fille
Au Rasoir/ La Saison Des Pluies/ Elaeudanla
Teiteia/ Scenic Railway/ Le Temps Des Yoyos/
Amour Sans Amour/ No No Thanks No/ Maxim's/
Negative Blues*

1964 **GAINSBOURG CONFIDENTIAL**
(LP, 12" Philips)
*Joanna/ Là-bas C'est Naturel/ Pauvre Lola/ Quand
Mon 6.35 Me Fait Les Yeux Doux/ Machins Choses/
Les Sambassadeurs/ New York USA/ Couleur Café/
Marabout/ Ces Petits Riens/ Tatou Jrmie/ Coco And Co*

1965 **Brigitte Bardot**
Bubble Gum (Single, Philips)

1965 **France Gall**
Poupée De Cire, Poupée De Son
(Eurovision Song Contest)

1966 QUI EST 'IN' QUI EST 'OUT' (EP, Philips)
*Qui Est 'In' Qui Est 'Out'/ Marilu/ Docteur Jekyll Et
Monsieur Hyde/ Shu Ba Du Ba Loo Ba*

1967 ANNA (Soundtrack LP, Philips)
*Sous Le Soleil Exactement (instrumental)/ Sous Le
Soleil Exactement / C'est La Cristallisation Comme
Dit Stendahl/ Pas Mal Pas Mal Du Tout/ J'Etais Fait
Pour Les Sympathies/ Photographies Et Religieuses/
Rien Rien J'Disais a Comme a/ Un Jour Comme Un
Autre/ Boomerang/ Un Poison Violent C'est a
L'Amour/ De Plus En Plus, De Moins En Moins/
Roller Girl/ Ne Dis Rien/ Pistolet Jo/ G.I Jo/ Je
N'Avais Qu'Un Mot A Lui Dire*

**1968 Brigitte Bardot & Serge Gainsbourg
BRIGITTE BARDOT ET SERGE GAINSBOURG**
(LP, Philips)
*Bonnie And Clyde/ Bubble Gum/ Comic Strip/
Pauvre Lola/ L'Eau A La Bouche/ La Javanaise/
Intoxicated Man/ Baudelaire/ Docteur Jekyll Et
Monsieur Hyde*

**1968 Brigitte Bardot & Serge Gainsbourg
INITIALS B.B** (LP, Philips)
*Initials B.B/ Comic Strip/ Bloody Jack/ Docteur
Jekyll Et Monsieur Hyde/ Torrey Canyon/ Shu Ba Du
Ba Loo Ba/ Ford Mustang/ Bonnie And Clyde/
Black And White/ Qui Est 'In' Qui Est 'Out'/ Hold-
up/ Marilu*

**1969 Serge Gainsbourg and Jane Birkin
La Chanson De Slogan** (Single, Philips)

**1969 Jane Birkin and Serge Gainsbourg
Je T'Aime, Moi Non Plus** (Single, Fontana)

**1969 Jane Birkin and Serge Gainsbourg
JANE BIRKIN-SERGE GAINSBOURG**
(LP, Fontana)
*Je T'Aime, Moi Non Plus/ L'Anamour/ Orang-
Outan/ Sous Le Soleil Exactement/ 18-39/ 69
Année Erotique/ Jane B./ Le Canari Est Sur Le
Balcon/ Les Sucettes/ Manon*

1971 HISTOIRE DE MELODY NELSON
(LP, Philips)
*Melody/ Ballade De Melody Nelson/ Valse De
Melody/ Ah! Melody/ L'Hotel Particulier/ En
Melody/ Cargo Culte*

**1973 Jane Birkin
DI DOO DAH** (LP, Philips)
*Di Doo Dah/ Help Camionneur/ Encore Lui/ Les
Capotes Anglaises/ Leur Plaisir Sans Moi/ Mon
Amour Baiser/ Banana Boat/ Kawasaki/ La Cible
Qui Bouge/ La Baigneuse De Brighton/ C'est La Vie
Qui Veut a*

1973 VU DE L'EXTERIEUR (LP, Philips)
*Je Suis Venu Te Dire Que Je M'En Vais/ Vu De
L'Exterieur/ Panpan Cucul/ Par Hasard Et Pas Ras/
Des Vents Des Pets Des Poums/ Titicaca/ Pamela
Popo/ La Poupée Qui Fait/ L'Hippodame/ Sensuelle
Et Sans Suite*

1975 ROCK AROUND THE BUNKER
(LP, Philips)
*Nazi Rock/ Tata Teutonne/ J'Entends Des Voix Off/
Eva/ Smoke Gets In Your Eyes/ Zig Zig Avec Toi/
Est-ce Est-ce Si Bon/ Yellow Star/ Rock Around The
Bunker/ S.S In Uruguay*

1976 JE T'AIME, MOI NON PLUS
(Soundtrack LP, Philips)

1976 L'HOMME A TETE DE CHOU (LP, Philips)
*L'Homme A Tête De Chou/ Chez Max Coiffeur Pour
Hommes/ Marilou Reggae/ Transit A Marilou/
Flash-Forward/ Aéroplanes/ Premiers Symptômes/
Ma Lou Marilou/ Variations Sur Marilou/ Meurtre A
L'Extincteur/ Marilou Sous La Neige/ Lunatic Asylum*

1978 Les Bronzés (Soundtrack single, Philips)
Sea Sex And Sun/ Mister Iceberg

**1978 Jane Birkin
EX-FAN DES SIXTIES** (LP, Fontana)

1979 AUX ARMES ETCAETERA (LP, Philips)
*Javanaise Remake/ Aux Armes Et Caetera/ Les
Locataires/ Des Laids Des Laids/ Brigade Des
Stups/ Vieille Canaille 'You Rascal You'/ Lola*

Rastaquoure/ Relax Baby Be Cool/ Daisy Temple/
Eau Et Gaz A Tous Les Etages/ Pas Long Feu/
Marilou Reggae Dub

1980 AU THEATRE LE PALACE (Live LP, Philips)

**1980 Jacques Dutronc
GUERRE ET PETS** (LP, Gaumont)

**1981 Alain Bashung
PLAY BLESSURES** (LP, Philips)

1981 MAUVAISE NOUVELLES DES ETOILES
(LP, Philips)
Overseas Telegram/ Ecce Homo/ Mickey Maousse/
Juif Et Dieu/ Shush Shush Charlotte/ Toi Mourir/ La
Nostalgie Camarade/ Bana Basadi Balado/
Evguénie Sokolov/ Negusa Nagast/ Strike/ Bad
News From The Stars

**1981 Catherine Deneuve
SOUVIENS-TOI DE M'OUBLIER** (LP, Philips)

**1983 Jane Birkin
BABY ALONE IN BABYLONE** (LP, Philips)

**1983 Isabelle Adjani
ISABELLE ADJANI** (LP, Philips)

1984 LOVE ON THE BEAT (LP, Philips)
Love On The Beat/ Sorry Angel/ Hmm Hmm Hmm/
Kiss Me Hardy/ No Comment/ I'm The Boy/ Harley
David Son Of A Bitch/ Lemon Incest

1986 LIVE (LP, Philips)

**1986 Brigitte Bardot & Serge Gainsbourg
Je T'Aime, Moi Non Plus** (Single, Philips)

**1986 Bambou
Lulu** (Single, Philips)

**1986 Charlotte Gainsbourg
CHARLOTTE FOREVER** (LP, Philips)
Charlotte Forever/ Ouvertures Eclair/ Oh Daddy
Oh/ Don't Forget To Forget Me/ Plus Doux Avec
Moi/ Pour Ce Que Tu N'Etais Pas/ Elastique/ Zéro
Point Vers L'Infini

**1987 Jane Birkin
LOST SONG** (LP, Philips)

1987 YOU'RE UNDER ARREST (LP, Philips)
You're Under Arrest/ Five Easy Pisseuses/ Suck
Baby Suck/ Baille Baille Samantha/ Gloomy
Sunday/ Aux Enfants De la Chance/ Shotgun/
Glass Securité/
Dispatch Box/ Mon Légionnaire

**1987 Jane Birkin
AU BATACLAN** (Live LP, Philips)
1989 LE ZENITH DE GAINSBOURG
(Live LP, Philips)

**1989 Bambou
MADE IN CHINA** (LP, Philips)

1989 DE GAINSBOURG A GAINSBARRE
(207-song box set, Philips)

**1990 Vanessa Paradis
VARIATIONS SUE LE MEME T'AIME**
(LP, Polydor)

**1990 Jane Birkin
AMOURS DES FEINTES** (LP, Philips)
Et Quand Bien Même/ Des Ils Et Des Elles/ Litanie
En Lituanie/ L'Impression Du Déjà Vu/ Asphalte/
Tombe Des Nues/ Un Amour Peut En Cacher Un
Autre/ 32 Farenheit/ Love Fifteen/ Amour Des
Feintes

Serge Gainsbourg Discography 1958 - 2000
(with thanks to Christian Eudeline)

ALBUMS

1958

Serge Gainsbourg
DU CHANT A LA UNE! (10") France
(CD rerelease Dial Phonogram 900 517-2)   LP

Serge Gainsbourg
OPUS 109 LES 3 BAUDETS *Le Poinçonneur
des lilas* [Philips Réalités V 16] France (included
on compilation)   LP

1959

Serge Gainsbourg
NO. 2 (10") [Philips 840.903 BZ] (CD rerelease
Dial Phogram 900 518-2) France   LP

1960

Serge Gainsbourg
L'AMOUR A LA PAPA Volume 3 (Compilation)
[Fontana 680.073TL] France   LP

1961

Serge Gainsbourg
L'ETONNANT SERGE GAINSBOURG (10")
[CD rerelease Dial Phonogram 900 519-2]
France   LP

1962

Serge Gainsbourg
NO. 4 (10") CD rerelease
[Dial Phonogram 900 520-2] France   LP

1963

Serge Gainsbourg
GAINSBOURG CONFIDENTIEL
[Philips B 77.980 L] France   LP
(Rerelease) [Philips 812 824-1] France   LP
(Rerelease) [Philips BL] Japan   LP

Serge Gainsbourg 1958 – 1963 16 tracks
[Philips 8128231]   LP

1964

Serge Gainsbourg
GAINSBOURG PERCUSSIONS
[Philips B 77.842 L] France   LP

Serge Gainsbourg
GAINSBOURG PERCUSSIONS (Rerelease) [Philips
B 77.842 L] Japan   LP

1966

Serge Gainsbourg
LES PLUS BELLES CHANSONS 1966
[Philips P70.370] *Qui est in qui est out* France
(included on compilation)   LP

1967

Serge Gainsbourg ANNA [Philips 70.391]
Canada   LP

1968

Serge Gainsbourg
BONNIE AND CLYDE [Philips 885.529 MY]
France   LP

1969

Serge Gainsbourg JANE BIRKIN SERGE
& Jane Birkin   GAINSBOURG
[Fontana 6325 337] France   LP

Serge Gainsbourg
LES TUBES TERRIBLES N°1 [Philips SCDP-PF001/
GB]-GB *Elisa* Brazil (included on compilation)   LP

Serge Gainsbourg
JE T'AIME BEAUTIFUL LOVE
[Fontana 67610] USA   LP

1970

Serge Gainsbourg
GRANDES CHANSONS DE GAINSBOURG
(Compilation) [Philips 6620 016] France   Double

Serge Gainsbourg
LE DISQUE D'OR (Compilation)
[Philips 6332 198] France   LP

1971

Serge Gainsbourg
HISTOIRE DE MELODY NELSON (1st pressing)
[Philips 6397 020] France   LP

Serge Gainsbourg
HISTOIRE DE MELODY NELSON (2nd pressing,
1st sleeve) [Philips 6325 071] France   LP

Serge Gainsbourg
HISTOIRE DE MELODY NELSON (2nd pressing,
2nd sleeve) [Philips 6325 071] France   LP

Serge Gainsbourg
HISTOIRE DE MELODY NELSON
[Philips 6325 071] Japan   LP

Serge Gainsbourg
HISTOIRE DE MELODY NELSON (Normal) [Philips
532 073-2] France   CD

1973

Serge Gainsbourg VU DE L'EXTERIEUR
[Philips 6499731] France   LP

Serge Gainsbourg VU DE L'EXTERIEUR
[Philips 532 075-2] France   CD

1976

Serge Gainsbourg
JE T'AIME MOI NON PLUS (soundtrack)
[Philips 9101 030] France   LP

Serge Gainsbourg
L'HOMME A TETE DE CHOU (1st pressing)
[Philips 9101 097] France   LP

Serge Gainsbourg
JE T'AIME MOI NON PLUS (soundtrack)
[Barclay 80265] Canada   LP

Serge Gainsbourg
JE T'AIME MOI NON PLUS (BOF/Rerelease)
[Philips 9101 030] Japan   LP

1977

Serge Gainsbourg
MADAME CLAUDE (soundtrack)
[Philips 9101 144] France   LP

1979

Serge Gainsbourg
AUX ARMES ET CAETERA [Philips 9101 218]
France   LP

Serge Gainsbourg
ENREGISTREMENT PUBLIC AU THEATRE
LE PALACE [Philips 6681 013] France   Double

Serge Gainsbourg
AUX ARMES ET CAETERA [Philips 9120-384]
Canada   LP

Serge Gainsbourg
AUX ARMES ET CAETERA [Philips 91 20 384]
Spain   LP

Serge Gainsbourg
FRENCHROCKMANIA *Relax Baby Be Cool
(with Bijou)* [Phonogram 6444 746] France
(included on compilation)   LP

1980

Serge Gainsbourg
GAINSBOURG EN CONCERT LE PALACE
80 [Polygram 830 599-1] France   LP

Serge Gainsbourg
LA CHANSON DE PREVERT (Compilation)
Rerelease de GRANDES CHANSONS
[Philips 6620 016] France   Double

Serge Gainsbourg
PROGRAMME PLUS (Compilation)
[Impact 824 125-1] France   LP

Serge Gainsbourg
PROGRAMME PLUS Volume 2 (Compilation)
[Impact 826 623-1] France   LP

Serge Gainsbourg
OU ES-TU MELODY? [Vent d'Ouest] France Promo

Serge Gainsbourg
LABEO / DE WOLFE
[Labeo Synthesise SYS 125] *Cabou Cadin*
France (included on compilation)   LP

1983

Serge Gainsbourg
GAINSBOURG 1958-1983 25 ans (Compilation)
[Philips 812 877-1] France   LP

1984

Serge Gainsbourg
LOVE ON THE BEAT Interview de Gainsbourg par
Philippe Manoeuvre [Philips 6863 241] France
Promo

Serge Gainsbourg LOVE ON THE BEAT
[Philips 822 849-1] France   LP

Serge Gainsbourg LOVE ON THE BEAT
[Philips 822849-1] Argentine   LP

Serge Gainsbourg LOVE ON THE BEAT
[Phonogram 82 849 2] Canada   LP

Serge Gainsbourg LOVE ON THE BEAT
[Philips 822849] USA   LP

Serge Gainsbourg LOVE ON THE BEAT
[Philips 28PP93] Japan   LP

1986

Serge Gainsbourg
SERGE GAINSBOURG LIVE (3, 4 & 5 Oct 1985,
Casino de Paris) [Philips 826 721-1] France
Double

Serge Gainsbourg
TENUE DE SOIREE (soundtrack)
[WEA Apache 240921-1] France   LP

Serge Gainsbourg
LOVE ON THE BEAT [Mercury 822 849-1 M-1]
USA Promo   CD

Serge Gainsbourg
LEMON INCEST + 3 audio titles
[Philips 080 418-2] France   Laser video

Serge Gainsbourg
MON LEGIONNAIRE + 4 audio titles [Philips 080
544-2] France   Laser video

Serge Gainsbourg
HEY MAN AMEN + 4 audio titles
[Philips 080 696-2] France   Laser video

Serge Gainsbourg CONFIDENTIAL
[Philips 8112051] France   CD

1987

Serge Gainsbourg
YOU'RE UNDER ARREST [Philips 834 034-1]
France   LP

1989

Serge Gainsbourg
LE ZENITH DE GAINSBOURG
[Philips 838 162-1] France   Double

Serge Gainsbourg
LE ZENITH DE GAINSBOURG
[Polygram 080 690.1] France   Laser video

Serge Gainsbourg
PENTEL DES PROMOS QUI VOUS CHANTENT
[Label blanc] (TV film soundtrack) *Pentex*
France (included on compilation)   LP

1990

Serge Gainsbourg
BONNIE AND CLYDE [Philips 885.529 MY] Japan
LP

Serge Gainsbourg
DE GAINSBOURG A GAINSBARRE (Compilation)
[Philips 842 489-1] France   Double

1995

Serge Gainsbourg
BEST OF FRANCE [Versailles 14-984 820-10]
L'Anamour France (included on compilation)   CD

1996

Serge Gainsbourg
DE SERGE GAINSBOURG A GAINSBARRE
(Compilation) [Philips 532 221-2]
France   Double CD

Serge Gainsbourg
DU JAZZ DANS LE RAVIN [Philips 522 629-2]
France   CD

1998

Serge Gainsbourg ANNA (Digipack)
[Philips 558 837-2] France   CD

Serge Gainsbourg ANNA Japan
[Philips pHCA-1060] France   CD

Serge Gainsbourg
JANE BIRKIN SERGE GAINSBOURG
[Philips 558 830-2] France   CD

Serge Gainsbourg
HISTOIRE DE MELODY NELSON (Digipack)
[Philips 532 073-2] France   CD

Serge Gainsbourg
CLASSE X LES 20 CHANSONS LES PLUS
"SEXE" DE GAINSBOURG (Compilation)
[Philips 558 429-2] France   CD

Serge Gainsbourg
GAINSBOURG DU POINCONNEUR...
AU LEGIONNAIRE [Polygram 056 874-1]
France (included on compilation)   Laser video
L'ORIGINAL CD sampler 1 [Polygram 6977]
Javanaise Remake France   promo CD
L'ORIGINAL CD sampler 2 [Polygram 6978]
Ballade de Melody Nelson Remake
France   promo CD

2000

Serge Gainsbourg
SES PLUS BELLES CHANSONS (Compilation)
Volume 4 [Universal] France   CD
LES PAPILLONS NOIRS RELAX BABY BE COOL
AVEC BIJOU [Philips 548 310-2]
(included on compilation) France   LP

7-INCH SINGLES, 12-INCH SINGLES EPS & CD SINGLES

1958

Serge Gainsbourg
Le Poinçonneur des lilas/Douze belles dans la
peau/La Femme des uns.../Du jazz dans le ravin
[Philips 432.307 BE] France   EP

Serge Gainsbourg
La Jambe de bois (Friedland) / Le Charleston... /
La Recette de l'amour fou / Ronsard 58
[Philips 432 325 BE] France   EP

Serge Gainsbourg
SERGE GAINSBOURG N°2
[Philips 840.903 BZ] France

1959

Serge Gainsbourg
Le Claqueur de doigts / Indifférente /
Adieu, créature ! / L'Amour à la papa
[Philips 432.397 BE] France   EP

Serge Gainsbourg
L'Anthracite / Mambo miam miam /
La Nuit d'octobre /Jeunes femmes et vieux
messieurs [Philips 432.398 BE] France   EP

Serge Gainsbourg
No 2 (8 tracks) [Philips 76473] France   EP

1960

Serge Gainsbourg
Cha cha cha du loup / Sois belle et tais-toi /
Judith / Laissez-moi tranquille
[Philips 432 437 BE] France   EP

Serge Gainsbourg
Sois belle et tais-toi / Cha Cha Cha du loup
[Philips B 372.773] France   SP

Serge Gainsbourg
Judith / Laissez-moi tranquille
[Philips B 372.774 F] France   SP

Serge Gainsbourg
LES LOUPS DANS LA BERGERIE (soundtrack)
[Philips 432 447 BE] France   EP

Serge Gainsbourg
L'EAU A LA BOUCHE (soundtrack)
[Philips 432 492 BE] B&W sleeve France   EP

Serge Gainsbourg
L'EAU A LA BOUCHE (soundtrack) colour sleeve
[Philips 432 492 BE] France   EP

Serge Gainsbourg
Judith / L'Eau à la bouche
[Philips B 372.731 F] France   SP

1961

Serge Gainsbourg
La Chanson de Prévert / En relisant ta lettre /
Viva Villa / Le Rock de Nerval
[Philips 432 533 BE] France   EP

Serge Gainsbourg
La Chanson de Prévert / Viva Villa
[Philips B 372.848 F] France   SP

1962

Serge Gainsbourg
Les Goémons / Black trombonne / Quand
tu t'y mets / Baudelaire [Philips 432.771 BE]
France   EP

Serge Gainsbourg
Les Goémons / Black trombonne
[Philips P 372.992 F] France   SP

Serge Gainsbourg
Vilaine fille, mauvais garçon /
L'Appareil à sous / La Javanaise/ Un Violon,
un jambon [Philips 432 862 BE] France   EP

Serge Gainsbourg
STRIP-TEASE (soundtrack) [Philips 432.898 BE]
France   EP

Serge Gainsbourg
No 4 [Philips B76553R]   ?

1963

Serge Gainsbourg
Chez les yé-yé / Le Temps des yoyos / Eleudanla
teiteïa / Scenic-Railway
[Philips 434.888 BE] France   EP

Serge Gainsbourg
Chez les yé-yé / Eleudanla teiteïa
[Philips B 373 294 F] France   SP

Serge Gainsbourg
Scenic Railway / Le Temps des yoyos
[Philips B 373.295 F] France   SP

1964

Serge Gainsbourg
Couleur café / Tatoué Jérémie /Joanna /
New York USA [Philips 434 994 BE] France   EP

Serge Gainsbourg
Couleur café / Machins choses
[SP Philips B 373 459 F] France   SP

Serge Gainsbourg
Joanna / Pauvre Lola [Philips B 373 460 F] France
SP

Serge Gainsbourg
New York USA / Tatoué Jérémie
[Philips B 373 468 2 F] France   SP

1965

Serge Gainsbourg
& Brigitte Bardot   Bubble Gum
[Philips 437125] France   ?

1966

Serge Gainsbourg
Qui est in qui est out / Marilu / Docteur Jekyll
et Monsieur Hyde/ Sha badu ba loo ba
[Philips 437 165 2E] France   EP

Serge Gainsbourg
Docteur Jekyll et Monsieur Hyde /
Qui est in qui est out [Philips 373 728 2F] France
SP

Serge Gainsbourg
Marilu / Docteur Jekyll et Monsieur Hyde
[Philips 373 730 2F] France   SP

1967

Serge Gainsbourg ANNA (soundtrack)
[Philips 437 279 BE] France   EP

Serge Gainsbourg VIDOCQ (soundtrack)
[Philips 437 290 BE] France   EP

Serge Gainsbourg
Comic Strip / Torrey Canyon / Chatterton /
Hold-Up [Philips 437 355 BE] France   EP

Serge Gainsbourg Comic Strip
[Philips HC 8.7.1967] France   Promo

Serge Gainsbourg
& Brigitte Bardot Bonnie And Clyde.
[Fontana 460.247 ME] France   EP

1968

Serge Gainsbourg
LE PACHA (soundtrack) [Philips 370 617 F] France
SP

Serge Gainsbourg
Bonnie And Clyde / Comic Strip / Bubble Gum
[Philips 460 247] France

Serge Gainsbourg
CE SACRE GRAND-PERE (soundtrack)
[Philips B 370 650 F] France   SP

Serge Gainsbourg
MICHEL SIMON L'Herbe Tendre (soundtrack)
[Philips 437.488 BE] France   EP

Serge Gainsbourg
Initials B.B. / Bloody Jack / Ford Mustang / Black
And White [Philips 437 431 BE] France   EP

Serge Gainsbourg
Initials B.B. / Ford Mustang
[Philips B 370 699 F] France   SP

Serge Gainsbourg
SLOGAN (soundtrack) [Philips B 336 217 F]
France   SP

Serge Gainsbourg
SLOGAN (soundtrack) [Philips 336 217 BE]
Germany   SP

Serge Gainsbourg
Bonnie And Clyde / Comic Strip /
Bubble Gum [Fontana 460.247 ME] Spain   EP

1969

Serge Gainsbourg
L'Anamour / 69 année érotique
[Philips 370 759 F] France   SP

Serge Gainsbourg
Elisa / Les sucettes [Philips 370 777 F] France   SP

Serge Gainsbourg Je t'aime... Moi non plus /
& Jane Birkin   Jane B [Fontana 260 196 MF]
France   SP

Serge Gainsbourg Je t'aime... Moi non plus /
& Jane Birkin   Jane B [Disc'AZ SG 113]
France   SP

Serge Gainsbourg Je t'aime... Moi non plus /
& Jane Birkin   Jane B (Rerelease)
[Warner Bros 16447] France   SP

Serge Gainsbourg Je t'aime... Moi non plus /
& Jane Birkin   Jane B [Fontana 260.196 MF]
Germany   SP

Serge Gainsbourg Je t'aime... Moi non plus /
& Jane Birkin   69 année érotique
(blue lettering) [Fontana MF 260 241] Belgium SP

Serge Gainsbourg Je t'aime... Moi non plus /
& Jane Birkin   Jane B (without picture sleeve)
[Philips cs 139.034] Brazil   Promo

Serge Gainsbourg Je t'aime... Moi non plus /
& Jane Birkin   Jane B (without sleeve)
[Philips cs 139.034] Brazil   SP

Serge Gainsbourg Je t'aime... Moi non plus /
& Jane Birkin   Jane B [Fontana 260.196]
Canada   SP

Serge Gainsbourg Je t'aime... Moi non plus /
& Jane Birkin   Jane B [Fontana 260.196 TF]
Denmark   SP

Serge Gainsbourg Je t'aime... Moi non plus /
& Jane Birkin   Jane B [Antic K 11511] GB   SP

Serge Gainsbourg Je t'aime Moi non plus /
& Jane Birkin   Requiem pour un con / Jane B
(white sleeve) [Phonodor 74033] Israel   EP

Serge Gainsbourg Je t'aime... Moi non plus /
& Jane Birkin   Requiem pour un con / Jane B
(red sleeve) [Phonodor 74033] Israel   EP

Serge Gainsbourg Je t'aime... Moi non plus /
& Jane Birkin   Jane B [Oméga OM 36.141]
Holland   SP

Serge Gainsbourg Je t'aime... Moi non plus /
& Jane Birkin   Jane B [Fontana 260.496 TF]
Holland   SP

Serge Gainsbourg Je t'aime... Moi non plus /
& Jane Birkin   Jane B [Fontana F-1665] USA SP

Serge Gainsbourg
Je t'aime... Moi non plus / Jane B
[Fontana 260.196 TF] Sweden   SP

1971

Serge Gainsbourg
La Décadanse / La Décadanse
[Fontana 6837 050] France   Promo

Serge Gainsbourg
Decadanse/ Les Langues De Chats
[Fontana 6010054] Canada   SP

Serge Gainsbourg
Decadanse/ Les Langues De Chats
[Fontana 6010054] France   SP

Serge Gainsbourg
Decadanse/ Les Langues De Chats
[Fontana 6010054] Portugal   SP

Serge Gainsbourg
Ballade de Melody Nelson / Valse de Melody
[Philips 6118014] France   SP

Serge Gainsbourg
UN PETIT GARCON APPELE CHARLIE BROWN
(soundtrack) [Philips 6009 104 1] France   SP

Serge Gainsbourg
La Décadanse / Je t'aime... Moi non plus [Philips
FD-1725] Japan   SP

1972

Serge Gainsbourg
TROP JOLIES POUR ETRE HONNETES
(soundtrack) Moogy Woogy / Close combat
[Philips 6009 286 1] France   SP

Serge Gainsbourg
La Décadanse / Les Langues de chat
(without sleeve) Philips 6009 201] Brazil   SP

Serge Gainsbourg
La Décadanse / Les Langues de chat [Fontana
6010 054] Italy   SP

Serge Gainsbourg
La Décadanse / Je t'aime... Moi non plus
[Philips 6PP-1022] Japan   SP

Serge Gainsbourg
Yo Te Amo? Yo Tampoco (Je t'aime... Moi non plus)
/ Jane B [Disc'AZ Gamma G922]
Mexico   SP

1973

Serge Gainsbourg
Je suis venu te dire que je m'en vais /Vu de
l'extérieur [Philips 6837 167] France   Promo

Serge Gainsbourg
Je suis venu te dire que je m'en vais /
Vu de l'extérieur [Philips 6009 459 France   SP

Serge Gainsbourg
SEX SHOP (soundtrack) Sex Shop /
Quand le sexe te chope (without sleeve)
[Fontana 6010 071] Brazil   SP

1974

Serge Gainsbourg
Je t'aime... Moi non plus / Jane B
[WB F16447] Italy   SP

Serge Gainsbourg
Je t'aime... Moi non plus / Jane B
[Disc'AZ SG 113] Sweden   SP

1975

Serge Gainsbourg
Nazi Rock / Tata teutonne [Philips 6837 250]
France   Promo

Serge Gainsbourg
L'Ami caouette / Le Cadavre exquis
[Philips 6009.678] France   SP

Serge Gainsbourg
Rock Around The Bunker / Nazi Rock
[Philips 6009 631] Italy   SP

Serge Gainsbourg
Rock Around The Bunker/ Nazi Rock
[Philips 6009631) France   SP

Serge Gainsbourg
Je t'aime... Moi non plus / La Décadanse
[Philips FD-2004] Japan   SP

1976

Serge Gainsbourg
Marilou sous la neige / Ma lou Marilou
[Philips 6042 272] France   SP

Serge Gainsbourg
Marilou sous la neige / L'Homme à tête de
chou [Philips 6837 387] France   Promo

Serge Gainsbourg
Je t'aime... Moi non plus / Jane B
[Fontana 260 196 MF] Spain   SP

1977

Serge Gainsbourg
MADAME CLAUDE (soundtrack) Yesterday,
Yes A Day / Dusty Lane [Philips 6172 009]
France   SP

Serge Gainsbourg
My Lady Héroïne / Trois millions de Joconde
[Philips 6172 026] France   SP

Serge Gainsbourg
VOUS N'AUREZ PAS L'ALSACE ET LA
LORRAINE (soundtrack) [Déesse DPX 727]
France   SP

Serge Gainsbourg
Je t'aime... Moi non plus / Jane B
[Warner Bros 45-1506] Spain   S

Serge Gainsbourg
MADAME CLAUDE (soundtrack)
[Philips SFL-2192] Japan   SP

Serge Gainsbourg
MADAME CLAUDE (soundtrack) Yesterday,
Yes A Day / Dusty Lane [Philips 6042 320]
Holland   SP

1978

Serge Gainsbourg
Sea Sex And Sun / Mister Iceberg
[Philips 6172 147] France   SP

Serge Gainsbourg
LES BRONZES (soundtrack) [Philips 6172 187]
France   SP

Serge Gainsbourg
Sea Sex And Sun / Sous le soleil exactement
[Philips 812 034-7] France   SP

Serge Gainsbourg
Sea Sex And Sun / Mister Iceberg
[Philips 6042 412]Germany   SP

Serge Gainsbourg
Sea Sex and Sun/ Mister Iceberg
[Philips 6042412] UK   SP

1979

Serge Gainsbourg
Des Laids des laids / Aux armes et caetera [Philips
6172250] France   SP

Serge Gainsbourg
TAPAGE NOCTURNE (soundtrack)
Tapage nocturne / Jolielaide
[Philips 6172 266] France   SP

Serge Gainsbourg
Vieille canaille / Daisy Temple
[Philips 6172 287] France   SP

Serge Gainsbourg
MUSIQUE & SON Comic Strip / L'Eau à la
bouche [Phonogram 16077917] France   Promo

Serge Gainsbourg
Daisy Temple / Aux armes et caetera
[Philips 6042 475] Germany   SP

Serge Gainsbourg
Daisy Temple/ Aux Armes Et Cetera
[Philips 6042 475] Germany   SP

Serge Gainsbourg
Aux armes et caetera / Lola rastaquouoère [Philips
6042 469] Spain   SP

Serge Gainsbourg
Aux Armes Et Cetera / Lola Rastaquorore
[Philips 6837549] France   SP

Serge Gainsbourg
Daisy Temple / Vieille canaille
[Philips 6042 477] Holland   SP

1980

Serge Gainsbourg
Harley Davidson / Docteur Jekyll et Monsieur Hyde
[Philips 6172 316] France   SP

Serge Gainsbourg
JE VOUS AIME (soundtrack) Je vous salue
Marie + Gérard Depardieu
[Philips 6837 678] France   Promo

Serge Gainsbourg
JE VOUS AIME (soundtrack) Dieu fumeur de
havanes avec Catherine Deneuve / La Fautive
[Philips 6010 291] France   SP

Serge Gainsbourg
DU CHANT A LA UNE (Rerelease)
[Philips Mono 6313 150] France   10-inch

1981

Serge Gainsbourg
Requiem pour un twisteur / Intoxicated Man
(Re-release) [Philips 6010 255] France   SP

Serge Gainsbourg
Souviens-toi de m'oublier avec Catherine Deneuve
[Philips 6010 360] France   SP

Serge Gainsbourg
La Nostalgie camarade / Ecce Homo
[Philips 6837 717] France   Promo

Serge Gainsbourg
Ecce Homo / La Nostalgie camarade
[Philips 6010 448] France   SP

Serge Gainsbourg
LE PHYSIQUE ET LE FIGURE (soundtrack) [Gaumont
751.814] France   SP

Serge Gainsbourg
La Nostalgie Camarade / Ecce Homo /
Eugenie Sokolov / Mickey Maousse
[Philips 6863 171] France   Promo Maxi single

1982

Serge Gainsbourg
Bana Basadi Balalo/ Negula Nagast
[Philips 6010 555] France   SP

1984

Serge Gainsbourg
Lemon Incest (avec Charlotte) / Hmm
Hmm Hmm Hmm [Philips 6863 264]
France   Promo Maxi single

Serge Gainsbourg
Love On The Beat / Harley David Son Of
A Bitch / Sorry Angel [Philips 6863 240]
France   Promo Maxi single

Serge Gainsbourg
Love On The Beat / Harley David Son Of
A Bitch [Philips 880 538.1] France   Maxi single

Serge Gainsbourg
Je t'aime moi non plus / Bonnie & Clyde
[Philips 884 240-1] 2 Titres France   Maxi single

Serge Gainsbourg
Love On The Beat Part 1/ Part 2
[Philips 6837851] France   SP

Serge Gainsbourg
No Comment/ Kiss Me Hardy
[Philips 8806201] France   12"

Serge Gainsbourg
No Comment/ Kiss Me Hardy
[Philips 8806201] France   SP

1985

Serge Gainsbourg
Je t'aime moi non plus/ Bonnie & Clyde
[Philips 8848402] France   12"

Serge Gainsbourg
Des Laids et Des Laids/ Aux Armes Et Cetera
[Philips 6042485] Canada   SP

Serge Gainsbourg
My Lady Heroine (Live) / Je Suis Venu...
[Philips 6837880] France   SP

1986

Serge Gainsbourg
Vieille canaille avec Eddy Mitchell /
Lola Rastaquouere [Philips 884 590-7] France   SP

Serge Gainsbourg
Charlotte For Ever / Pour ce que tu n'étais
pas (with Charlotte) [Philips 888 165-1]
France   Maxi single

Serge Gainsbourg
Sorry Angel (Live) / Bonnie & Clyde (Live) [Philips
8844447] France   SP

1987

Serge Gainsbourg
You're Under Arrest / Baille baille Samantha
[Philips 6837 933] France   SP

Serge Gainsbourg
Gloomy Sunday / Five Easy Pisseuses
[Philips 6837 969] France   Promo

Serge Gainsbourg
Aux enfants de la chance / Shotgun
[Philips 570 174-7] France   SP

Serge Gainsbourg
You're Under Arrest [Philips 870 002-2]
France   CD single

Serge Gainsbourg
You're Under Arrest [Philips 870 002-2]
France   CD single

Serge Gainsbourg
Mon légionnaire / Dispatch (picture)
[Philips 870 510-7] France   SP

Serge Gainsbourg
Mon légionnaire / Dispatch (photo)
[Philips 870 510-7]France   SP

1988

Serge Gainsbourg
AUX ENFANTS DE LA CHANCE / SHOTGUN
[Philips 870 174-2] France   CD single

Serge Gainsbourg
Mon Legionaire/ Dispatch Box
[Philips 6837949] France   SP

Serge Gainsbourg
MON LEGIONNAIRE (picture)
[Philips 870 510-2] France   CD single

1989

Serge Gainsbourg
Hey Man Amen / Bonnie And Clyde
[Philips 872 256-7] France   SP

Serge Gainsbourg
Couleur café / Les Dessous chics
[Philips 874 988-7] France   SP

Serge Gainsbourg
HEY MAN AMEN [Philips 872 257-2]
France   CD single

Serge Gainsbourg
COULEUR CAFE [Philips 874 989-2]
France   CD single

Serge Gainsbourg
LE ZENITH DE GAINSBOURG
[Philips 6863 382] France   Promo

Serge Gainsbourg
Mon Legionaire/ Dispatch Box
[Philips 870511] France   SP

1990

Serge Gainsbourg
STAN THE FLASHER (soundtrack) Stan The Flasher
/Elodie [Philips 875 046-7] France   SP

Serge Gainsbourg
Gainsbourg Medley [Philips 1243] France   Promo

Serge Gainsbourg
Old Gold Je t'aime... Moi non plus / Jane B
(Rerelease) [Fontana Records OG 992] GB   SP

Serge Gainsbourg
LA NOYÉE (04/11/1972) [Vade Retro]
France   CD single

1991

Serge Gainsbourg
Requiem pour un con (Remix 91) / Requiem
pour un con [Philips 878 904-7] France   SP

Serge Gainsbourg
Requiem pour un con (Remix 91) / Requiem pour
un con [Philips 878 906-7] France   Picture

Serge Gainsbourg
Le Pacha / Toutes folles de lui
[Hortensia S404] France   SP

Serge Gainsbourg
Sex Shop / Si j'étais un espion
[Hortensia S603] France   SP

Serge Gainsbourg
SEX SHOP (soundtrack) Sex Shop / Quand le sexe
te choppe [Fontana 6010 071] Portugal   SP

1994

Serge Gainsbourg
DU CHANT A LA UNE (Re-release)
[Dial Phonogram 900 517-2] France   CD

Serge Gainsbourg
SERGE GAINSBOURG N°2 (Rerelease)
[Dial Phonogram 900 518-2] France   CD

Serge Gainsbourg
L'ETONNANT SERGE GAINSBOURG (Rerelease)
[Dial Phonogram 900 519-2] France   CD

Serge Gainsbourg
SERGE GAINSBOURG N°4 (Rerelease)
[Dial Phonogram 900 520-2 France   CD

Serge Gainsbourg
AUX ARMES ET CAETERA / LOLA RASTAQUOUÈRE
[Philips 858 422-2] France   CD single

Serge Gainsbourg
MON LÉGIONNAIRE / YOU'RE UNDER
ARREST [Philips 858 450-2] France   CD single

Serge Gainsbourg
LEMON INCEST / HEY MAN AMEN
[Philips 858 454-2] France   CD single

Serge Gainsbourg
LOVE ON THE BEAT / NO COMMENT
[Philips 858 456-2] France   CD single

1995

Serge Gainsbourg ELISA [Mercury 1969]
France   Promo

1996

Serge Gainsbourg
Les Papillons Noirs avec Michèle Arnaud
[EMI 2002] France   Promo

Serge Gainsbourg
Pauvre Lola / Ces petits riens [Philips 2631]
France   Promo

Serge Gainsbourg
Coco And Co / Black Trombonne
[Philips 2630] France   Promo

Serge Gainsbourg
L'Anamour / Ford Mustang [Philips 2632]
France   Promo

Serge Gainsbourg
Black Trombone/ Coco and co [Philips 2630]
France

1998

Serge Gainsbourg
LE POINÇONNEUR DES LILAS / LE
POINÇONNEUR DES LILAS /
LE POINÇONNEUR DES LILAS
[Polygram Video 4540] France   CD singles

1999

Serge Gainsbourg
INITIALS B.B. / BLOODY JACK / FORD
MUSTANG / BLACK AND WHITE (n°217)
[Mercury 9245] France   CD singles

2000

Serge Gainsbourg
Single: Amnesty International picture disc GB   SP

RECORDINGS BY OTHER ARTISTS 1958 – 2000

Isabelle ADJANI

Pull marine. (Serge Gainsbourg / Isabelle Adjani)
(SP Philips 880 010-7) France

Beau oui comme Bowie. (Serge Gainsbourg)
ISABELLE ADJANI (LP Philips 814 827-1) France
(1983)

ISABELLE ADJANI (CD Philips 814 827-2) France
(1983)

Le Bonheur c'est malheureux. (Serge Gainsbourg /
Isabelle Adjani) [Philips 880 010-7] France SP

ISABELLE ADJANI (LP Philips 814 827-1) France

ISABELLE ADJANI (CD Philips 814 827-2) France

C'est rien je m'en vais c'est tout. (Serge Gainsbourg)

D'Un taxiphone. (Serge Gainsbourg /
Isabelle Adjani)

Entre autre pas en traître. (Serge Gainsbourg)

Et moi chouchou. (Serge Gainsbourg /
Isabelle Adjani)

Je t'aime idiot. (Serge Gainsbourg /
Isabelle Adjani)

Le Mal intérieur. (Serge Gainsbourg)

Ohio. (Serge Gainsbourg)

Ok pour plus jamais. (Serge Gainsbourg /
Isabelle Adjani)

Pull marine. (Serge Gainsbourg / Isabelle Adjani)
ISABELLE ADJANI (LP Philips 814 827-1) France

ISABELLE ADJANI (CD Philips 814 827-2) France

IL LES FAIT CHANTER (LP Polygram 834 378-1)
France (1983)

L'ALSACIENNE

Poupée de cire, poupée de son. Orchestre de la
Discothèque de Paris (EP Chanson et Play-Backs de
l'Alsacienne Album 3) France

Michele ARNAUD

Douze belles dans la peau. (Serge Gainsbourg)
MICHELE ARNAUD Vol.4 (25 cm Ducretet Thomson
260 V 093) France

La Femme des uns sous le corps des autres.
(Serge Gainsbourg) (EP Ducretet Thomson
260 V 432) France (1958)

La Femme des uns sous le corps des autres /
La Recette de l'amour fou [Philips B 372.586 F]
France SP (1958)

Jeunes femmes et vieux messieurs.
(Serge Gainsbourg) (EP Ducretet Thomson 260
V 432) France (1958)

La Recette de l'amour fou. (Serge Gainsbourg)
MICHELE ARNAUD Vol.4 (25 cm Ducretet Thomson
260 V 093) France (1958)

Ballade des oiseaux de croix. (Serge Gainsbourg) (EP
Pathé Marconi EG 951) France

Les Papillons noirs. (Serge Gainsbourg)

Ne dis rien. (Serge Gainsbourg) (EP Pathé Marconi EG
951) France (1967)

Ballade des oiseaux de croix. (Serge Gainsbourg)

La Chanson de Prévert. (Serge Gainsbourg)

Les Goémons. (Serge Gainsbourg)

Il était une oie. (Serge Gainsbourg)

La Javanaise. (Serge Gainsbourg)

Jeunes femmes et vieux messieurs. (Serge
Gainsbourg)

Ne dis rien. (Serge Gainsbourg)

La Recette de l'amour fou.

Rêves et caravelles. (Serge Gainsbourg)

Ronsard 58. (Serge Gainsbourg)

GAINSBOURG CHANTE PAR... (CD EMI 854 067 2)
France (1996)

Claire d'ASTA

La Chanson de Prévert. (Serge Gainsbourg) (SP
Philips 6010 372) France (1981)

IL LES FAIT CHANTER (LP Polygram 834 378-1)
France (1981)

Isabelle AUBRET

Pour aimer il faut être trois. (EP Polydor 27 172) France

Vicky AUTIER.

La Chanson de Prévert. (Serge Gainsbourg)
GAINSBOURG CHANTE PAR... (CD EMI 854 067 2)
France (1996)

BABY BIRKIN

Mélo mélo. (Serge Gainsbourg) (SP Dishy Records
DISHY 29) GB (1996)

Orang outan. (Serge Gainsbourg) (SP Damaged
Records DAMGOOD 130) GB (1997)

BALLABILI DURIUM

Je t'aime... Moi non plus. (Serge Gainsbourg) (SP
Durium LdA 7642) Italie (1969)

BAMBOU

Aberdeen e Kowloon. (Serge Gainsbourg) (SP
Philips 874 230-7) France (1989)

Entre l'âme et l'amour. (Serge Gainsbourg) (SP Philips 876 218-7) France (1989)

Hey Mister Zippo. (Serge Gainsbourg) (SP Philips 876 218-7) France (1989)

Nuits de Chine. (Serge Gainsbourg) (SP Philips 874 230-7) France (1989)

Ghetto Blaster. (Serge Gainsbourg) (SP Philips 875 602-7) France (1990)

J'ai pleuré le Yang Tsé. (Serge Gainsbourg) (SP Philips 875 602-7) France (1990)

Lulu. (Serge Gainsbourg) IL LES FAIT CHANTER (LP Polygram 834 378-1) France (1989)

BARBARA

En relisant ta lettre. (Serge Gainsbourg) EN LIBERTE SUR EUROPE 1.(CD Philips 5354) France

BASHUNG

C'est comment qu'on freine. (Serge Gainsbourg/Bashung)

Lavabo. (Serge Gainsbourg/Bashung)

Martine boude. (Serge Gainsbourg/Bashung)

Scène de manager. (Serge Gainsbourg)

Trompé d'érection. (Serge Gainsbourg/Bashung)

Volontaire. (Serge Gainsbourg/Bashung) Duo avec Noir Désir

PLAY BLESSURES (LP Philips 829 606-1) France

PLAY BLESSURES (LP Philips 6313 426) France

BASHUNG (CD Barclay 517 221-2) France

J'croise aux hébrides. (Serge Gainsbourg/ Bashung)

J'envisage. (Serge Gainsbourg/Bashung, Bashung)

PLAY BLESSURES (LP Philips 829 606-1) France

PLAY BLESSURES (LP Philips 6313 426) France

Martine boude. (Serge Gainsbourg/Bashung)

Volontaire. (Serge Gainsbourg/Bashung) Duo with Noir Désir

LIVE TOUR 85 (LP Philips 826 435-1) France (1985) Version live

CONFESSIONS PUBLIQUES (CD Barclay 529 241-2) France (1995) Version live

C'est comment qu'on freine. (Serge Gainsbourg/ Bashung)

CLIMAX (CD Barclay 543 648 2) France (2000)

Eszter BALINT

Un poison violent, c'est ça l'amour. (Serge Gainsbourg)

GREAT JEWISH MUSIC : SERGE GAINSBOURG (CD Tzadik TZ 7116) USA (1997)

Cyro BAPTISTA

Là-bas c'est naturel. (Serge Gainsbourg)

GREAT JEWISH MUSIC : SERGE GAINSBOURG (CD Tzadik TZ 7116) USA (1997)

Brigitte BARDOT

L'Appareil à sous. (Serge Gainsbourg) (EP Philips 432.874 BE) France (1963)

Contact. (Serge Gainsbourg)

Harley Davidson. (Serge Gainsbourg) (SP Disc'AZ AZ 10 346) France (1967)

Bubble Gum. (Serge Gainsbourg) (EP Fontana 460.247 ME) France (1967)

INITIALES BB (Serge Gainsbourg)

Je t'aime... Moi non plus. (Serge Gainsbourg)

Les Omnibus. (Serge Gainsbourg / Alain Goraguer) (Sampler CD Philips 5760) France (3 CD box set Philips 514 673-2) France

L'Appareil à sous. (Serge Gainsbourg) (EP Philips 432.874 BE) France

BRIGITTE BARDOT (CD Philips 536 276-2) France

INITIALES BB (Serge Gainsbourg)

BRIGITTE BARDOT (LP Polygram 830 296-1) France (Rerelease) (1963)

BRIGITTE BARDOT (LP Disc'AZ AZ/2 332) France (1980)

BONNIE AND CLYDE LP Fontana 885 529 (1968)

Je t'aime... Moi non plus (Remix 86).

Bonnie And Clyde (Remix 86).

BRIGITTE BARDOT (LP Polygram 830 296-1) France (Rerelease) (1996)

La Belle et les blues. (Serge Gainsbourg / Claude Bolling)

INITIALES BB (3 CD box set Philips 514 673-2) France (1993)

Je me donne à qui me plait. (Serge Gainsbourg)

BRIGITTE BARDOT (CD Philips 536 276-2) France

BONNIE AND CLYDE LP Fontana 885 529 MY / Rerelease (Japan)

Je t'aime... Moi non plus. (Serge Gainsbourg)

IL LES FAIT CHANTER (LP Polygram 834 378-1)
France (1993)

BRIGITTE BARDOT SHOW (CD Magic MAM 003)
France (1999) Two different versions

Minouche BARELLI

Boum Badamou. (Serge Gainsbourg) (SP CBS
DP 2659) France (1967)

Steve BERESFORD

Couleur café. (Serge Gainsbourg)

GREAT JEWISH MUSIC : SERGE GAINSBOURG (CD
Tzadik TZ 7116) USA (1997)

BIJOU

Betty Jane rose. (Serge Gainsbourg) Version studio
(SP Philips 6172 192) France (1978)

Les Papillons noirs. (Serge Gainsbourg) Duo
with Serge Gainsbourg

OK CAROLE (LP Philips 9101 178) France (1978)

Les Papillons noirs with Bijou Album
[Philips 9101 178] Ok Carole France LP

Les Papillons noirs with Bijou Album
[Philips 9101 178] Ok Carole Re-release
France LP (1978)

Tapage nocturne. (Serge Gainsbourg) Bande
Originale de Film Tapage

Nocturne (SP Philips 6172 266) France (1979)

Jolie laide Cool. (Serge Gainsbourg) film sound track
Tapage

Nocturne (SP Philips 6172 266) France

Relax Baby Be Cool. (Serge Gainsbourg) Duo
with Serge Gainsbourg

FRENCHROCKMANIA (LP Phonogram 6444 746)
France 1979

Betty Jane rose. (Serge Gainsbourg) live version

EN PUBLIC (LP Philips 6313 059) France 1980

Les Papillons noirs. (Serge Gainsbourg) Duo with
Serge Gainsbourg

OK CAROLE (CD Philips 536 791-2) France 1998

Betty Jane rose. (Serge Gainsbourg) studio version

Betty Jane rose. (Serge Gainsbourg) studio version

Jolie laide Cool. (Serge Gainsbourg)

Les Papillons noirs. (Serge Gainsbourg) Duo
with Serge Gainsbourg

Relax Baby Be Cool. (Serge Gainsbourg) Duo
with Serge Gainsbourg

Tapage nocturne. (Serge Gainsbourg)

Jane BIRKIN

Singles

Bébé gai. (Serge Gainsbourg)

My chérie Jane. (André Popp, Serge Gainsbourg) (SP
Fontana 6010 102) France (1974)

La Fille aux claquettes. (Serge Gainsbourg)
(SP Fontana 6010 114) France (1975)

Rien pour rien. (Serge Gainsbourg, Philippe Labro)
(SP Fontana 6010 114) France (1975)

Ballade de Johnny-Jane. (Serge Gainsbourg)
(SP Fontana 6010 118) France

Raccrochez c'est une horreur. (Serge Gainsbourg) (SP
Fontana 6010 118) France (1975)

Apocalypstick. (Serge Gainsbourg) (SP Fontana 6172
762) France

Ex fan des sixties. (Serge Gainsbourg) (SP Fontana
6172 761) France

Mélo mélo. (Serge Gainsbourg) SP Fontana 6172
761) France

Nicotine (Il est parti chercher des cigarettes). (Serge
Gainsbourg) (SP Fontana 6172 762) France
(1978)

Amour des feintes. (Serge Gainsbourg)
(SP Philips 878 026-7) France (1990)

Asphalte. (Serge Gainsbourg) (SP Philips 878
026-7) France (1990)

Litanie en Lituanie. (Serge Gainsbourg) (CD SP Philips
868 747-2) France (1990)

Tombée des nues. (Serge Gainsbourg) (CD SP Philips
868 747-2) France

Love Fifteen. (Serge Gainsbourg) (SP Philips
868 746-7) France (1991)

Tombée des nues. (Serge Gainsbourg) (SP Philips
868 746-7) France (1991)

La Chanson de Prévert. (Serge Gainsbourg)
(CD SP Philips 866 860-2) France Version
live au Casino de Paris

Je suis venu te dire que je m'en vais. (Serge
Gainsbourg) (CD SP Philips 866 421-2) France
(1992) Version live au Casino de Paris

Sous le soleil exactement. (Serge Gainsbourg)
(CD SP Philips 866 860-2) France (1992) Version
live au Casino de Paris

LPs

JANE BIRKIN SERGE GAINSBOURG (LP Fontana
6325 337) France

JE T'AIME (LP Fontana SRF 67610) USA (1971)

18-39. (Serge Gainsbourg) JE T'AIME... MOI NON PLUS / DI DOO DAH (CD Philips 514 122-2) France Part of the box set INTEGRALE JANE.B (1992)

32 Fahrenheit. (Serge Gainsbourg)

Amour des feintes. (Serge Gainsbourg)

Asphalte. (Serge Gainsbourg)

Des Ils et des elles. (Serge Gainsbourg)

Et quand bien même. (Serge Gainsbourg)

L'Impression du déjà vu. (Serge Gainsbourg)

Litanie en Lituanie. (Serge Gainsbourg)

Love Fifteen. (Serge Gainsbourg)

Tombée des nues. (Serge Gainsbourg)

Un Amour peut en cacher un autre. (Serge Gainsbourg)

AMOUR DES FEINTES (CD Philips 846 521-2) France (1990)

32 Fahrenheit. (Serge Gainsbourg)

Amour des feintes. (Serge Gainsbourg)

JE SUIS VENU TE DIRE QUE JE M'EN VAIS... (CD Philips 510 972-2) France Concert au Casino de Paris

32 Fahrenheit. (Serge Gainsbourg)

Amour des feintes. (Serge Gainsbourg)

Asphalte. (Serge Gainsbourg)

L'Amour de moi. (Traditionnel arrangé par Serge Gainsbourg)

Un Amour peut en cacher un autre. (Serge Gainsbourg)

AMOUR DES FEINTES / LOST SONG (CD Philips 514 125-2) France Part of the box set INTEGRALE JANE.B

Apocalypstick. (Serge Gainsbourg)

EX FAN DES SIXTIES (CD Fontana 536 802-2) France

EX-FAN DES SIXTIES / BABY ALONE IN BAYLONE (CD Philips 514 124-2)

L'Aquoiboniste. (Serge Gainsbourg)

EX FAN DES SIXTIES (CD Fontana 536 802-2) France

EX-FAN DES SIXTIES / BABY ALONE IN BAYLONE (CD Philips 514 124-2) France Part of the box set INTEGRALE JANE.B

EX FAN DES SIXTIES (CD Fontana 536 802-2) France

JE SUIS VENU TE DIRE QUE JE M'EN VAIS... (CD Philips 510 972-2) France Concert au Casino de Paris

EX-FAN DES SIXTIES / BABY ALONE IN BAYLONE (CD Philips 514 124-2) France Part of the box set INTEGRALE JANE.B

Asphalte. (Serge Gainsbourg)

JE SUIS VENU TE DIRE QUE JE M'EN VAIS... (CD Philips 510 972-2) France (1992) Concert au Casino de Paris

Baby Alone In Babylone. (Serge Gainsbourg based on the 2nd movement of Symphony n° 3 by Brahms)

BABY ALONE IN BABYLONE (CD Philips 814 524-2) France

IL LES FAIT CHANTER (LP Polygram 834 378-1) France

JE SUIS VENU TE DIRE QUE JE M'EN VAIS... (CD Philips 510 972-2) France Concert au Casino de Paris

EX-FAN DES SIXTIES / BABY ALONE IN BAYLONE (CD Philips 514 124-2) France Part of the box set INTEGRALE JANE.B

Baby lou. (Serge Gainsbourg, Alain Chamfort/ Michel Pealy)

BABY ALONE IN BABYLONE (CD Philips 814 524-2) France

EX-FAN DES SIXTIES / BABY ALONE IN BAYLONE (CD Philips 514 124-2) France Part of the box set INTEGRALE JANE.B

La Baigneuse de Brighton. (Serge Gainsbourg)

IL LES FAIT CHANTER (LP Polygram 834 378-1) France

JE T'AIME... MOI NON PLUS / DI DOO DAH (CDPhilips 514 122-2) France Part of the box set INTEGRALE JANE.B

Ballade de Johnny-Jane. (Serge Gainsbourg)

JE SUIS VENU TE DIRE QUE JE M'EN VAIS... (CD Philips 510 972-2) France Concert au Casino de Paris

BALLADE DE JOHNY-JANE / LOLITA GO HOME (CD Philips 514 123-2) France Part of the box set INTEGRALE JANE.B

Banana Boat. (Serge Gainsbourg)

IL LES FAIT CHANTER (LP Polygram 834 378-1) France

JE T'AIME... MOI NON PLUS / DI DOO DAH (CD Philips 514 122-2) France Part of the box set INTEGRALE JANE.B

Bébé gai. (Serge Gainsbourg)

BALLADE DE JOHNY-JANE / LOLITA GO HOME (CD Philips 514 123-2) France Part of the box set INTEGRALE JANE.B

Bébé Song. (Serge Gainsbourg, Philippe Labro)

LOLITA GO HOME (CD Fontana 538 832-2) France

BALLADE DE JOHNY-JANE / LOLITA GO HOME (CD Philips 514 123-2) France Part of the box set INTEGRALE JANE.B

Le Canari est sur le balcon. (Serge Gainsbourg)

JE T'AIME... MOI NON PLUS / DI DOO DAH
(CD Philips 514 122-2) France
Part of the box set INTEGRALE JANE.B

Les Capotes anglaise. (Serge Gainsbourg)

IL LES FAIT CHANTER (LP Polygram 834 378-1) France

JE T'AIME... MOI NON PLUS / DI DOO DAH
(CD Philips 514 122-2) France
Part of the box set INTEGRALE JANE.B

C'est la vie qui veut ça. (Jean-Claude Vannier, Serge
Gainsbourg)

IL LES FAIT CHANTER (LP Polygram 834 378-1) France

JE T'AIME... MOI NON PLUS / DI DOO DAH
(CD Philips 514 122-2) France (1992)
Part of the box set INTEGRALE JANE.B

AMOUR DES FEINTES / LOST SONG
(CD Philips 514 125-2) France (1992) Part
of the box set INTEGRALE JANE.B Version n°2

La Chanson de Prévert. (Serge Gainsbourg)

JE SUIS VENU TE DIRE QUE JE M'EN VAIS...
(CD Philips 510 972-2) France Concert au Casino
de Paris

La Chanson de slogan. (Serge Gainsbourg)
Duo with Serge Gainsbourg

JE T'AIME (LP Fontana SRF 67610) USA

JE T'AIME... MOI NON PLUS / DI DOO DAH
(CD Philips 514 122-2) France Part of the box set
INTEGRALE JANE.B

Une Chose entre autres. (Serge Gainsbourg)

AMOUR DES FEINTES / LOST SONG
(CD Philips 514 125-2) France
Part of the box set INTEGRALE JANE.B

La Cible qui bouge. (Jean-Claude Vannier /
Serge Gainsbourg)

IL LES FAIT CHANTER (LP Polygram 834 378-1) France

JE T'AIME... MOI NON PLUS / DI DOO DAH
(CD Philips 514 122-2) France
Part of the box set INTEGRALE JANE.B

Classé x. (Serge Gainsbourg)

EX FAN DES SIXTIES (CD Fontana 536 802-2) France

EX-FAN DES SIXTIES / BABY ALONE IN BAYLONE
(CD Philips 514 124-2) France (1992)
Part of the box set INTEGRALE JANE.B

Con c'est con ces conséquences.(Serge Gainsbourg)

BABY ALONE IN BABYLONE
(CD Philips 814 524-2) France

EX-FAN DES SIXTIES / BABY ALONE IN BAYLONE
(CD Philips 514 124-2) France (1992) Part of the
box set INTEGRALE JANE.B

Le Couteau dans le Play. (Serge Gainsbourg)

AMOUR DES FEINTES / LOST SONG (CD Philips
514 125-2) France (1992) Part of the box set

INTEGRALE JANE.B

La Décadanse. (Serge Gainsbourg) Duo with
Serge Gainsbourg

JE T'AIME... MOI NON PLUS / DI DOO DAH
(CD Philips 514 122-2) France (1992)
Part of the box set INTEGRALE JANE.B

Dépressive. (Serge Gainsbourg)

EX FAN DES SIXTIES (CD Fontana 536 802-2)
France

EX-FAN DES SIXTIES / BABY ALONE IN BAYLONE

(CD Philips 514 124-2) France
Part of the box set INTEGRALE JANE.B

Les Dessous chics. (Serge Gainsbourg)

BABY ALONE IN BABYLONE (CD Philips 814 524-2)
France

JE SUIS VENU TE DIRE QUE JE M'EN VAIS...
(CD Philips 510 972-2) France Concert au Casino
de Paris

EX-FAN DES SIXTIES / BABY ALONE IN BAYLONE
(CD Philips 514 124-2) France Part of the box set
INTEGRALE JANE.B

Di Doo Dah. (Serge Gainsbourg)

DI DOO DAH (CD Fontana 558 829-2) France

JE SUIS VENU TE DIRE QUE JE M'EN VAIS...
(CD Philips 510 972-2) France Concert au Casino
de Paris

JE T'AIME... MOI NON PLUS / DI DOO DAH
(CD Philips 514 122-2) France Part of the box set
INTEGRALE JANE.B

Encore lui. (Jean-Claude Vannier, Serge Gainsbourg)

IL LES FAIT CHANTER (LP Polygram 834 378-1)
France

JE T'AIME... MOI NON PLUS / DI DOO DAH (CD
Philips 514 122-2) France Part of the box set INTE-
GRALE JANE.B

En rire de peur d'être obligée d'en pleurer. (Serge
Gainsbourg)

BABY ALONE IN BABYLONE (CD Philips 814 524-2)
France

EX-FAN DES SIXTIES / BABY ALONE IN BAYLONE
(CD Philips 514 124-2) France (1992)
Part of the box set INTEGRALE JANE.B

Etre ou ne pas naître. (Serge Gainsbourg)

AMOUR DES FEINTES / LOST SONG (CD Philips
514 125-2) France (1992) Part of the box set
INTEGRALE JANE.B

Et quand bien même. (Serge Gainsbourg)

JE SUIS VENU TE DIRE QUE JE M'EN VAIS...
(CD Philips 510 972-2) France (1992) Concert au
Casino de Paris

AMOUR DES FEINTES / LOST SONG (CD Philips
514 125-2) France (1992) Part of the box set
INTEGRALE JANE.B

Exercice en forme de z. (Serge Gainsbourg)

EX-FAN DES SIXTIES / BABY ALONE IN BAYLONE
(CD Philips 514 124-2) France
Part of the box set INTEGRALE JANE.B

Ex fan des sixties. (Serge Gainsbourg)

EX FAN DES SIXTIES (CD Fontana 536 802-2)
France (CD SP Philips 866 421-2) France (1992)
Version live au Casino de Paris

JE SUIS VENU TE DIRE QUE JE M'EN VAIS...
(CD Philips 510 972-2) France (1992)
Concert au Casino de Paris

EX-FAN DES SIXTIES / BABY ALONE IN BAYLONE
(CD Philips 514 124-2) France (1992)
Part of the box set INTEGRALE JANE.B

Ex fan des sixties. (Serge Gainsbourg) English version

BALLADE DE JOHNNY-JANE / LOLITA GO HOME
(CD Philips 514 123-2) France
Part of the box set INTEGRALE JANE.B

La Fille aux claquettes. (Serge Gainsbourg) (

LOLITA GO HOME (CD Fontana 538 832-2) France

BALLADE DE JOHNNY-JANE / LOLITA GO HOME
(CD Philips 514 123-2) France
Part of the box set INTEGRALE JANE.B

French graffiti. (Serge Gainsbourg, Philippe Labro)

LOLITA GO HOME (CD Fontana 538 832-2) France

BALLADE DE JOHNNY-JANE / LOLITA GO HOME
(CD Philips 514 123-2) France
Part of the box set INTEGRALE JANE.B

Fuir le bonheur de peur qu'il ne se sauve.
(Serge Gainsbourg)

BABY ALONE IN BABYLONE (CD Philips 814
524-2) France

IL LES FAIT CHANTER (LP Polygram 834 378-1)
France (CD SP Philips 866 421-2) France (1992)
Version live au Casino de Paris

JE SUIS VENU TE DIRE QUE JE M'EN VAIS...
(CD Philips 510 972-2) France
Concert au Casino de Paris

EX-FAN DES SIXTIES / BABY ALONE IN BAYLONE
(CD Philips 514 124-2) France
Part of the box set INTEGRALE JANE.B

Haine pour aime. (Serge Gainsbourg)

BABY ALONE IN BABYLONE (CD Philips 814
524-2) France

EX-FAN DES SIXTIES / BABY ALONE IN BAYLONE
(CD Philips 514 124-2) France (1992)
Part of the box set INTEGRALE JANE.B

Help camionneur. (Serge Gainsbourg)

IL LES FAIT CHANTER (LP Polygram 834 378-1) France

JE T'AIME... MOI NON PLUS / DI DOO DAH
(CD Philips 514 122-2) France Part of the box set
INTEGRALE JANE.B

Des Ils et des elles. (Serge Gainsbourg)

JE SUIS VENU TE DIRE QUE JE M'EN VAIS...
(CD Philips 510 972-2)
France (1992) Concert au Casino de Paris

AMOUR DES FEINTES / LOST SONG (CD Philips
514 125-2) France (1992) Part of the box set
INTEGRALE JANE.B

L'Impression du déjà vu. (Serge Gainsbourg)

JE SUIS VENU TE DIRE QUE JE M'EN VAIS...
(CD Philips 510 972-2) France (1992)
Concert au Casino de Paris

AMOUR DES FEINTES / LOST SONG (CD Philips
514 125-2) France (1992)
Part of the box set INTEGRALE JANE.B

Je suis venu te dire que je m'en vais.
(Serge Gainsbourg) (CD SP Philips 866 421-2)
France (1992) Version live au Casino de Paris

JE SUIS VENU TE DIRE QUE JE M'EN VAIS...
(CD Philips 510 972-2) France (1992)
Concert au Casino de Paris

Je t'aime... Moi non plus. (Serge Gainsbourg)
Duo with Serge Gainsbourg

JE T'AIME... MOI NON PLUS / DI DOO DAH
(CDPhilips 514 122-2) France (1992)
Part of the box set INTEGRALE JANE.B

Just Me And You. (Serge Gainsbourg, Philippe Labro)

LOLITA GO HOME (CD Fontana 538 832-2) France

BALLADE DE JOHNNY-JANE / LOLITA GO HOME
(CD Philips 514 123-2) France (1992)
Part of the box set INTEGRALE JANE.B

Kawasaki. (Serge Gainsbourg)

IL LES FAIT CHANTER (LP Polygram 834 378-1)
France

JE T'AIME... MOI NON PLUS / DI DOO DAH
(CD Philips 514 122-2) France (1992)
Part of the box set INTEGRALE JANE.B

Les Langues de chat. (Jean-Claude Vannier,
Serge Gainsbourg)

JE T'AIME... MOI NON PLUS / DI DOO DAH
(CD Philips 514 122-2) France (1992)
Part of the box set INTEGRALE JANE.B

Leur plaisir sans moi. (Jean-Claude Vannier,
Serge Gainsbourg)

IL LES FAIT CHANTER (LP Polygram 834 378-1)
France

JE T'AIME... MOI NON PLUS / DI DOO DAH
(CD Philips 514 122-2) France (1992)
Part of the box set INTEGRALE JANE.B

AMOUR DES FEINTES / LOST SONG
(CD Philips 514 125-2) France (1992)
Part of the box set INTEGRALE JANE.B

Litanie en Lituanie. (Serge Gainsbourg)

JE SUIS VENU TE DIRE QUE JE M'EN VAIS...
(CD Philips 510 972-2) France (1992)
Concert au Casino de Paris

AMOUR DES FEINTES / LOST SONG
(CD Philips 514 125-2) France
Part of the box set INTEGRALE JANE.B

Lolita Go Home. (Serge Gainsbourg, Philippe Labro)

LOLITA GO HOME (CD Fontana 538 832-2) France

BALLADE DE JOHNY-JANE / LOLITA GO HOME
(CD Philips 514 123-2) France (1992) Part of the
box set INTEGRALE JANE.B

Lost Song. (Grieg – Peer Gynt suite n°2 op.55
arranged by Serge Gainsbourg)

AMOUR DES FEINTES / LOST SONG
(CD Philips 514 125-2) France (1992)
Part of the box set INTEGRALE JANE.B

Love Fifteen (Serge Gainsbourg)

JE SUIS VENU TE DIRE QUE JE M'EN VAIS...
(CD Philips 510 972-2) France (1992)
Concert au Casino de Paris

AMOUR DES FEINTES / LOST SONG
(CD Philips 514 125-2) France (1992)
Part of the box set INTEGRALE JANE.B

Manon. (Serge Gainsbourg)

JE SUIS VENU TE DIRE QUE JE M'EN VAIS...
(CD Philips 510 972-2) France (1992)
Concert au Casino de Paris

Marilou sous la neige. (Serge Gainsbourg)

JE SUIS VENU TE DIRE QUE JE M'EN VAIS...
(CD Philips 510 972-2) France (1992)
Concert au Casino de Paris

Mélodie interdite. (Serge Gainsbourg)

EX FAN DES SIXTIES (CD Fontana 536 802-2) France

EX-FAN DES SIXTIES / BABY ALONE IN BAYLONE
(CD Philips 514 124-2) France (1992)
Part of the box set INTEGRALE JANE.B

Mélo mélo. (Serge Gainsbourg)

EX FAN DES SIXTIES (CD Fontana 536 802-2) France

EX-FAN DES SIXTIES / BABY ALONE IN BAYLONE
(CD Philips 514 124-2) France (1992)
Part of the box set INTEGRALE JANE.B

Mister Iceberg. (Serge Gainsbourg) English version

BALLADE DE JOHNY-JANE / LOLITA GO HOME (CD
Philips 514 123-2) France (1992)
Part of the box set INTEGRALE JANE.B

Le Moi et le je. (Serge Gainsbourg)

JE SUIS VENU TE DIRE QUE JE M'EN VAIS...
(CD Philips 510 972-2) France (1992)
Concert au Casino de Paris

AMOUR DES FEINTES / LOST SONG
(CD Philips 514 125-2) France (1992)
Part of the box set INTEGRALE JANE.B

Mon amour baiser. (Serge Gainsbourg)

IL LES FAIT CHANTER (LP Polygram 834 378-1) France

JE T'AIME... MOI NON PLUS / DI DOO DAH
(CDPhilips 514 122-2) France (1992)
Part of the box set INTEGRALE JANE.B

My chérie Jane. (André Popp, Serge Gainsbourg)

BALLADE DE JOHNY-JANE / LOLITA GO HOME (CD
Philips 514 123-2) France

Nicotine (Il est parti chercher des cigarettes). (Serge
Gainsbourg)

EX FAN DES SIXTIES (CD Fontana 536 802-2) France

JE SUIS VENU TE DIRE QUE JE M'EN VAIS...
(CD Philips 510 972-2) France (1992)
Concert au Casino de Paris

EX-FAN DES SIXTIES / BABY ALONE IN BAYLONE
(CD Philips 514 124-2) France (1992)
Part of the box set INTEGRALE JANE.B

Norma Jean Baker. (Serge Gainsbourg)

BABY ALONE IN BABYLONE (CD Philips 814 524-2)
France

EX-FAN DES SIXTIES / BABY ALONE IN BAYLONE
(CD Philips 514 124-2) France (1992)
Part of the box set INTEGRALE JANE.B

Orang outan. (Serge Gainsbourg)

JE T'AIME... MOI NON PLUS / DI DOO DAH
(CD Philips 514 122-2) France (1992)
Part of the box set INTEGRALE JANE.B

Overseas Telegram. (Serge Gainsbourg)

BABY ALONE IN BABYLONE (CD Philips 814 524-2)
France

EX-FAN DES SIXTIES / BABY ALONE IN BAYLONE
(CD Philips 514 124-2) France (1992)
Part of the box set INTEGRALE JANE.B

Partie perdue. (Serge Gainsbourg)

BABY ALONE IN BABYLONE (CD Philips 814 524-2)
France

EX-FAN DES SIXTIES / BABY ALONE IN BAYLONE
(CD Philips 514 124-2) France (1992)
Part of the box set INTEGRALE JANE.B

Physique et sans issue. (Serge Gainsbourg)
AMOUR DES FEINTES / LOST SONG
(CD Philips 514 125-2) France (1992)
Part of the box set INTEGRALE JANE.B

Puisque je te le dis. (Serge Gainsbourg)
IL LES FAIT CHANTER (LP Polygram 834 378-1)
France

JE T'AIME... MOI NON PLUS / DI DOO DAH
(CD Philips 514 122-2) France (1992)
Part of the box set INTEGRALE JANE.B

Quoi. (Serge Gainsbourg)
IL LES FAIT CHANTER (LP Polygram 834 378-1) France

JE SUIS VENU TE DIRE QUE JE M'EN VAIS...
(CD Philips 510 972-2) France (1992)
Concert au Casino de Paris

EX-FAN DES SIXTIES / BABY ALONE IN BAYLONE
(CD Philips 514 124-2) France (1992)
Part of the box set INTEGRALE JANE.B

Raccrochez c'est une horreur. (Serge Gainsbourg)
BALLADE DE JOHNNY-JANE / LOLITA GO HOME
(CD Philips 514 123-2) France (1992)
Part of the box set INTEGRALE JANE.B

Rien pour rien. (Serge Gainsbourg, Philippe Labro)
LOLITA GO HOME (CD Fontana 538 832-2) France
BALLADE DE JOHNNY-JANE / LOLITA GO HOME
(CD Philips 514 123-2) France (1992)
Part of the box set INTEGRALE JANE.B

Rocking Chair. (Serge Gainsbourg)
EX FAN DES SIXTIES (CD Fontana 536 802-2) France
EX-FAN DES SIXTIES / BABY ALONE IN BAYLONE
(CD Philips 514 124-2) France (1992)
Part of the box set INTEGRALE JANE.B

Rupture au miroir. (Serge Gainsbourg)
BABY ALONE IN BABYLONE
(CD Philips 814 524-2) France

EX-FAN DES SIXTIES / BABY ALONE IN BAYLONE
(CD Philips 514 124-2) France (1992)
Part of the box set INTEGRALE JANE.B

Si ça peut te consoler. (Serge Gainsbourg,
Philippe Labro)
LOLITA GO HOME (CD Fontana 538 832-2) France
BALLADE DE JOHNNY-JANE / LOLITA GO HOME
(CD Philips 514 123-2) France
Part of the box set INTEGRALE JANE.B

Sous le soleil exactement. (Serge Gainsbourg)
JE SUIS VENU TE DIRE QUE JE M'EN VAIS...
(CD Philips 510 972-2) France Concert au Casino
de Paris

Tombée des nues. (Serge Gainsbourg)
JE SUIS VENU TE DIRE QUE JE M'EN VAIS...
(CD Philips 510 972-2) France (1992)
Concert au Casino de Paris

AMOUR DES FEINTES / LOST SONG
(CD Philips 514 125-2) France (1992)
Part of the box set INTEGRALE JANE.B

Valse de Mélody. (Serge Gainsbourg)
JE SUIS VENU TE DIRE QUE JE M'EN VAIS...
(CD Philips 510 972-2) France (1992)
Concert au Casino de Paris

Le Velours des vierges. (Serge Gainsbourg)
EX FAN DES SIXTIES (CD Fontana 536 802-2) France
EX-FAN DES SIXTIES / BABY ALONE IN BAYLONE
(CD Philips 514 124-2) France (1992)
Part of the box set INTEGRALE JANE.B

Vie mort et résurrection d'un amour passion.
(Serge Gainsbourg)
EX FAN DES SIXTIES (CD Fontana 536 802-2) France
EX-FAN DES SIXTIES / BABY ALONE IN BAYLONE
(CD Philips 514 124-2) France (1992)
Part of the box set INTEGRALE JANE.B

Yesterday Yes A Day. (Serge Gainsbourg)
BALLADE DE JOHNNY-JANE / LOLITA GO HOME
(CD Philips 514 123-2) France (1992)
Part of the box set INTEGRALE JANE.B

Aux Enfants de la chance. (Serge Gainsbourg)
Ce mortel ennui. (Serge Gainsbourg)
Ces petits riens. (Serge Gainsbourg)
Comment te dire adieu. (Serge Gainsbourg)
Couleur café. (Serge Gainsbourg)
Dépression au-dessus du jardin.
(Serge Gainsbourg)
Elaeudanla Téïtéïa. (Serge Gainsbourg)
Elisa. (Serge Gainsbourg)
Exercice en forme de z. (Serge Gainsbourg)
Ford Mustang. (Serge Gainsbourg)
L'Anamour. (Serge Gainsbourg)
La Gadoue. (Serge Gainsbourg)
Le Mal intérieur. (Serge Gainsbourg)
Physique et sans issue. (Serge Gainsbourg)
Sorry Angel. (Serge Gainsbourg)
VERSIONS JANE (CD Philips 532 140-2- France
(1996)

Exercice en forme de z. (Serge Gainsbourg)
EX FAN DES SIXTIES (CD Fontana 536 802-2)
France (1996)

Honor BLACKMAN

Men Will Deceive You (Serge Gainsbourg, Stellman)
(English language adaptation of 'La Javanaise')
Trad (LP EVERYTHING I'VE GOT, London LL.3408)
USA (1965)

BLONDE REDHEAD

La Chanson de slogan (Serge Gainsbourg)
GREAT JEWISH MUSIC : SERGE GAINSBOURG (CD
Tzadik TZ 7116) USA (1997)

BLOWN

Je t'aime... Moi non plus. (Serge Gainsbourg)
JE T'AIME MOI NON PLUS
(CD Epic EPC 660279 2) France

The BOLLOCK BROTHERS

Harley David. (Serge Gainsbourg, McDonald)
Son Of A Bitch. (Serge Gainsbourg, McDonald)
(SP Play It Again Sam Records 7 BIAS 36) Belgium
(1987) (SP New Musidisc Play It Again Sam
Records 135 153) France (1987)

BOURVIL – Jacqueline MAILLAN

Ça (Je t'aime... Moi non plus) (Serge Gainsbourg)
(SP EMI Pathé 2 C006 11079) France
Pauvre Lola. (Serge Gainsbourg) (SP EMI Pathé 2
C006 11079) France (1996)
GAINSBOURG CHANTE PAR...
(CD EMI 854 067 2) France (1996)

Rodolphe BURGER + The Meteor Band + Philippe Poirirer

Les Petits papiers. (Serge Gainsbourg) LIBERTE DE
CIRCULATION (CD Naive NV 0540) France (1999)

Alain CHAMFORT

Joujou à la casse. (Serge Gainsbourg
Alain Chamfort / Jean-Noël Chaléat) (SP CBS
5791) France
Privé. (Serge Gainsbourg Alain Chamfort) (SP CBS
5791) France (1977)
Démodé. (Serge Gainsbourg Alain Chamfort / Jean-
Noël Chaleat) (SP CBS 8281) France (1979)
Manureva. (Serge Gainsbourg Alain Chamfort /
Jean-Noël Chaléat) (SP CBS 7497) France (1979)
Bambou. (Serge Gainsbourg Alain Chamfort) (SP
CBS A 1337) France (1981)
Poupée poupée. (Serge Gainsbourg Alain Chamfort)
(SP CBS A 1337) France (1981)
Baby lou. (Serge Gainsbourg Alain Chamfort /
Michel Pelay)

Disc-Jockey. (Serge Gainsbourg Alain Chamfort /
Michel Pelay)
Joujou à la casse. (Serge Gainsbourg Alain Chamfort
/ Jean-Noël Chaléat)
Lucette et Lucie. (Serge Gainsbourg Alain Chamfort /
Jean-Noël Chaléat)
Privé. (Serge Gainsbourg Alain Chamfort)
Rock'n Rose. (Serge Gainsbourg Alain Chamfort /
Jean-Noël Chaléat)
Sparadrap. (Serge Gainsbourg Alain Chamfort /
Jean-Noël Chaléat)
Tennisman. (Serge Gainsbourg Alain Chamfort /
Michel Pelay)
Le Vide au coeur. (Serge Gainsbourg Alain Chamfort
/ Michel Pelay)
ROCK'N ROSE (LP CBS 82377) France (1977)
Bébé Polaroid. (Serge Gainsbourg Alain Chamfort /
Jean-Noël Chaléat)
Démodé. (Serge Gainsbourg Alain Chamfort / Jean-
Noël Chaleat)
Manureva. (Serge Gainsbourg Alain Chamfort /
Jean-Noël Chaléat)
POSES (LP CBS 451025 1) France (1979)
Dieu fumeur de havanes Duo with Serge Gainsbourg
(Serge Gainsbourg)
IL LES FAIT CHANTER (LP Polygram 834 378-1)
France (1980)
Amour année zéro. (Serge Gainsbourg
Alain Chamfort)
Baby boum. (Serge Gainsbourg Alain Chamfort)
Bambou. (Serge Gainsbourg Alain Chamfort)
Chasseur d'ivoire. (Serge Gainsbourg
Alain Chamfort)
Jet Society. (Serge Gainsbourg Alain Chamfort)
Laide jolie laide. (Serge Gainsbourg Alain Chamfort)
Malaise en Malaisie. (Serge Gainsbourg
Alain Chamfort)
Poupée poupée. (Serge Gainsbourg
Alain Chamfort) (SP CBS A 1337) France (1981)
AMOUR ANNEE ZERO (LP CBS 451027 1)
France (1981)
Baby boum. (Serge Gainsbourg Alain Chamfort)
Bambou. (Serge Gainsbourg Alain Chamfort)
Bébé Polaroid. (Serge Gainsbourg Alain Chamfort /
Jean-Noël Chaléat)
Joujou à la casse. (Serge Gainsbourg
Alain Chamfort / Jean-Noël Chaléat)
Malaise en Malaisie. (Serge Gainsbourg
Alain Chamfort)
Manureva. (Serge Gainsbourg Alain Chamfort /
Jean-Noël Chaléat) (SP CBS 7497) France (1979)

BEST OF Ce N'Est Que Moi (CD Promo sampler Epic SAMPCS 78 522) France

BEST OF Ce N'Est Que Moi (CD Epic EPC 496466 2) France (1999)

Les CHARLOTS

Sois érotique. SP Vogue V45.1743) France (1986)

CIBO MATTO

Je t'aime, moi non plus. (Serge Gainsbourg)

GREAT JEWISH MUSIC : SERGE GAINSBOURG (CD Tzadik TZ 7116) USA (1997)

Anthony COLEMAN

Ce mortel ennui. (Serge Gainsbourg)

GREAT JEWISH MUSIC : SERGE GAINSBOURG (CD Tzadik TZ 7116) USA (1997)

JAMAIS DOMPTES (Box set Philips 548 310-2) France 2000

Petula CLARK

Les Incorruptibles/ La gadoue (Serge Gainsbourg) (EP Vogue EPL 8 386) France (1965)

Vilaine file, mauvais garçon. (Serge Gainsbourg)

RENDEZ VOUS AVEC PETULA Anthologie Vol 1 (CD Anthology's 3039572) France (1998)

La Gadoue. (Serge Gainsbourg)

Les Incorruptibles. (Serge Gainsbourg)

O O Shériff. (Serge Gainsbourg)

PETULA CLARK Anthologie Vol 4 (CD Anthology's 3051932) France (1999)

Etienne DAHO

Chez les Yé-Yé. (Serge Gainsbourg)

ED COLLECTION (CD Virgin CDV 30065) France (1987)

DALIDA

Je préfère naturellement. (Serge Gainsbourg) (EP Barclay 71 064) France

Dany CLAUDE & Marie Françoise

Laisse tomber les filles. (EP Disque Saphir LDP 5551) France

Daniel DARC

Comment te dire adieu. (Jack Gold/Harnold Goland, Serge Gainsbourg) Adaptation of the instrumental 'It Hurts To Say Goodbye')

SOUS INFLUENCE DIVINE (CD Play It Again Sam Records BIAS 111 CD) France

Mireille DARC

La Cavaleuse (Serge Gainsbourg)

COMPARTIMENT 23 / ACTRICES MIREILLE DARC (CD Philips 848 488-2) France

MIREILLE DARC CHANTE L'AMOUR (CD Philips PPD-4) Japan

IL LES FAIT CHANTER (LP Polygram 834 378-1) France

Le Drapeau noir (Serge Gainsbourg)

Hélicoptère (Serge Gainsbourg)

COMPARTIMENT 23 / ACTRICES MIREILLE DARC (CD Philips 848 488-2) France

DAUGA Philippe (ex Bijou)

J'en ai autant pour toi. (Philippe Dauga / Serge Gainsbourg) (SP Philips 6010 551) France (1982)

J'en ai autant pour toi. (Philippe Dauga / Serge Gainsbourg)

PILE OU FACE (CD Musidisc 170 142) France (1993)

Catherine DENEUVE

Dieu fumeur de havanes Duo with Serge Gainsbourg (Serge Gainsbourg) SP Philips 6010 291 France (1980)

Digital Delay. (Serge Gainsbourg)

Epsilon. (Serge Gainsbourg)

Marine band tremolo. (Serge Gainsbourg)

Monna Vanna et Miss Duncan. (Serge Gainsbourg)

Oh Soliman. (Serge Gainsbourg)

Overseas Telegram. (Serge Gainsbourg)

Souviens-toi de m'oublier. Duo with Serge Gainsbourg (Serge Gainsbourg)

What tu dis qu'est ce que tu say. (Serge Gainsbourg)

SOUVIENS-TOI DE M'OUBLIER LP Philips 6313 172 France (1981) 6313 172 France (1981)

Sacha DISTEL

Mamadou. (EP EMI EGF 839) France

DOMINIQUE

Poupée de cire, poupée de son. (EP Trianon 4531 ets) France

Diane DUFRESNE

Suicide. (Serge Gainsbourg, Claude Engel)

TURBULENCES (LP RCA NL 70206) France (1982)

Jacques DUTRONC

Le Bras mécanique. (Serge Gainsbourg, Jacques Dutronc) (SP Vogue 45 V 12126) France (1975)

L'Amour prison. (Serge Gainsbourg, Jacques Dutronc)

Le Bras mécanique. (Serge Gainsbourg, Jacques Dutronc) (SP Vogue 45 V 12126)

JACQUES DUTRONC (LP Vogue LDY. 28.033) France (1971)

Elle est si... (Serge Gainsbourg, Jacques Dutronc)

1972 (LP Vogue LDM. 30.114) France (1972)

L'Amour prison. (Serge Gainsbourg, Jacques Dutronc)

COMPLETEMENT DUTRONC (CD Vogue 614 007)
France (1991)

L'Ethylique. (Serge Gainsbourg, Jacques Dutronc)

GUERRE ET PETS (LP Gaumont Musique 753 801)
France (1980)

L'INTEGRALE DUTRONC LES ANNEES COLUMBIA
1980 1987 (Double CD Columbia
CO 472 940 2) France (1992)

L'Hymne à l'amour (moi l'nıud). (Serge Gainsbourg,
Jacques Dutronc) (SP de promotion
Gaumont 750 801) France (1980)
(SP Gaumont 751 809) France (1980)

GUERRE ET PETS (LP Gaumont Musique 753 801)
France (1980)

L'INTEGRALE DUTRONC LES ANNEES COLUMBIA
1980 1987 (Double CD Columbia
CO 472 940 2) France (1992)

DUTRONC AU CASINO (CD Columbia 472 834-2)
France (1992) Live version

DUTRONC AU CASINO (CD Livre Columbia 489
8143-2) France (1998) Live version

DUTRONC 33 ANS DE TRAVAIL Volume 2 Les
Années 80-90 (CD Columbia CO 491 101-2)
France (1997)

L'Ile enchanteresse. (Serge Gainsbourg, Jacques
Dutronc) (SP Vogue 45 V 12051) France (1975)

JACQUES DUTRONC (LP Vogue LDY. 28.033) France
(1971)

J'ai déjà donné. (Serge Gainsbourg, Jacques
Dutronc) (promo single Gaumont 750 801) France
(1980) (SP Gaumont 751 809) France (1980)

GUERRE ET PETS (LP Gaumont Musique 753 801)
France (1980)

L'INTEGRALE DUTRONC LES ANNEES COLUMBIA
1980 1987 (Double CD Columbia
CO 472 940 2) France (1992)

DUTRONC AU CASINO (CD Columbia 472 834-2)
France (1992) Version live

DUTRONC AU CASINO (CD book
Columbia 489 8143-2) France (1998) Live version

DUTRONC 33 ANS DE TRAVAIL Volume 2 Les
Années 80-90 (CD Columbia CO 491 101-2)
France (1997)

Mes idées sales. (Serge Gainsbourg, Jacques Dutronc)

GUERRE ET PETS (LP Gaumont Musique 753 801)
France (1980)

L'INTEGRALE DUTRONC LES ANNEES COLUMBIA
1980 1987 (Double CD Columbia
CO 472 940 2) France (1992)

Les Roses fanées. (Serge Gainsbourg)
(SP Vogue 45 V 12051) France (1975)

JACQUES DUTRONC (LP Vogue LDY. 28.033) France
(1971)

DUTRONC AU CASINO (CD Columbia 472 834-2)
France (1992) Live version

DUTRONC AU CASINO (CD book Columbia 489
8143-2) France (1998) Live version

Les DUTRONC

Je ne t'aime pas... Moi aussi. (A.Godlean, Serge
Gainsbourg)

DUTRONC ! DUTRONC ! DUTRONC ! (CD Garden
Records DAMGOOD CD-70) GB (1995)

Franca DUVAI

Arc-en-ciel. (Serge Gainsbourg) EP COD 504. (France)

Les ENFOIRES

Aux Armes etc. / La Marseillaise. (Rouget de Lisle,
adaptation Serge Gainsbourg) Emanuel Petit,
Bixente Lizarazu, Fabien Barthez, Alain
Boghossian, Lilian Thuram, Christian Karembeu,
Roch Voisine, Patrick Bruel, Patrick Fiori, Renaud,
Michael Jones, Jean-Jacques Goldman, Fabrice
Luchini, Marc Lavoine, Laetitia Casta, Elie Seimoun
et Alain Chabat.

LES ENFOIRES Xxe siècle (CD BMG 74321703612)
France (1999)

Dis lui toi que je l'aime. (Serge Gainsbourg) Trio with
Vanessa Paradis, Etienne Daho et Ian Lanty.

LES ENFOIRES Xxe siècle (CD BMG 74321703612)
France (1999)

ENSEMBLE VOCAL GARNIER

Les Sucettes. (Serge Gainsbourg)
(SP Vogue 45V1128) France (1978)

Je t'aime, moi non plus. (Serge Gainsbourg)
(SP Vogue 45V1128) France (1978)

Chris EVANS

Roller Girl. (Serge Gainsbourg) (CD promo single Pin
Up Records HC 501) France (1993)

DANS TOUS TES ETATS (CD Pin Up Records
CD 101) France (1993)

Robert FAREL

Les Petits boudins. (Serge Gainsbourg) (SP Barclay
885 626-7) France (1987)

Elysian FIELDS

Les Amours perdues. (Serge Gainsbourg)

GREAT JEWISH MUSIC : SERGE GAINSBOURG
(CD Tzadik TZ 7116) USA (1997)

Claude FRANÇOIS
Hip Hip Hurrah. (EP Philips 437.357 BE) France

Les FRERES JACQUES
Le Poinçonneur des lilas. (Serge Gainsbourg)
(EP Philips 432.267 BE) France (1958) (SP de
promotion Philips 28/10/1958) France (1958)
TOUS LES SUCCES DU RECITAL A LA COMEDIE DES
CHAMPS-ELYEES (LP Philips B77.317 L) France (195 ?)

Fred FRITH
The Ballad of Melody Nelson. (Serge Gainsbourg)
GREAT JEWISH MUSIC : SERGE GAINSBOURG (CD
Tzadik TZ 7116) USA (1997)

Charlotte GAINSBOURG
Elastique. (Serge Gainsbourg)
IL LES FAIT CHANTER (LP Polygram 834 378-1) France
IL LES FAIT CHANTER (LP Polygram 834 378-1)
France (1986)
Charlotte For Ever / Pour ce que n'etais pas [Philips
8881657] France SP (1986)

Lemon Incest (Duet with Serge Gainsbourg)/ *Hmm
Hmm Hmm* (Charlotte) [Philips 8841297] France
SP (1984)

Les Galeries Lafayette
Comment te dire adieu. (EP Cocktail Super Hit
Parade) France

France GALL
Attends ou va t'en. (Serge Gainsbourg)
POUPEE DE CIRE, POUPEE DE SON (Double LP
Philips 6620 048) France
SACRE CHARLEMAGNE (CD Dial 900 111-2)
France (1990)
POUPEE DE SON (CD Polydor 849 296-2) France
POUPEE DE SON (4 CD box setPolydor 849
296-2) France 1992
Baby Bop. (Serge Gainsbourg)
POUPEE DE CIRE, POUPEE DE Son (Double LP Philips
6620 048) France
SACRE CHARLEMAGNE (CD Dial 900 111-2)
France (1990)

POUPEE DE SON (CD Polydor 849 296-2) France
POUPEE DE SON (4 CD box set
Polydor 849 296-2) France 1992
Frankenstein. (Serge Gainsbourg)
GAINSBOURG CHANTE PAR...
(CD EMI 854 067 2) France (1996)
Laisse tomber les filles. (Serge Gainsbourg)
POUPEE DE CIRE, POUPEE DE Son (Double LP Philips
6620 048) France
SACRE CHARLEMAGNE (CD Dial 900 111-2) France
(1990)
POUPEE DE SON (CD Polydor 849 296-2) France
POUPEE DE SON (4 CD box set Polydor 849 296-2)
France 1992
N'écoute pas les idoles. (Serge Gainsbourg)
(EP Philips 434.874 BE) France
POUPEE DE CIRE, POUPEE DE Son (Double LP Philips
6620 048) France
SACRE CHARLEMAGNE (CD Dial 900 111-2) France
(1990)
POUPEE DE SON (CD Polydor 849 296-2) France
POUPEE DE SON (4 CD box set
Polydor 849 296-2) France 1992
Néfertiti. (Serge Gainsbourg)
POUPEE DE SON (4 CD box set
Polydor 849 296-2) France 1992
Nous ne sommes pas des anges. (Serge Gainsbourg)
SACRE CHARLEMAGNE (CD Dial 900 111-2) France
(1990)
POUPEE DE SON (CD Polydor 849 296-2) France
POUPEE DE SON (4 CD box set
Polydor 849 296-2) France 1992
Les Petits ballons. (Serge Gainsbourg)
GAINSBOURG CHANTE PAR...
(CD EMI 854 067 2) France (1996)
Poupeé de cire, poupée de son. (Serge Gainsbourg)
(SP Philips 328 036 JF) Pays-Bas
POUPEE DE CIRE, POUPEE DE Son (Double LP Philips
6620 048) France
SACRE CHARLEMAGNE (CD Dial 900 111-2) France
(1990)
POUPEE DE SON (CD Polydor 849 296-2) France
POUPEE DE SON (4 CD box set
Polydor 849 296-2) France 1992
Les Sucettes. (Serge Gainsbourg)
POUPEE DE CIRE, POUPEE DE SON (Double LP
Philips 6620 048) France
SACRE CHARLEMAGNE (CD Dial 900 111-2) France
(1990)
POUPEE DE SON (CD Polydor 849 296-2) France

POUPEE DE SON (4 CD box set Polydor 849 296-2)
  France (1992)

IL LES FAIT CHANTER (LP Polygram 834 378-1) France

Teenie Weenie Boppie. (Serge Gainsbourg)

POUPEE DE CIRE, POUPEE DE Son (Double LP Philips
  6620 048) France

SACRE CHARLEMAGNE (CD Dial 900 111-2) France
  (1990)

POUPEE DE SON (CD Polydor 849 296-2) France

POUPEE DE SON (4 CD box set
  Polydor 849 296-2) France (1992)

GAMINE

Harley Davidson. (Maxi 45 Tours Surfin' Bird
  SURF 1004) France (1984)

Groupe d'Information et de Soutien des Immigrés
  (GISTI)

Les Petits Papiers. (Serge Gainsbourg) with Jeanne
  Balibar, France Cartigny, Femmouzes, Dadou et
  Diésel de KDD, Noir Désir, Akosh S., Rodolphe
  Burger, Théo Hakola, Blankass et Grégoire Simon.

LIBERTE DE CIRCULATION (CD Naïve NV 0540)
  France (1999)

Juliette GRECO

Accordéon. (Serge Gainsbourg) (EP Philips
  432.711 BE) France

JULIETTE GRECO A L'OLYMPIA (CD promo sampler
  Philips 1538) France (1992)

JULIETTE GRECO A L'OLYMPIA (CD Philips
  512 366-2) France (1992) Version live

L'Amour à la papa. (Serge Gainsbourg)

L'AMOUR A LA PAPA (LP Fontana 680.073 TL)
  France 1963

BONJOUR TRISTESSE (LP Philips 844.791 BY) France

La Javanaise. (Serge Gainsbourg)

CELEBRATION (EP Philips 437.470) France

L'AMOUR A LA PAPA (LP Fontana 680.073 TL)
  France 1963

JULIETTE GRECO A L'OLYMPIA (CD Philips
  512 366-2) France (1992) Version live

La Recette de l'amour fou. (Serge Gainsbourg)

BONJOUR TRISTESSE (LP Philips 844.791 BY) France

Françoise HARDY

L'Anamour. (Serge Gainsbourg) (EP Vogue
  EPL 8 652) France (1968)

COMMENT TE DIRE ADIEU (CD Virgin
  7243 8 40638 2 5) France

Comment te dire adieu. (Jack Gold/
  Harnold Goland, Serge Gainsbourg)

Instrumental adaptation of 'It Hurts To Say Goodbye'
  (EP Vogue EPL 8 652) France (1968)

COMMENT TE DIRE ADIEU (CD Virgin 7243 8
  40638 2 5) France

BLUES 1962 1993 (CD Vogue 7432 1 1569 1 2)
  France (1993) Enregistrement.

GAINSBOURG CHANTE PAR...
  (CD EMI 854 067 2) France (1996)

Mick HARVEY

69 Erotic Year (69 année érotique). (Serge
  Gainsbourg)

INTOXICATED MAN (CD Mute Records
  74321217902) France (1995) (CD promo single
  Mute Records PCDSTUMM 157)
  Australia/GB (1997)

Anthracite. (Serge Gainsbourg)

PINK ELEPHANTS (CD Mute Records
  724384514723) Australia/GB (1997)

*Ballad Of Melody Nelson The (La Ballade de Melody
  Nelson)* (Serge Gainsbourg) (CD SP Mute Records
  CDMUTE 187) Australia/GB (1995)

PINK ELEPHANTS (CD Mute Records
  724384514723) Australia/GB (1997)

*The Barrel Of My 45 (Quand mon 6.35 me fait les
  yeux doux).* (Serge Gainsbourg)

INTOXICATED MAN (CD Mute Records
  74321217902) France (1995) (CD SP Mute
  Records CDMUTE 187) GB (1995)

Black Seaweed (Les Goémons). (Serge Gainsbourg)

PINK ELEPHANTS (CD Mute Records
  724384514723) GB (1997)

Bonnie & Clyde. (Serge Gainsbourg)

INTOXICATED MAN (CD Mute Records
  74321217902) France (1995)

Chatterton. (Serge Gainsbourg)

INTOXICATED MAN (CD Mute Records
  74321217902) France (1995)

Comic Strip. (Serge Gainsbourg)

PINK ELEPHANTS (CD Mute Records
  724384514723) GB (1997)

Ford Mustang. (Serge Gainsbourg)

INTOXICATED MAN (CD Mute Records
  74321217902) France (1995)

Harley Davidson. (Serge Gainsbourg)

INTOXICATED MAN (CD Mute Records
  74321217902) France (1995) (CD promo single
  Mute Records PCDSTUMM 157) GB (1997)

Hotel Specific (Hôtel particulier). (Serge Gainsbourg)

PINK ELEPHANTS (CD Mute Records
  724384514723) GB (1997)

I Have Come To Tell You I'm Going (Je suis venu te dire que je m'en vais). (Serge Gainsbourg)
INTOXICATED MAN (CD Mute Records 74321217902) France (1995)

I Love You... Nor I Do (Je t'aime... Moi non plus). Duo with Anita Lane and Nick Cave. (Serge Gainsbourg)
PINK ELEPHANTS (CD Mute Records 724384514723) GB (1997)

Initials BB. (Serge Gainsbourg)
INTOXICATED MAN (CD Mute Records 74321217902) France (1995) (CD SP Mute Records CD MUTE 187) GB (1995)

Intoxicated Man. (Serge Gainsbourg)
INTOXICATED MAN (CD Mute Records 74321217902) France (1995)

The Javanaise (La Javanaise). (Serge Gainsbourg)
PINK ELEPHANTS (CD Mute Records 724384514723) GB (1997) (CD SP de promotion Mute Records PCDSTUMM 157) GB (1997)

Jazz In The Ravine (Du jazz dans le ravin). (Serge Gainsbourg)
INTOXICATED MAN (CD Mute Records 74321217902) France (1995)

Lemon Incest. (Serge Gainsbourg)
INTOXICATED MAN (CD Mute Records 74321217902) France (1995)

Manon. (Serge Gainsbourg)
PINK ELEPHANTS (CD Mute Records 724384514723) GB (1997)

New York USA. (Serge Gainsbourg)
INTOXICATED MAN (CD Mute Records 74321217902) France (1995)

Non Affair (L'Anamour). (Serge Gainsbourg)
PINK ELEPHANTS (CD Mute Records 724384514723) GB (1997)

Overseas Telegram. (Serge Gainsbourg)
INTOXICATED MAN (CD Mute Records 74321217902) France (1995)

Requiem... (Requiem pour un...). (Serge Gainsbourg)
PINK ELEPHANTS (CD Mute Records 724384514723) GB (1997) (CD promo single Mute Records PCDSTUMM 157) GB (1997)

Scenic Railway. (Serge Gainsbourg)
PINK ELEPHANTS (CD Mute Records 724384514723) GB (1997)

Sex Shop. (Serge Gainsbourg)
INTOXICATED MAN (CD Mute Records 74321217902) France (1995)

The Songs Of Slurs (La Chanson de slogan). (Serge Gainsbourg)

INTOXICATED MAN (CD Mute Records 74321217902) France (1995)

The Sun Directly Overhead (Sous le soleil exactement). (Serge Gainsbourg)
INTOXICATED MAN (CD Mute Records 74321217902) France (1995)

The Ticket Puncher. (Le Poinçonneur des lilas). (Serge Gainsbourg)
PINK ELEPHANTS (CD Mute Records 724384514723) GB (1997)

To All The Lucky Kids (Aux enfants de la chance). (Serge Gainsbourg)
PINK ELEPHANTS (CD Mute Records 724384514723) GB (1997)

Torrey Canyon. (Serge Gainsbourg) (CD SP Mute Records CDMUTE 187) GB (1995)
PINK ELEPHANTS (CD Mute Records 724384514723) GB (1997)

Who Is In Who Is Out (Qui est in, qui est out). (Serge Gainsbourg)
PINK ELEPHANTS (CD Mute Records 724384514723) GB (1997)

Shelley HIRSCH
Comic Strip. (Serge Gainsbourg)
GREAT JEWISH MUSIC : SERGE GAINSBOURG (CD Tzadik TZ 7116) USA (1997)

Wayne HORVITZ & Robin HOLCOMB
Bonnie & Clyde. (Serge Gainsbourg)
GREAT JEWISH MUSIC : SERGE GAINSBOURG (CD Tzadik TZ 7116) USA (1997)

HOT BUTTER
Love At First Sight (Adaptation of 'Je t'aime... Moi non plus')
POP CORN (LP Barclay 920 399) France (1975)

Les INFIDELES
Je suis venu te dire que je m'en vais. (Mini LP Réflexes FAB 2059) France (1989)

JAD WIO
Contact. (Serge Gainsbourg)
FLEUR DE METAL. (CD Squatt SQT 4710662) France (1992)

Zizi JEANMAIRE
Au risque de te déplaire. (Serge Gainsbourg)
GAINSBOURG CHANTE PAR... (CD EMI 854 067 2) France (1996)

Bloody Jack. (Serge Gainsbourg) (EP Disc'AZ EP 1199) France

Ciel de plomb (Stormy Weather). (Serge Gainsbourg)
GAINSBOURG CHANTE PAR...
  (CD EMI 854 067 2) France (1996)
Elisa. (Serge Gainsbourg) (SP CBS 8008) France
Merde à l'amour. (Serge Gainsbourg)
GAINSBOURG CHANTE PAR...
  (CD EMI 854 067 2) France (1996)
Mesdames, Mesdemoiselles, mes yeux. (Serge Gainsbourg)
GAINSBOURG CHANTE PAR...
  (CD EMI 854 067 2) France (1996)
Rétro Song. (Serge Gainsbourg)
GAINSBOURG CHANTE PAR...
  (CD EMI 854 067 2) France (1996)
Tic Tac Toe. (Serge Gainsbourg)
GAINSBOURG CHANTE PAR...
  (CD EMI 854 067 2) France (1996)
Tout le monde est musicien. (Serge Gainsbourg)
  (SP CBS 8008) France
Vamp et vampire. (Serge Gainsbourg)
GAINSBOURG CHANTE PAR...
  (CD EMI 854 067 2) France (1996)
Yes Man. (Serge Gainsbourg)
GAINSBOURG CHANTE PAR...
  (CD EMI 854 067 2) France (1996)

JON

Les Sucettes. (Serge Gainsbourg)
GREAT JEWISH MUSIC : SERGE GAINSBOURG (CD
  Tzadik TZ 7116) USA (1997)

JUDGE DREAD

Je T'Aime, Moi Non Plus (Serge Gainsbourg) (1975) GB

Janie JURKA

Poupée de cire, poupée de son.
  (Serge Gainsbourg) (EP Succès du Jour 3.338)
  France (EP Pergola 450.164 PAE) France

Eyvind KANG

Sous le soleil exactement. (Serge Gainsbourg)
GREAT JEWISH MUSIC : SERGE GAINSBOURG (CD
  Tzadik TZ 7116) USA (1997)

KARINA

Muneca De Cera (Poupée de cire, poupée de son)
  (Serge Gainsbourg) (EP Hispavox 27 535) Spain
Oh, oh shériff. (Serge Gainsbourg) (EP Hispavox HH
  17.331) Spain

Anna KARINA

De plus en plus, de moins en mois.
  (Serge Gainsbourg) Duo with Jean-Claude Brialy

ANNA (LP Philips P 70.391 L) Canada (1967)
ANNA (LP Philips P 70.391 L) Japan (Reissue 1998)
G.I. Jo. (Serge Gainsbourg)
ANNA (LP Philips P 70.391 L) Canada (1967)
ANNA (LP Philips P 70.391 L) Japan (Reissue 1998)
Je n'avais qu'un seul mot à lui dire. (Serge Gainsbourg)
ANNA (LP Philips P 70.391 L) Canada (1967)
ANNA (LP Philips P 70.391 L) Japan (Reissue 1998)
Un Jour comme un autre. (Serge Gainsbourg)
ANNA (LP Philips P 70.391 L) Canada (1967)
ANNA (LP Philips P 70.391 L) Japan (Reissue 1998)
Pistolet Jo. (Serge Gainsbourg)
ANNA (LP Philips P 70.391 L) Canada (1967)
ANNA (LP Philips P 70.391 L) Japan (Reissue 1998)
Rien rien j'disais ça comme ça. (Serge Gainsbourg)
  Duo with Serge Gainsbourg
ANNA (LP Philips P 70.391 L) Canada (1967)
ANNA (LP Philips P 70.391 L) Japan (Reissue 1998)
Roller Girl. (Serge Gainsbourg)
ANNA (LP Philips P 70.391 L) Canada (1967)
ANNA (LP Philips P 70.391 L) Japan (Reissue 1998)
Sous le soleil exactement. (Serge Gainsbourg)
ANNA (LP Philips P 70.391 L) Canada (1967)
ANNA (LP Philips P 70.391 L) Japan (Reissue 1998)
IL LES FAIT CHANTER (LP Polygram 834 378-1)
  France

KRAMER

69 année érotique. (Serge Gainsbourg)
GREAT JEWISH MUSIC : SERGE GAINSBOURG (CD
  Tzadik TZ 7116) USA (1997)

Valérie LAGRANGE

La Guerilla. (EP Philips 437.055 BF) France

Anita LANE

I Love You... Nor I Do (Je t'aime... Moi non plus).
  Duet with Nick Cave. (Serge Gainsbourg)
  (CD SP Mute Records CDMUTE 177) Australia /
  GB (1995)

Gloria LASSO

La Chanson de Prévert. (Serge Gainsbourg)
GAINSBOURG CHANTE PAR...
  (CD EMI 854 067 2) France (1996)

Viktor LAZLO

Amour puissance six. (Serge Gainsbourg,
  Viktor Lazlo/G.B.Cadière/Claude Bofane)
  (SP Polydor 871 90-7) France (1989)

Jo LEMAIRE + FLOUZE

Je suis venu te dire que je m'en vais. (Serge
  Gainsbourg) (SP Vertigo 602 1 38) France (1981)
IL LES FAIT CHANTER (LP Polygram 834 378-1) France

LIO

Baby Lou. (Serge Gainsbourg) (SP Arabella
  104.6885) France (1982)

The LITTLE RABBITS

Roller Girl. (Serge Gainsbourg)
YEAH ! (CD Rosebud promo 7016) France (1998)
YEAH ! (CD Rosebud 557 214.2) France (1998)

The LONDON SOUND DANCE ORCHESTRA

La Gadoue. (Serge Gainsbourg) (SP Bagatelle n°103)
  France
Les P'tits papiers. (Serge Gainsbourg) (SP Bagatelle
  n°103) France

April MARCH

Brainwash Part II ("Chez les Yé-yé"). (Serge
  Gainsbourg / Plank)
PARIS IN APRIL! (CD SFTRI 456) USA (1997)
GAINSBOURSION! (CD Eurovision EURO 001)
  France (1998)
La Chanson de Prévert. (Serge Gainsbourg)
EP SFTRI 346 USA (1996)
PARIS IN APRIL! (CD SFTRI 456) USA (1997)
GAINSBOURSION! (CD Eurovision EURO 001)
  France (1998)
Chez les Yé-yé. (Serge Gainsbourg)
GAINSBOURSION! (CD Eurovision EURO 001)
  France (1998)
Chick Habit ("Laisse tomber les filles"). (Serge
  Gainsbourg / Blake)
EP SFTRI 346 USA (1996)
PARIS IN APRIL! (CD SFTRI 456) USA (1997)
GAINSBOURSION! (CD Eurovision EURO 001)
  France 1998
LESSONS OF APRIL MARCH (CD Ideal Records
  IPR0009-2) USA (1998)
Laisse tomber les filles. (Serge Gainsbourg) EP SFTRI
  346 USA (1996)
PARIS IN APRIL! (CD SFTRI 456) USA (1997)
GAINSBOURSION! (CD Eurovision EURO 001)
  France (1998)
The Land Of Go ("Le Temps des yoyos").
  (Serge Gainsbourg Blake / Atwell)
PARIS IN APRIL! (CD SFTRI 456) USA (1997)

GAINSBOURSION! (CD Eurovision EURO 001)
  France (1998)
Pauvre Lola. (Serge Gainsbourg)
PARIS IN APRIL! (CD SFTRI 456) USA (1997)
GAINSBOURSION! (CD Eurovision EURO 001)
  France (1998)
Poor Lola/"Pauvre Lola" (Serge Gainsbourg/Blake)
PARIS IN APRIL! (CD SFTRI 456) USA (1997)
GAINSBOURSION! (CD Eurovision EURO 001)
  France (1998)
Le Temps des yoyos. (Serge Gainsbourg)
PARIS IN APRIL! (CD SFTRI 456) USA (1997)
GAINSBOURSION! (CD Eurovision EURO 001)
  France (1998)

MARTIN CIRCUS

USSR/USA. (Serge Gainsbourg, S.Pauchard) (SP
  Vogue101 313) France (1980)

Doudou MASTA

Requiem pour un con. (Serge Gainsbourg)
L'HIP-HOPEE (CD Black Door 7243 5 25663 2 7)
  France (2000)

Medeski, Martin & Wood

Intoxicated Man. (Serge Gainsbourg)
GREAT JEWISH MUSIC : SERGE GAINSBOURG (CD
  Tzadik TZ 7116) USA (1997)

MIKADO

Attends ou vas-t'en. (Serge Gainsbourg)
MIKADO FOREVER (CD Le Village Vert 3036792)
  France (1998)

Misty OLDLAND

A Fair Affair. (Misty Oldland, Serge Gainsbourg)
  Sample from Je t'aime moi non plus. (CD promo
  single Columbia XPCD 363) GB (1993)

Eddy MITCHELL

Base-Ball (Serge Gainsbourg)
ET MAINTENANT (CD Polydor 523 094 2) France
  (1994)

Iku MORI

Pauvre Lola. (Serge Gainsbourg)
GREAT JEWISH MUSIC : SERGE GAINSBOURG (CD
  Tzadik TZ 7116) USA (1997)

NATHALIE et SERGE

Je t'aime... Moi non plus. (Serge Gainsbourg)
EROTICA (LP mfp 2 M 026-18240) France (1977)

OBERKAMP

Poupée de cire, poupée de son (Serge Gainsbourg)
COULEUR SUR PARIS (Maxi 45 Tours) France 1981
Requiem pour un con (Serge Gainsbourg)
P.L.C. (LP O3 New-Rose NR 335) France 1983

Vanessa PARADIS

L'Amour à deux. (Serge Gainsbourg, Frank Langolff)
VARIATIONS SUR LE MEME T'AIME (LP Polydor 843
447-1) France (1990)

L'Amour en soi. (Serge Gainsbourg, Frank Langolff)
(SP Polydor 879 868-7) France (1990)
VARIATIONS SUR LE MEME T'AIME (LP Polydor 843
447-1) France (1990)

Amour jamais. (Serge Gainsbourg, Frank Langolff)
VARIATIONS SUR LE MEME T'AIME (LP Polydor 843
447-1) France (1990)

Ardoise. (Serge Gainsbourg, Frank Langolff)
(SP Polydor 879 110-7) France (1990)
VARIATIONS SUR LE MEME T'AIME (LP Polydor 843
447-1) France (1990)

Au charme non plus. (Serge Gainsbourg, Frank Langolff)
VARIATIONS SUR LE MEME T'AIME
(LP Polydor 843 447-1) France (1990)

Dis lui toi que je l'aime. (Serge Gainsbourg, Frank
Langolff) (SP Polydor 879 110-7) France (1990)
VARIATIONS SUR LE MEME T'AIME
(LP Polydor 843 447-1) France (1990)

Flagrant délire. (Serge Gainsbourg, Frank Langolff)
(SP Polydor 879 868-7) France (1990)
VARIATIONS SUR LE MEME T'AIME
(LP Polydor 843 447-1) France (1990)

Ophélie. (Serge Gainsbourg, Frank Langolff)
(SP Polydor 877 302-7) France (1990)
VARIATIONS SUR LE MEME T'AIME
(LP Polydor 843 447-1) France (1990)

Tandem. (Serge Gainsbourg, Frank Langolff)
(SP Polydor 877 302-7) France (1990)
VARIATIONS SUR LE MEME T'AIME
(LP Polydor 843 447-1) France (1990)

La Vague à lames. (Serge Gainsbourg, Frank Langolff)
VARIATIONS SUR LE MEME T'AIME
(LP Polydor 843 447-1) France (1990)

Variations sur le même t'aime. (Serge Gainsbourg,
Frank Langolff)
VARIATIONS SUR LE MEME T'AIME
(LP Polydor 843 447-1) France (1990)

Jean-Claude PASCAL

L'Appareil à sous. (Serge Gainsbourg)
(EP La Voix de son Maître EGF 643) France

GAINSBOURG CHANTE PAR...
(CD EMI 854 067 2) France (1996)
Douze belles dans la peau. (Serge Gainsbourg)
GAINSBOURG CHANTE PAR...
(CD EMI 854 067 2) France (1996)
En relisant ta lettre. (Serge Gainsbourg)
(EP La Voix de son Maître EGF 529) France (1961)
GAINSBOURG CHANTE PAR...
(CD EMI 854 067 2) France (1996)
Les Oubliettes. (Serge Gainsbourg) (EP La Voix de
son Maître EGF 529) France (1961)
GAINSBOURG CHANTE PAR...
(CD EMI 854 067 2) France (1996)
Le Poinçonneur des lilas. (Serge Gainsbourg)
GAINSBOURG CHANTE PAR...
(CD EMI 854 067 2) France (1996)
La Recette de l'amour fou. (Serge Gainsbourg)
GAINSBOURG CHANTE PAR...
(CD EMI 854 067 2) France (1996)

Mike PATTON

Ford Mustang. (Serge Gainsbourg)
GREAT JEWISH MUSIC : SERGE GAINSBOURG (CD
Tzadik TZ 7116) USA (1997)

PSYCHIC TV

Je t'aime (Je t'aime... Moi non plus). (Serge
Gainsbourg) (Double EP Temple Records
TOPYD 23) GB (1986)
THE BEST OF PSYCHIC TV / BEAUTY FROM THEE
BEAST (CD Visionary VICD 006) GB (1995)

Serge REGGIANI

Maxim's . (Serge Gainsbourg)
ALBUM N°2 BOBINO (LP Jacques Canetti
48 819 GU) France
Quand j'aurai du vent dans mon crâne.
(Boris Vian, Serge Gainsbourg)
ALBUM N°2 BOBINO (LP Jacques Canetti
48 819 GU) France

REGINE

Capone et sa p'tite phyllis. (Serge Gainsbourg)
(promo single Pathé Marconi) France
REGINE (LP Pathé Marconi SPTX 340.553)
Il s'appelle reviens. (Serge Gainsbourg)
REGINE (LP Emidisc C 048-50633) France (EP Pathé
Marconi EG 899) France
Ouvre la bouche, ferme les yeux. (promo single
Pathé Marconi) France (EP Pathé Marconi
EG 1070) France

Pourquoi un pyjama ? (EP Pathé Marconi EG 948)
France

Les Petits papiers. (EP Pathé Marconi EG 899) France

Si t'attends qu'les diamants t'sautent au cou.
(Serge Gainsbourg)
REGINE (LP Emidisc C 048-50633) France

Tic Tac Toe. (promo single CBS 6580) France (1978)

Marc RIBOT

Black Trombonne. (Serge Gainsbourg)
GREAT JEWISH MUSIC: SERGE GAINSBOURG
(CD Tzadik TZ 7116) USA (1997)

RUINS

L'Homme à tête de chou. (Serge Gainsbourg)
GREAT JEWISH MUSIC : SERGE GAINSBOURG (CD
Tzadik TZ 7116) USA (1997)

SAINT TROPEZ

Je t'aime / Je t'aime... Moi non plus.
(Serge Gainsbourg) (LP Butterfly Records FLY 002)
France (1977)

Catherine SAUVAGE

L'Assassinat de Franz Lehar.
CATHERINE SAUVAGE CHANTE GAINSBOURG
(EP Philips 432.784 BE) France

Baudelaire. (Serge Gainsbourg)
CATHERINE SAUVAGE CHANTE GAINSBOURG
(EP Philips 432.784 BE) France

Black trombonne. (Serge Gainsbourg)
CATHERINE SAUVAGE CHANTE GAINSBOURG (EP
Philips 432.784 BE) France

Les Goémons. (Serge Gainsbourg)
CATHERINE SAUVAGE CHANTE GAINSBOURG
(EP Philips 432.784 BE) France

Le Cirque. (Serge Gainsbourg)
GAINSBOURG CHANTE PAR...
(CD EMI 854 067 2) France (1996)

Les Nanas au paradis. (Serge Gainsbourg)
GAINSBOURG CHANTE PAR...
(CD EMI 854 067 2) France (1996)

Les SCARLETT

Vilaine fille, mauvais garçon. (EP Panorama MH
117) France

David SHEA

Initiales BB. (Serge Gainsbourg)
GREAT JEWISH MUSIC: SERGE GAINSBOURG (CD
Tzadik TZ 7116) USA (1997)

Michel SIMON

L'Herbe tendre. (Serge Gainsbourg) Duet with Serge
Gainsbourg (SP Philips B 370.650) France (EP
Philips 437.488 BE) France

Jimmy SOMMERVILLE

Featuring Junes Miles Kingston
Comment te dire adieu. (SP London 886 768-7) France

Les SOUCOUPES VIOLENTES

Les Roses fanées. (Serge Gainsbourg)
ET POUR UN OUI, ET POUR UN NON (Maxi 45
Tours New Rose NEW 134) France

SOUNDS NICE

*Love At First Sight (Adaptation of 'Je t'aime... Moi
non plus')* 1969 GB

STARSHOOTER

Le Poinçonneur des lilas.
GAINSBOURG CHANTE PAR...
(CD EMI 854 067 2) France (1996)
. STARSHOOTER (LP Pathé Marconi C006 14588)
France (198)
STARSHOOTER (Fan Club FC 039) France (Reissue
1988)

Stomy BUGSY

No Comment. (Serge Gainsbourg)
L'HIP-HOPEE (CD Black Door 7243 5 25663 2 7)
France (2000)

DONNA SUMMER

Je T'Aime, Moi Non Plus. (Serge Gainsbourg) 1978
USA

Jacky TERRASSON

La Javanaise. (Serge Gainsbourg)
JAZZ A SAINT-GERMAIN
(CD Virgin 7243 8 451522 5) France (1997)

TOUBIB

Cuti-réaction. (Serge Gainsbourg)
GAINSBOURG CHANTE PAR...
(CD EMI 854 067 2) France (1996)
Le Vieux rocker. (Serge Gainsbourg)
GAINSBOURG CHANTE PAR...
(CD EMI 854 067 2) France (1996)

Franz TREICHLER

Requiem pour un con. (Serge Gainsbourg)
GREAT JEWISH MUSIC: SERGE GAINSBOURG (CD
Tzadik TZ 7116) USA (1997)

TRUMPET BOY

Le Claqueur de doigts. (EP Philips 424.151 PE)
France

Joelle URSULL

White And Black Blues. (Serge Gainsbourg, Joelle
Ursull) (SP CBS 655 951 7) France (1990)
BLACK FRENCH (LP CBS466 854 1) France (1990)
White And Black Blues. (Serge Gainsbourg, Joelle
Ursull) instrumental version (SP CBS 655 951 7)
France (1990)

Marie-Blanceh VERGNE

Au risque de te déplaire. (Serge Gainsbourg)
(EP Pathé Marconi ESRF 1855) France (1967)
GAINSBOURG CHANTE PAR...
(CD EMI 854 067 2) France (1996)

Dominique WALTER

Je suis capable de n'importe quoi. (Serge Gainsbourg)
(EP Disc'AZ EP 1163) France (1967)
Johnsyne et Kossigone. (Serge Gainsbourg) (EP
Disc'AZ EP 1163) France (1967)
Les Petits boudins. (Serge Gainsbourg) (EP Disc'AZ EP
1106) France (1967) (SP Disc'AZ 10 299) France (1967)
Plus dur sera le chut. (Serge Gainsbourg)
SP Disc'AZ SG 36 France (1968)

John ZORN

Contact. (Serge Gainsbourg)
GREAT JEWISH MUSIC : SERGE GAINSBOURG (CD
Tzadik TZ 7116) USA (1997)

Pirate CDs

GAINSBOURG INEDITS France   CD

MONSIEUR GAINSBOURG [Kiss 006] France   CD
Poste Restante (RTL) – with Jean-Bernard Hebey
06/06/79 France   CD
Interview by Philippe Manœuvre 01/08/90
France   CD
CONFIDENTIEL [Carre Blanc 001]
France   Pirate CD Compilations
10 ANS DES VICTOIRES DE LA MUSIQUE
France   Promo

Non-French 33 rpm

INITIALS B.B. [Philips 844 784] Canada   LP
Philips P 70.391 LANNA (Rerelease) Japan   LP
Fontana SRF 67610 JE T'AIME / BEAUTIFUL LOVE
USA   LP
Dial 900521-2 GAINSBOURG CONFIDENTIEL
(Digipack) France   CD
Dial 900522-2 GAINSBOURG PERCUSSIONS
(Digipack) France   CD
Philips 538 606-2 GAINSBOURG PERCUSSIONS
(Digipack) France   CD
Dial 900524-2 INITIALS B.B. (Digipack) France   CD
Philips 546 534-2 INITIALS B.B. (Digipack)
France   CD
Dial 900523-2 BONNIE AND CLYDE (Digipack)
France   CD

SERGE GAINSBOURG FILMOGRAPHY

AS DIRECTOR (FULL-LENGTH FEATURES)

1976

Je t'aime, moi non plus
... aka *I Love You No More* (1975)
... aka *I Love You, I Don't* (1975) (USA)
Released : 10th March 1976, Paris
Production : President Fils/ Renn Productions
(Jacques-Eric Strauss & Claude Berri
Running time : 90 minutes
Music: Serge Gainsbourg
Cast: Jane Birkin (Johnny), Joe Dalessandro (Krassky,
alias Krass), Hugues Quester (Padovan), Rene
Kolldehoff (Boris), Gerard Depardieu (un paysan a
cheval), Michel Blanc (un ouvrier)

1983

Équateur
Released: 17th August 1983, Paris
Production: Corso, TF1, Gaumont
Running time: 85 minutes
Music: Serge Gainsbourg
Cast: Barbara Sukowa (Adele), Francis Huster
(Timar), Rene Kolldehoff (Eugene), Francois Dyrek
(the commissioner), Jean Boise, Julien Guiomar
(Bouilloux).

1986

Charlotte forever
Released : 10th December 1986, Paris
Production: G.P.F.I.
Running time: 94 minutes
Music: Serge Gainsbourg
Cast: Roland Bertin (Leon), Sabeline Campo
(Therese), Roland Dubillard (Herman), Charlotte
Gainsbourg (Charlotte), Serge Gainsbourg (Stan),
Anne Le Guernec (Adelaide), Anne Zaberlan (Lola)

1990

Stan the Flasher
Released: 7th March, 1990, Paris
Production: Francois Ravard for R. Fils/Canal +
Running Time 65 minutes
Music: Serge Gainsbourg

Cast: Claude Berri (Stan),
Aurore Clement (Aurore),
Richard Bohringer (David),
Elodie (Natacha),
Lucie Cabanis (Rosalie),
Daniel Duval (the father),
Michel Robin (), Mark
Stokle (Jojo), Jacques
Wolfsohn (friend of David)

AS DIRECTOR (TV, SHORTS AND VIDEO CLIPS)

1981

Le Physique et le figuré
Released 1981
Production: French confederation of beauty products
Running time: 5 minutes
Music: Serge Gainsbourg
Cast: Alexandra (the model)

1982

Marianne Faithfull
Two clips in London for *Les Enfants du Rock* TV series

1982

Scarface (TV)
Production: FR3
Running Time: 5 minutes
Transmitted 15th April 1982
Cast: Jane Birkin (Cesca), Daniel Duval (Toni)

1984

Renaud "Morgane de Toi"
Clip

1985

Total
Released: May 1985
Running time: 12 minutes
Circulated privately

Bubble gum
Released : June 1985, Paris
Running time: 1 minute 12 seconds

Lemon Incest
Video clip

1987

Springtime in Bourges (TV)
Transmitted July 1987 on FR3

Charlotte Forever
Video Clip

Indochine "Tes Yeux noirs"
Video clip

1990

Jane Birkin "Amour des feintes"
Video clip

WRITER

Stan the Flasher (1990)
Charlotte forever (1986)
Équateur (1983)
Scarface (1981) (TV)

ACTOR

1959

Voulez-vous danser avec moi? as Leon
    ... aka *Come Dance with Me* (UK)
    ... aka *Come Dance with Me!* (1960) (USA)
    ... aka *Do You Want to Dance with Me?* (1959)
    (International: English title)
    ... aka *Sexy girl* (1959) (Italy)
Directed by Michel Boisrond
Running time: 90 inutes
Cast:, Brigitte Bardot, Henri Vidal, Dawn
    Addams,Noel Roquevert, Dario Moreno, Phillipe
    Nicaud, Serge Gainsbourg, Paul Frankeur.

1961

Rivolta degli schiavi, La (1961) as Corvino
    ... aka *Rebelión de los esclavos, La* (1961) (Spain)
    ... aka *Revolt of the Slaves, The* (1961)
    ... aka *Révolte des esclaves, La* (1961)
    ... aka *Sklaven Roms, Die (1961)* (West Germany)
Directed by Nunzio Malasoma
Running time: 90 minutes
Cast: Dario Moreno, Rhonda Fleming, Wandisa
    Guida, Gino Cervi, Serge Gainsbourg

Furia di Ercole, La (1961)
    ... aka *Fury of Hercules, The* (1961) (USA)
    ... aka *Fury of Samson* (1961) (USA: TV title)
    ... aka *Samson* (1961/II)
    ... aka *Sansone* (1961) (Italy: alternative title)
Directed by: Gianfranco Parolini and Victor Scega
Running time: 93 minutes
Cast; Brad Harris, Serge Gainsbourg, Brigitte Corey,
    Mara Berni,Carlo Tamberlani

1963

Strip-tease (1963/I) as the piano player
    ... aka *Ragazza nuda, Una* (1963) (Italy)
    ... aka *Sweet Skin* (1963) (USA)
Directed by: Jacques Poirenaud
Music: Serge Gainsbourg
Inconnue de Hong Kong, L' (1963)
    ... aka *Stranger from Hong-Kong* (1963) (USA)
Directed by Jacques Poirenaud
Running time: 90 minutes

1965

Jardinier d'Argenteuil, Le (1965)
    ... aka *Blüten, Gauner und die Nacht von Nizza*
    (1965) (West Germany)
Directed by Jean-Paul Le Chanois
Music: Serge Gainsbourg

1966

Noël à Vaugirard (TV)
Estouffade à la Caraïbe (1966) as Clyde
    ... aka *Avventurieri per una rivolta* (1966) (Italy)
    ... aka *Gold Robbers* (1966)
    ... aka *Looters, The* (1966) (UK)
    ... aka *Pagati per morire* (1966) (Italy)
Directed by : Jacques Besnard
Cast : Jean Seberg, Frederick Stafford, Maria-Rosa
    Rodriquez, Serge Gainsbourg, Paul Crauchet

1967

Anna
Directed by Pierre Koralnik
Music: Serge Gainsbourg
Cast: Anna Karina (Anna), Jean-Claude Brialy
    (Serge), Serge Gainsbourg (Serge's friend),
    Marianne Faithfull (the girl)
Valmy (TV) as Marquis de Sade

1968

Vivre la nuit as Mathieu
Directed by: Paul Androeta
Cast: Jacques Perrin, Catherine Jourdan,
    Estella Blain, Georges Geret, Serge Gainsbourg.
Ce sacré grand-père as Rémy
    ... aka *Marriage Came Tumbling Down, The*
    (1967) (USA)
Directed by: Jacques Poitrenaud
Music: Serge Gainsbourg
Running time: 90 minutes
Cast: Michel Simon, Marie Dubois, Yyves Lefebvre,
    Serge Gainsbourg
L'Inconnu de Shandigor
Directed by: Jean-Luis Roy
Music: Serge Gainsbourg & Alphone Roy
Cast: Jacques Dufilho, Marie-France Boyer, Ben
    Carruthers, Serge Gainsbourg
Lapin de Noël, Le (TV)
Pacha, Le (as Himself)
    ... aka *Fredda alba del commissario Joss, La*
    (Italy)
    ... aka *Pasha* (International: English title)
Directed by: Georges Lautner
Running time: 100 minutes
Music: Serge Gainsbourg
Cast: Jean Gabin, Dany Carrel, Jean Gaven, Andre
    Pousse, Serge Gainsbourg
Released: 14th March 1968

Saint-Tropez priez pour eux (TV) as Le grand prêtre

Naissance d'une chanson, La (TV) as Himself

Erotissimo

1969

Paris n'existe pas
Directed by: Robert Benayoun
Music: Serge Gainsbourg
Running time: 100 minutes
Cast: Serge Gainsbourg, Richard Leduc, Daniele
   Gaubert, Tamra Belnekki, Monique Lejeune.

Mister Freedom as M. Drugstore

Slogan as Serge

Chemins de Katmandou, Les as Ted
   ... aka *Road to Katmandou, The* (1969)

1970

Cannabis
Directed by: Pierre Kralnik
Music: Serge Gainsbourg
Running time: 90 minutes
Cast: Jane Birkin, Serge Gainsbourg,
   Paul Nicholas, Curt Jurgens, Gabrielle Ferzetti,
   Rita Renoir, Marcel Lupovici

1971

*Le Roman d'un Voleur de Chevaux (Romance of a
   Horse Thief)*
Directed by: Abraham Polonsky
Music: Mort Shuman, with a song by Serge
   Gainsbourg *(La Noyee)*
Running time: 104 minutes
Cast: Yul Brynner, Eli Wallach, Jane Birkin, Oliver
   Tobias, Laine Kazan, Serge Gainsbourg.

Le Traitre aka *19 jeunes filles et le matelot*
Directed by: Milutin Kosvac
Music: Serge Gainsbourg
Cast: Serge Gainsbourg, Jane Birkin, Spela Rozin,
   Diana Rutic, Milos Kandic, Mira Nikolic.

1972

Trop jolies pour etre honnete
Directed by: Robert Balducci
Music: Serge Gainsbourg
Cast: Jane Birkin, Bernadette Lasfont, Elisabeth
   Wiener, Daniel Ceccaldi, Serge Gainsbourg

Le Derniere Violette
Directed by: Andre Hardellet, inspired by his novel,
   Le Tueuer de Vielles
Music: Serge Gainsbourg

1973

Sex-shop

Morte negli occhi del gatto, La (1973)
   ... aka *Diablesses, Les* (1973/I) (France)
   ... aka *Seven Deaths in the Cat's Eye* (1973)
   (USA)
   ... aka *Sieben Tote in den Augen der Katze* (1973)
   (West Germany)

1974

Les Diablesses
Directed by Anthony M Dawson
Music Riz Ortolani
Cast: Jane Birkin, Hiram Keller, Francois Christophe,
   Venantino Venantini, Serge Gainsbourg

1975

Serieux comme le plaisir
Directed by Robert Benayoun
Music: Michael Berger
Cast: Jane Birkin, Richard Leduc, Georges Mansart,
   Michel Lonsdale, Roland Dubillard, Jean-Luc
   Bideau, Andrea Ferreol, Serge Gainsbourg

1980

Je vous aime
Directed by Claude Berri
Music: Serge Gainsbourg
Running time: 103 minutes
Cast: Catherine Deneuve, Jean-Louis Trintignant,
   Gerard Depardieu, Alain Souchon, Serge
   Gainsbourg

1981

Le Grand Pardon
Directed by Alexander Arcady
Cast: Roger Hanin, Clio Goldsmith, Richard Berry,
   Serge Gainsbourg

Reporters
Directed by Raymond Depardon
Cast: Serge Gainsbourg

1986

Charlotte Forever
Directed and written by Serge Gainsbourg
Released 10th December 1996, Paris
Running time: 94 minutes
Music: Serge Gainsbourg
Cast: Roland Bertin, Sabeline Campo, Roland
   Dubillard, Charlotte Gainsbourg, Serge
   Gainsbourg, Anne Le Guernec, Anne Zamberlan.

1987

Jane B. par Agnes V
Directed by Agnes Varda
Music: Serge Gainsbourg
Cast: Jane Birkin, Jean-Pierre Leaud, Farid Chopel,
   Laura Betti, Charlotte Gainsbourg, Serge
   Gainsbourg

COMPOSER

Eau à la bouche, L' (1959)
... aka Game for Six Lovers, A (1959)

Loups dans la bergerie, Les (1960)

Loups dans la bergerie, Les (1960)

Lettre dans un taxi, La (1962) (TV)

Strip-tease (1963/I)
... aka Ragazza nuda, Una (1963) (Italy)
... aka Sweet Skin (1963) (USA)

Dix grammes d'arc-en-ciel (1963)

Comment trouvez-vous ma soeur? (1963)

Plus belles escroqueries du monde, Les (1964)
... aka Beautiful Swindlers, The (1964)
... aka Più belle truffe del mondo, Le (1964) (Italy)
... aka World's Greatest Swindles (1964)
... aka World's Most Beautiful Swindlers, The (1964)

Jardinier d'Argenteuil, Le (1965)
... aka Blüten, Gauner und die Nacht von Nizza (1965) (West Germany)

Anna (1965)

Defector, The (1966)
... aka Espion, L' (1966) (France)
... aka Lautlose Waffen (1966)

Coeurs verts, Les (1966)
... aka Naked Hearts (1966

Carré de dames pour un as (1966)
... aka Demasiadas mujeres para Layton (1967) (Spain)
... aka Layton... bambole e karatè (1966) (Italy)

"Vidocq" (1967) TV Series

Une et l'autre, L' (1967)
... aka Other One, The (1967) (USA)

Toutes folles de lui (1967)

Si j'étais un espion (1967)
... aka If I Were a Spy (1967) (USA)

Pacha, Le (1967)
... aka Fredda alba del commissario Joss, La (1967) (Italy)
... aka Pasha (1967) (International: English title)

Inconnu de Shandigor, L' (1967)

Horizon, L' (1967)

Ce sacré grand-père (1967)
... aka Marriage Came Tumbling Down, The (1967) (USA)

Anatomie d'un mouvement (1967)

Manon 70 (1968)
... aka Hemmungslose Manon (1968) (West Germany)

Paris n'existe pas (1968)

Naissance d'une chanson, La (1968) (song "Initials BB")

Mini-midi (1968)

Mister Freedom (1969)

Boy Named Charlie Brown, A (1969) (song "Un petit garçon nommé Charlie Brown for French version")
... aka Boy Called Charlie Brown, A (1969) (UK)

Une veuve en or (1969) (song "La fille qui fait tchic ti tchic")

Slogan (1969)

Horse, La (1969)
... aka Clan degli uomini violenti, Il (1970) (Italy)
... aka Erbarmungslos (1969) (West Germany)

Chemins de Katmandou, Les (1969)
... aka Road to Katmandu, The (1969)

Cannabis (1969)
... aka Cannabis - Engel der Gewalt (1970) (West Germany)
... aka French Intrigue (1969)
... aka Mafia Wants Your Blood, The (1969) (USA)
... aka New York Parigi per una condanna a morte (1969)

Piggies (1970) (TV) (Italy)

Romance of a Horsethief (1971) (song "La noyée")
... aka Roman d'un voleur de chevaux, Le (1971) (France)

19 djevojaka i Mornar (1971)

Trop jolies pour être honnêtes (1972)
... aka Demasiado bonitas para ser honestas (1974) (Spain)
... aka Perchè mammà ti manda solo? (1972) (Italy)
... aka Too Pretty to Be Honest (1972)

Dernière violette, La (1972)

Sex-shop (1973)

Projection privée (1973)
... aka Private Projection (1973)

Je t'aime, moi non plus (1975)
... aka I Love You No More (1975)
... aka I Love You, I Don't (1975) (USA)

Madame Claude (1977)
... aka French Woman, The (1977) (USA)

Goodbye, Emmanuelle (1977)
... aka Emmanuele (1977)

Vous n'aurez pas l'Alsace et la Lorraine (1977)

Aurais dû faire gaffe... le choc est terrible (1977)

Bronzés, Les (1978)
    ... aka French Fried Vacation (1978)
Tapage nocturne (1979)
    ... aka Nocturnal Uproar (1979) (International:
    English title
Melancholy Baby (1979)
Je vous aime (1980)
    ... aka I Love You All (1980)
Physique et le figuré, Le (1981)
Équateur (1983)
Boy Meets Girl (1984)
Mode en France (1985)
Tenue de soirée (1986)
    ... aka Evening Dress (1986)
    ... aka Ménage (1986) (USA)

Charlotte forever (1986)
Jane B. par Agnès V. (1987)
    ... aka A.V. sur J.B. (1987)
    ... aka Jane B. by Agnes V. (1987)
    ... aka Jane B. for Agnes V. (1987) (International:
    English title)
    ... aka Jane B. sur Agnes V. (1987)
Stan the Flasher (1990)
Élisa (1995) (theme)
En avoir (ou pas) (1995)
    ... aka To Have (or not) (1995)

DIRECTOR, COMPOSER & ACTOR IN FILM & TV COMMERCIALS

1976-1977 **Woolite**
Cast: Jane Birkin, Brigitte Fossey, Marlene Jobert
Product: Washing powder for wool
1980 **Bayard**
Cast: Serge Gainsbourg
Product: Suits
1980 **Brandt**
Product: Dish-washer

1980 **Roudor Saint-Michel**
Cast: Serge Gainsbourg
Product: Biscuits
1982 **Lee Cooper**
Cast: Serge Gainsbourg
Product: Jeans
1982 **Renault 9**
Cast: Serge Gainsbourg
Product: Cars
1982 **Maggi**
Product: Soup
1982-84 **Gini**
Three films
Cast: Serge Gainsbourg
Product: Lemonade

1983 **Orelia**
Product: Orange Juice

1984 **Roumillat**
Product: Cheese

1984 **Faure**
Product: Cookers

1984 **Anny Blatt**
Product: Woollens

1984 **Babyliss**
Product: Curling tongs

1984 **Palmolive**
Product: Shampoo

1984 **Spring Court**
Product: Tennis shoes

1985 **Danone aux fruits**
Product: Yoghurt

1985: **Konica**
Product: Photographic film

1985-86 **Saba**
Product: TVs and videos

1986 **Connexion**
Cast: Serge Gainsbourg
Product: Hi-fi

1986 **Pepsodent**
Product: Toothpaste

1986 **Sagamore de Lancome**
Product: Perfume

1987 **Pentex**
Product: Corrector

1988 **Tutti Free**
Cast: Helena
Product: Sweeteners

SERGE GAINSBOURG BIBLIOGRAPHY

Chanson Cruelles (Tchou) 1968

Melody Nelson (Ed. Eric Losfeld) 1971

Bambou Et Les Poupées (Filipacchi) 1981

Black-Out (graphic novel, with Jacques Armand) (Les Humanoîdes Associés) 1983

Où Es-Tu Melody? (graphic novel with Iusse) (Vents D'Ouest) 1987

Evguénie Sokolov (Gallimard) 1980

Mon Propre Rôle 1 – Textes 1958-75 (Denoël) 1987

Mon Propre Rôle 2 – Textes 1976-87 (Denoël) 1987

Movies (textes) (Ed. Franck Lhomeau) 1994

Dernières Nouvelles Des Étoiles (complete lyrics) (Plon) 1994

About the author

Sylvie Simmons is one of Britain's best-known rock writers. A lifelong music obsessive who even filed her nursery rhymes in alphabetical order, she left for Los Angeles on a musical pilgrimage in the late '70s and wound up as correspondent for then-leading rock weekly *Sounds*. Since then, living at various times in America, her native London, and France, her interviews and reviews have appeared in countless books and publications, from legendary U.S. magazine *Creem* to U.K.'s *MOJO*, for whom she still writes today.

Other Titles available from Helter Skelter and Firefly Publishing and SAF.

Coming Soon from Helter Skelter:

Summer 2001

Calling Out Around the World: A Motown Reader
Edited by Kingsley Abbott £13.99
With a foreword by Martha Reeves, this is a unique collection of articles which tell the story of the rise of a black company in a white industry, and its talented stable of artists, musicians, writers and producers. Included are rare interviews with key figures such as Berry Gordy, Marvin Gaye, Smokey Robinson and Florence Ballard as well as reference sources for collectors and several specially commissioned pieces.

Razor Edge: Bob Dylan and The Never-ending Tour
Andrew Muir £12.99
Respected Dylan expert Andrew Muir documents the ups and downs of this unprecedented trek, and finds time to tell the story of his own curious meeting with Dylan.
   Muir also tries to get to grips with what exactly it all means – both for Dylan and for the Bobcats: dedicated Dylan followers, like himself, who trade tapes of every show and regularly cross the globe to catch up with the latest leg of The Never Ending Tour.

The Beach Boys' *Pet Sounds*: The Greatest Album of the Twentieth Century
By Kingsley Abbott £12.99
Pet Sounds is the 1966 album that saw The Beach Boys graduate from lightweight pop like "Surfin' USA", et al, into a vehicle for the mature compositional genius of Brian Wilson. The album was hugely influential, not least on The Beatles. This full story of the album's background, its composition and recording, its contemporary reception and its enduring legacy.

The Return of The Last Gang in Town: The Story and Myth of the Clash
By Marcus Gray £14.99
Revised, updated and completely overhauled, mammoth history of the greatest rock 'n' roll band of the modern rock era, that is also a detailed and erudite history of punk and the punk fall out years.
   "If you're a music fan … it's important you read this book." *Record Collector*
   "A valuable document for anyone interested in the punk era." *Billboard*

Autumn 2001

Ashley Hutchins: The Guvnor and the Rise of Folk Rock – Fairport Convention, Steeleye Span and the Albion Band
By Geoff Wall and Brian Hinton £12.99
As founder of Fairport Convention and Steeleye Span, Ashley Hutchins is the pivotal figure in the history of folk rock. This book draws on hundreds of hours of interviews with Hutchins and other folk-rock artists and paints a vivid picture of the scene that also produced Sandy Denny, Richard Thompson, Nick Drake, John Martyn and Al Stewart.

Gram Parsons: God's Own Singer
By Jason Walker £12.99
Brand new biography of the man who pushed The Byrds into country-rock territory on *Sweethearts of The Rodeo*, and then quit to form the acclaimed Flying Burrito Brothers. Parsons' second solo record, *Grievous Angel*, is a haunting masterpiece of country soul. By the time the album was released, Parsons had been dead for 4 months. He was 26 years old.

King Crimson: Track by Track
By Sid Smith £14.99
King Crimson's 1969 masterpiece In The Court Of The Crimson King, was a huge U.S. chart hit. The band followed it with 40 further albums of consistently challenging, distinctive and innovative music. Drawing on hours of new interviews, and encouraged by Crimson supremo Robert Fripp, the author traces the band's turbulent history year by year, track by track.

I've Been Everywhere: A Johnny Cash Chronicle
By Peter Lewry £12.99
A complete chronological illustrated diary of Johnny Cash's concerts, TV appearances, record releases, recording sessions and other milestones. From his early days with Sam Phillips in Memphis to international stardom, the wilderness years of the mid-sixties, and on to his legendary prison concerts and his recent creative resurgence with the hugely successful 2000 release, *American Recording III: Solitary Man*.

Sandy Denny: No More Sad Refrains
By Clinton Heylin £12.99
Paperback edition of the highly acclaimed biography of the greatest female singer-songwriter this country has ever produced.

Currently Available from Helter Skelter:

Emerson Lake and Palmer: The Show That Never Ends
George Forrester, Martin Hanson and Frank Askew £14.00
Prog-rock supergroup Emerson Lake and Palmer, were one the most successful acts of the seventies and, in terms of sound, artistic vision and concept, operated on a scale far in excess of any rivals.
Drawing on years of research, the authors have produced a gripping and fascinating document of one of the great rock bands of the seventies.

Animal Tracks: The Story of The Animals
Sean Egan £12.99
Sean Egan, author of the acclaimed Verve biography, *Starsailor* (Omnibus, 1998) has enjoyed full access to surviving Animals and associates and has produced a compelling portrait of a truly distinctive band of survivors.

Like a Bullet of Light: The Films of Bob Dylan
CP Lee £12.99
In studying in-depth an often overlooked part of Dylan's oeuvre, *Like A Bullet of Light* forms a compelling portrait of an enigmatic artist as keen to challenge perceptions in the visual medium as in his better known career in music.

Rock's Wild Things: The Troggs Files
Alan Clayson and Jacqueline Ryan £12.99
Respected rock writer Alan Clayson has had full access to the band and traces their history from 60s Andover rock roots to 90s covers, collaborations and corn circles. The Troggs Files also features the first ever publication of the full transcript of the legendary "Troggs Tapes," said to have inspired the movie *This is Spinal Tap*, together with an exhaustive discography and many rare photos

Waiting for the Man: The Story of Drugs and Popular Music
by Harry Shapiro UK Price £12.99
Fully revised edition of the classic story of two intertwining billion dollar industries. "Wise and witty." *The Guardian*

The Sharper Word: A Mod Reader
Edited by Paolo Hewitt (available November 1999) UK price:£12.99
Hugely readable collection of articles documenting one of the most misunderstood cultural movements

Dylan's Daemon Lover: The Tangled Tale of a 450-Year Old Pop Ballad
by Clinton Heylin UK price £12.00
Written as a detective story, Heylin unearths the mystery of why Dylan knew enough to return "The House Carpenter" to its 16th century source.

Get Back: The Beatles' *Let It Be* Disaster
by Doug Sulpy & Ray Schweighardt UK price £12.99
No-holds barred account of the power struggles, the bickering, and the bitterness that led to the break-up of the greatest band in the history of rock 'n' roll. "One of the most poignant Beatles books ever." *Mojo*

XTC: Song Stories – The Exclusive & Authorised Story
by XTC and Neville Farmer UK Price £12.99
"A cheerful celebration of the minutiae surrounding XTC's music with the band's musical passion intact … high in setting-the-record-straight anecdotes. Superbright, funny, commanding." *Mojo*

Like The Night: Bob Dylan and the Road to the Manchester Free Trade Hall
by CP Lee UK Price £12.00
In 1966 at the height of Dylan's protest-singing popularity he plugged in an electric guitar to the outrage of folk fans who booed and jeered. Finally, in Manchester, fans branded him Judas. "Essential Reading" *Uncut*

Born in the USA: Bruce Springsteen and the American Tradition
by Jim Cullen UK Price £9.99
"Cullen has written an excellent treatise expressing exactly how and why Springsteen translated his uneducated hicktown American-ness into music and stories that touched hearts and souls around the world." *Q****

Back to the Beach: A Brian Wilson and the Beach Boys Reader
Ed Kingsley Abbott UK Price £12.99
"A detailed study and comprehensive overview of the BBs' lives and music, even including a foreword from Wilson himself by way of validation. Most impressively, Abbott manages to appeal to both die-hard fans and rather less obsessive newcomers." *Time Out* "Rivetting!" **** *Q* "An essential purchase." *Mojo*

A Journey Through America with the Rolling Stones
by Robert Greenfield UK Price £9.99
Featuring a new foreword by Ian Rankin
   This is the definitive account of their legendary '72 tour.
   "Filled with finely-rendered detail ... a fascinating tale of times we shall never see again" *Mojo*

Bob Dylan
by Anthony Scaduto UK Price £9.99
The first and best biography of Dylan. "The best book ever written on Dylan" *Record Collector* "Now in a welcome reprint it's a real treat to read the still-classic Bobography". *Q*****

Coming Soon from Firefly Publishing:

To Hell and Back with Catatonia
by Brian Wright UK price £12.99
Fronted by the brassy, irrepressible Cerys Matthews, Catatonia exploded onto the British pop scene in 1998. Author Brian Wright has been an ardent Catatonia supporter since their earliest days. Drawing on first hand experience, new interviews and years of research, he charts their struggle from obscure 1993 Cardiff pub gigs to the Top Ten.

U2: The Complete Encyclopedia
by Mark Chatterton UK Price £14.99
Here at last is the book that all completists, fans and U2 reference hounds have been waiting for. Hot on the heels of the huge success of Firefly's ultimate guide to all things Genesis, we can now announce the publication of the complete A to Z of the career of U2. Fully up-to-date, it documents the band's historical details from their early days in Dublin, to the current world tour.

Currently Available from Firefly Publishing:

Poison Heart: Surviving The Ramones
by Dee Dee Ramone and Veronica KofmanUK Price £11.95
Dee Dee's crushingly honest account of life as junkie and Ramone. A great rock story!

Minstrels In The Gallery: A History Of Jethro Tull
by David Rees UK Price £12.99
At Last! To coincide with their 30th anniversary, a full history of one of the most popular and inventive British bands.

DANCEMUSICSEXROMANCE: Prince – The First Decade
by Per Nilsen UK Price £12.99
A portrait of Prince's reign as the most exciting black performer to emerge since James Brown and Jimi Hendrix.

Soul Sacrifice: The Santana Story
by Simon Leng UK Price £12.99
In depth study of seventies Latin guitar legend whose career began at Woodstock through to a 1999 number one US album.

Opening The Musical Box: A Genesis Chronicle
by Alan Hewitt UK Price £12.99
Drawing on hours of new interviews and packed with insights, anecdotes and trivia, here is the ultimat compendium to one of the most successful and inventive bands of the modern rock era.

Blowin' Free: Thirty Years Of Wishbone Ash
by Gary Carter and Mark Chatterton UK Price £12.99
Packed with memorabilia, rare photos, a definitive discography and utilising unprecedented access to band members and associates, Gary Carter and Mark Chatterton have charted the long and turbulent career of one of England's premier rock outfits.

Coming soon from SAF Publishing:

The Zombies: Hung Up On A Dream
by Claes Johansen UK Price: £16.99 (limited edition hardback)
Formed in 1963, The Zombies featured Rod Argent and Colin Blunstone. Their undenied masterpiece, the album *Odessey & Oracle*, was recorded at Abbey Road during that famous Summer of 1967 and featured the classic "Time Of The Season" and recently made *Mojo's* best 100 LPs of all time.

Gentle Giant – Acquiring The Taste
by Paul Stump. UK Price: £16.99 (limited edition hardback)
Based around the Shulman brothers, Gentle Giant quickly acquired a large cult following the world over. Their music has endured over time and new generations are as entranced by their intricate sound as were audiences of 30 years ago.

Free At Last: The Story of Free and Bad Company
by Steven Rosen
One of the greatest rock blues outfits of the early seventies, Free peaked with the seminal hit "All Right Now", centred around the gravel-laden voice of Paul Rodgers and the hauntingly resonant guitar playing of troubled soul Paul Kossoff. When Free disbanded, Rodgers and Free drummer Simon Kirke went on to form one of the seventies best-known supergroups – Bad Company.
　　Steve Rosen's history with both bands goes back a long way – he once drove Paul Rodgers to an Elvis Presley concert in his Triumph Herald, as well as covering Bad Company's formation in *Rolling Stone*. Using old and new interviews with members and associates, here at last is a portrait of two of rock music's treasures.

Currently available from SAF Publishing:

Necessity Is... The Early Years of Frank Zappa and the Mothers of Invention
by Billy James UK Price: £12.95

No More Mr Nice Guy: The Inside Story of the Alice Cooper Group
By Michael Bruce and Billy James UK Price £11.99

Procol Harum: Beyond The Pale
by Claes Johansen UK Price £12.99

An American Band: The Story of Grand Funk Railroad
By Billy James UK Price £12.99

Wish The World Away: Mark Eitzel and American Music Club
by Sean Body UK Price £12.99

Go Ahead John! The Music of John McLaughlin
by Paul Stump UK Price £12.99

Lunar Notes: Zoot Horn Rollo's Captain Beefheart Experience
by Bill Harkleroad and Billy James UK Price £11.95

Meet The Residents: America's Most Eccentric Band
by Ian Shirley UK Price £11.95

Digital Gothic: A Critical Discography of Tangerine Dream
by Paul Stump UK Price £9.95

The One and Only – Homme Fatale: Peter Perrett & The Only Ones
by Nina Antonia UK Price £11.95

Plunderphonics, 'Pataphysics and Pop Mechanics
The Leading Exponents of Musique Actuelle
By Andrew Jones UK Price £12.95

Kraftwerk: Man, Machine and Music
By Pascal Bussy UK Price £12.95

Wrong Movements: A Robert Wyatt History
by Mike King UK Price £14.95

Wire: Everybody Loves A History
by Kevin Eden UK Price £9.95

Tape Delay: A Documentary of Industrial Music
by Charles Neal UK Price £15.99

Dark Entries: Bauhaus and Beyond
by Ian Shirley UK Price £11.95

Mail Order

All Helter Skelter, Firefly and SAF titles are available by mail order from the world famous Helter Skelter bookshop.

You can either phone or fax your order to Helter Skelter on the following numbers:

Telephone: +44 (0)20 7836 1151 or Fax: +44 (0)20 7240 9880
Office hours: Mon-Fri 10:00am – 7:00pm,
Sat: 10:00am – 6:00pm, Sun: closed.

Postage prices per book worldwide are as follows:

UK & Channel Islands	£1.50
Europe & Eire (air)	£2.95
USA, Canada (air)	£7.50
Australasia, Far East (air)	£9.00
Overseas (surface)	£2.50

You can also write enclosing a cheque, International Money Order, or registered cash. Please include postage. DO NOT send cash. DO NOT send foreign currency, or cheques drawn on an overseas bank. Send to:

Helter Skelter Bookshop,
4 Denmark Street, London, WC2H 8LL, United Kingdom.
If you are in London come and visit us, and browse the titles in person!!

Email: helter@skelter.demon.co.uk
Website: http://www.skelter.demon.co.uk